Liturgy Pastoral and Parochial

Liturgy
Pastoral and Parochial

Michael Perham

First published 1984
SPCK
Holy Trinity Church
Marylebone Road
London NW1 4DU

Third impression 1991

ACKNOWLEDGEMENTS

Biblical quotations are from the New English Bible,
second edition © 1970, and are used by permission of the
Oxford and Cambridge University Presses.

Extracts from *The Alternative Service Book 1980*
are reproduced by permission of the Central Board of Finance
of the Church of England.

British Library Cataloguing in Publication Data

Perham, Michael
    Liturgy pastoral and parochial.
    1. Church of England – Liturgy   2. Public worship
    I. Title
    264'.03   BX5141
    ISBN 0-281-04092-3

Printed in Great Britain at
Dotesios Limited, Trowbridge, Wiltshire

For
Dick and Bar Norburn
and for
The Clergy and People
of St Mary's, Addington, Croydon,
with affection and
gratitude

Contents

Foreword

A bishop of the Church of England has to have many of the qualities of an old theatrical trouper. He sets out on circuit with a hazy, unreliable memory of the peculiarities of the next 'house' in which he is to perform and wondering which version of the script they are expecting him to use. Yet, besides studying the whims of each audience and being 'all things to all men', he has to believe in what he is doing and satisfy himself that each detail serves the total effect that he wants to communicate.

So I consider myself to have been exceptionally lucky in having Michael Perham as my chaplain. Whether he is briefing me on my part in the service, or reconciling my preferences with those of a local vicar, or sharing in a post-mortem on the way home, he combines a keen eye for detail with an insistence that detail must be subservient to the clean, clear shape of the whole. He never loses sight of the ultimate objective of all worship, and of each act of worship in particular. So our discussion of some small point of order will almost always lead us back to the gospel, and to the spirituality that the gospel generates. This is not surprising, since I first encountered Michael as the Secretary of the Doctrine Commission of the Church of England and have seen him become also a consultant to the Liturgical Commission.

I am delighted, therefore, that this book will make his wisdom available to so many others. It is easy to read and should be enjoyed by lay men and women as well as church professionals. On every page there is common sense, humour and some striking fresh insight, so that it is hard to resist the temptation to dip here and there, as though it were an anthology. But the temptation ought to be resisted because the chapters hold together as lessons in a well-planned course.

Though it throws much light upon them, it is not an apologia for the Alternative Services, for the author is equally at home in the Book of Common Prayer. It is, rather, an invitation to lay people and priests together to seek intelligently and to find joyfully the forms of worship and the patterns of services that can most effectively serve their community. I hope it will have a wide sale and run into many editions.

June 1983   JOHN V. TAYLOR

Introduction

The publication of the *Alternative Service Book* in 1980 marked the close of a chapter in the liturgical renewal of the Church of England. But it was only a chapter, and perhaps not the most important chapter, in the story, still not completed, of that renewal. The ASB is about textual change. Other changes may flow from it, but in itself it is principally a provision of reformed texts. The task that now lies before the Church is to set those texts within an enriching setting, to give them an ethos, and a validity which can only be theirs when they have become, at a deep level, part of the devotion and spirituality of church members. This is a more difficult task, and one that cannot be done by synods, commissions or revision committees. It is something that must happen in every local Christian community. It is partly a matter of *understanding* the liturgy and the reforms that are being made. It is partly a matter of *presenting* the liturgy with such sensitivity and devotion that it regains its power to excite and to thrill, to move and to console. It is, above all, about *assimilating* the liturgy, so that its moods and cycles deepen our experience of life.

It is a task for the local church. Experiment, discussion, even conflict, all undergirded by prayer, will play their part. This book is offered to the Church as one way into the subject. It provides no rigid set of rules for the right conduct of worship, for no such set can exist. It does provide some guidelines and pointers and, on the whole, these are not of my devising, but would meet with the approval of many working in the field of liturgy. It is an invitation to think hard, and to be bold, in the use of the new freedom that the Alternative Service Book has given to English Anglicans. It is also a plea for excellence, for an end to slipshod liturgy, theologically ill thought out and pastorally insensitive. Above all, it is about the rediscovery of the power of worship to change lives. These are lofty aims and this is a very small contribution to their achievement.

Some will question whether an Anglican needed to undertake the task of writing a book such as this. Has not the Roman Church, with its far greater liturgical resources, done so much work in this field, and published so much material, that an Anglican contribution can add little? I can only answer by saying that, however indebted we may be to modern Roman scholarship – the ASB is undoubtedly deeply influenced by it – Anglican worship remains distinctive and the English temperament demands something at times quite different. The theological presuppositions behind the new services of the two Communions are at points different, and the devotional habits of members of the two churches are quite distinct. I do not believe that a slavish following of things Roman will always be satisfactory.

One particular point of difference is the Anglican expectation that some of the high points of the liturgical year, at least for some people who call themselves members of the Church of England, will be non-eucharistic. Sometimes we may bewail this, but the inescapable fact is that the English Church often reaches out most effectively to those on its fringes when it uses forms and styles for which the liturgical purist has no time. This book takes very seriously the great moments of the traditional liturgical year, but it treats with as much seriousness those opportunities of contact when liturgy needs to be, in the best sense of the word, *evangelical*. I believe the Church of England must acquire both the confidence and the breadth to enter into the celebration of the catholic liturgy in all its richness, and thereby to deepen the experience of worship of its people, and yet at the same time to believe in, and to practise effectively, those less formal or traditional quasi-liturgical occasions, whether they be services for Harvest Thanksgiving and Mothering Sunday, or passion plays and outdoor processions, which have been its genius in the past. I also believe in the evangelistic and pastoral opportunity afforded by every baptism, marriage or funeral, not just by the contact they make possible, but in the actual liturgy itself of these occasions.

My reticence has not therefore been about whether this task should be undertaken from a specifically Anglican viewpoint, but about whether it should be I who tackle the task. Others have treated, and will treat, all the subjects in this book in greater depth and with greater scholarship. But no one has, to my knowledge, brought together in one manageable book as much material as this for use in the parish. I recognize that what I have written will soon be superseded, probably by other books, but certainly by better ideas, for nearly everything written about pastoral liturgy at the present time is provisional, because we are living through a great ferment of ideas. No clergyman should be ordering liturgy by this book in a generation's time. I shall certainly not be doing so. I am aware how my ideas have developed in the five years since *The Eucharist*[1] was first published, and the next five years will no doubt see greater development. In particular my colleagues of the Liturgical Commission are bound to show me the error of some of my ways. But if books on liturgy had to wait for liturgists to be sure they had got it right, we should probably have to wait a very long time, and the final product might be lifeless and boring.

I have hesitated also because of the limitation of my experience of some of the many shades of Anglican tradition. My own upbringing and early experience have enabled me to discover the strengths both of the Catholic tradition and of that style that would call itself simply 'Anglican' without any more specific label. My recent experience, travelling around a great English diocese, has made me increasingly familiar with forms of worship that owe more to charismatic, Evangelical and ecumenical influences. I have been very struck by the fact that it has often been the churches where these influences have been strongest that have been full, and, not only full, but vibrant with life, with people on the tiptoe of expectation both to hear God's word and to express his lordship in worship. I am conscious that in what follows I am not able to show sufficiently deep knowledge of these traditions by which the whole Church is being enriched. Nevertheless I hope that Anglican Christians who identify more fully with these traditions than I do will find this book helpful and will translate it, where necessary, into terms in which they are more at home. I have tried, for instance,

[1] Published by SPCK (second edition 1981).

to be sensitive about Evangelical suspicion of words like 'offering', 'priest', and 'blessing' of objects. Yet since they are used quite freely by the majority of Anglicans, their use here is inevitable. But another term could be substituted mentally where this remains a source of unease. This is not a 'party' book and my hope is that those who emphasize freedom and spontaneity in worship will not find its suggestions restricting or stultifying.

This book is not meant only for the parish priest. The first chapter argues as strongly as possible that liturgy is too important to be left to clergymen. It should be in every parish the responsibility, and the real joy, of lay people to help to find the forms of worship and patterns of services that can most effectively serve that community. Of course this book *is* for the priest, and I hope he may find it useful, but if he keeps it in his study, and locks himself there, with or without this book open before him, to plan the liturgy in his church, then I have failed to make clearly one of the fundamental points in which I believe.

I will also have failed if I have given the impression that I believe worship to be the only important thing that the Church does. Of course it is true that worship is a primary task of the Church, and this is all the more so because worship turns out to be one of the most compelling ways into both mission and pastoral care. I do believe that there is a relationship between worship and every other Christian activity, but I do not believe that a Christian congregation is fulfilling its vocation simply by ensuring that at the centre of its life is found satisfying worship. 'Getting the liturgy right' could become, and has become in some parishes, an excuse to turn aside from all the social, moral, pastoral and evangelistic opportunities and problems to which an alert congregation should be ready to respond. 'Send us out in the power of the Spirit' are as vital as any words in the liturgy. The thoroughness of the treatment of worship here must not be taken as a blindness to the Church's other tasks.

Chapters 6 to 18 are about the various Christian rites, sacraments and seasons. Using the index, the reader may use this part of the book as a source of ideas for different occasions. He need not read all those chapters 'at one go', so to speak, though I hope some may do so to get the total picture. But the first five chapters, which present the major themes and emphases of the book, are a necessary preface to using this as a source book. The reader is urged to read them before 'delving' in the later chapters.

My particular thanks to individuals and communities must be recorded. Like every other younger liturgist in the Church of England, I owe a great debt to the constant encouragement of Dr Geoffrey Cuming. In a year in which others have honoured his sixty-fifth birthday with the publication of *Liturgy Reshaped*, I am happy to be able to associate myself with that tribute by this acknowledgement. The Reverend Charles Taylor, the Chaplain of Westminster Abbey, has been generous in sharing his insights with me in the preparation of several chapters. Many clergy of the Winchester Diocese have both encouraged me and made helpful suggestions. The Bishop of Winchester, with whom I share many a liturgical occasion, has influenced my thinking considerably, probably more than he or I realize. I record my thanks to all of these, as also to Mr Robin Brookes, the Senior Editor of SPCK, who in all our dealings over several years has unfailingly shown characteristic kindness and courtesy, to Mrs Jane Miall, my secretary through most of the time in which this book was written, who made sense cheerfully and speedily of a difficult manuscript, to Miss Mary Matthews, my secretary more recently, who has helped with all the tasks that fall to the author between first draft and publication, to Mr Timothy Fairbairn, who has once again given invaluable help with reading the proofs, and to my wife Alison, who, in the months immediately before and after our marriage, never complained about the time devoted to this book and encouraged its completion.

But a book on liturgy must include, among its acknowledgements, not only individuals, but whole Christian communities in which the author has experienced the power of Christian worship. I have found that in St John's Church, Winchester, where, during the early months of the writing of this book, I was acting as parish priest, and where now I continue to worship and minister when other duties allow. I have learned at St John's the particular constraints and opportunities of worshipping in a tiny church with a small, but deeply devout, congregation. I have found it also in Winchester Cathedral, where it is my privilege, almost daily, to share in the timeless experience of Christian worship, lovingly and carefully ordered. I have learned there truths about the beauty of God's holiness that somehow must be translated into the very different ethos of a parish church if our liturgy is not to lose its soul. But, above all, I owe more thanks than I can express to the people of St Mary's Church, Addington, in Croydon, among whom I served from 1976 to 1981, and with whom I discovered the better part of what is written in this book. To them and to The Very Reverend Richard Norburn, Vicar of Addington throughout that period, but now Dean of Gaborone, this book is dedicated with immeasurable thanks.

Winchester   MICHAEL PERHAM
November 1982

1
Community Celebration

Let the People Celebrate

A Christian community conveys more than it probably intends of its theology of the Church or of its self-understanding by the way it orders its worship. It is right that it should, for in worship the Church is doing its characteristic thing. In a way, worship both reflects the Church's life and constitutes that life. The church in which the leading of worship seems to be the prerogative of one man, the priest, is more often than not the church in which lay participation in every other area is small. The church in which, in the chancel, clergy, servers and choir seem to 'perform', while, in the nave, the congregation enjoys or endures the performance, often with a great gulf of a screen fixed between them, is all too often an unhappy church of divisions, frustrations and misunderstandings. This is to generalize dangerously, but of many churches such comments will ring true.

Sometimes, however, things will look better than they are. Very often a church may seem to have taken on board intelligent liturgical reforms, but it will emerge on questioning that there has been no real understanding, by people and sometimes by priest, of the reason for the reform. Where lay people now read the lessons or lead the Intercessions, all too often it is explained that this is 'to relieve the vicar who is so hard pressed on a Sunday, rushing from service to service'. The thought that lay involvement in the liturgy says something fundamental about the nature of the Church has never been developed. This is not cause for too much concern, for future generations growing up with a liturgical style in which lay people play an active role will unconsciously assimilate a healthier understanding of the nature of the Church, but it will be a pity if valuable insights have to take a whole generation to make their impact.

Liturgical principles should reflect theological truth. The

'liturgical assembly', the community gathered for worship, is an expression of the nature of the Church. In our own century there has been a renewed understanding of the 'body' language that St Paul employs. To 'discern the Lord's body' is to comprehend at more than one level the meaning of the phrase 'Body of Christ'. For the mystery of the Christian Eucharist is as much about *being* the Body as about *eating* the Body, and the two are inextricably linked. Only those who have been drawn together into the Body can perceive what they do, and understand what they re-present, in sharing the bread of the Eucharist. Conversely, only those whose fellowship has been deepened and enriched by sharing in the eucharistic experience can really say with conviction and understanding, 'We are the Body'. Paul's use of the 'body' concept points to a variety of functions, all of which contribute to the life of the whole. Each has his or her value and gift, each complements another, so that there is a completeness about the whole.

We are learning that afresh in the Church of today. We are recognizing our individual gifts, our interdependence, and our incompleteness separate from one another. Within the liturgy, when the Church is asserting its identity and its shape as it responds to its Lord, this same structure should be apparent. It is *the Church* at worship. It is not a series of individuals who, for convenience sake, have gathered under one roof. It is a community which recognizes its dependence not only on a Father, who is in heaven, but on brothers and sisters, who stand or kneel together. To symbolize that, within the Christian community, there are both different functions and differing gifts; various parts of the liturgy are normally the prerogative of particular 'orders' – the priest presides, the deacon reads the Gospel, the laity read the other Scriptures, offer certain prayers, present bread and wine. Perhaps the fact that not every lay person is willing to be called out to do these public things witnesses to the fact that many ministries in the Church are hidden, anonymous and unrecognized. He or she whose silent prayer, or quiet reflection, is unknown to the community exercises a gift or ministry as real as he or she who reads. Other less obviously liturgical ministries contribute to the community's worship. Bells are rung, anthems are sung, flowers are arranged, books are handed out and collected in, hands are shaken and words of welcome spoken. All of these are liturgical gifts and ministries, experiences in the Church's worship of what the Christian life is like every day outside the church's walls. Bringing help, beauty and friendship into human life is an extension of these liturgical ministries. Or, rather, the liturgy enables these daily offerings of the Christian life to be given liturgical expression, so that the worship of the Church can be indeed a marvellous dramatic celebration of the Church's nature and *raison d'être*.

Christian worship is therefore always the activity of a community. Sometimes, as in the private prayer at home of an individual Christian, that community is not visibly present, but even then it is prayer nurtured by the Church's life and fellowship. Even the prayer of one hostile to the community is the prayer of one whose faith has been handed on and shaped by the community.

It is important that those who come to church on Sunday recognize and experience that it is *they* who celebrate, that Christian liturgy is their business and concern. It is not, in the end, something they can leave to others to plan and order. It is too important for that. Every parish needs to discover its own way of involving the people, at least occasionally, in the discussion and design of worship, so that they may feel that it is *their* worship that is offered to God, that it reflects their needs and hopes. In too many parishes, worship has been the one area that the priest has kept firmly within his own compass. Of course in this area many clergy have a sensitivity and an expertise that will be invaluable in the parish's thinking and doing. But others have a contribution to make, some a specialist contribution of music or literature or visual sense, some simply the contribution of those who learn to articulate their spiritual needs and ask how they may be met. Worship is too important to be left to the professionals. It is the people whose celebration the liturgy must always be.

'Celebration' is the characteristic Christian activity in worship. We use the word in two senses. In the more limited sense, we mean that praise, thankfulness and joy will never be far below the surface, and often will burst into song, in Christian worship. In a wider sense, we know that even when worship appears to be chiefly concerned with some other

3

aspect of Christian experience – confession, reflection, intercession – it is all within the context of a trusting joyful faith,
founded on good news of salvation. There is the celebration of
the party for the prodigal son behind every act of sorrowful
confession and search for forgiveness. There is an *alleluia* deep
down in every reflection or meditation, however anxious, per-
plexed or uncertain it may be. Sometimes it is the celebration –
the confident joyful life – of the Church's worship that carries
individuals along through personal agonies or doubts. But,
tragically, the Church's worship all too often lets the individual
down. This vital ingredient of worship is all too often lost. The
pages that follow in this book are, as much as anything else, an
attempt to help the Church to rediscover the joy of *celebration* in
its worship.

It is the pre-eminence of celebration as an activity of the
whole community that argues most strongly against the
traditional description of the president at the Eucharist as
'the celebrant' and, even more, of other priests grouped around
the altar as 'the concelebrants'. Every worshipper is a celebrant,
and the misuse of the term for particular ministries within the
service weakens the impact of that truth.

Celebration is never a superficial jollity or heartiness. True
celebration has about it a deep thankfulness for the gospel. But
often celebration does call for *sparkle*. David danced before
the Lord with exuberance gone a little wild. Jesus radiated
a thankful joy in life, in people, in his Father. Of course
traditional formal liturgical styles have conveyed a sense of
thankfulness and joy, but very often there has been a restraint
that has robbed them of the sheer vitality that should sometimes break through.

Within the total celebration, other elements and emotions
will have their place. In our own day, emphasis has been placed
more and more on the sense of fellowship. It has proved difficult to find the right level. In some churches the message
has still not been fully understood. Talk of fellowship has
increased, but it has been seen principally as an activity *after*
worship. For all its very real value, the parish 'breakfast', or get-
together over coffee, has obscured the truth if it has allowed
people to think of fellowship as what happens when the service
is over. The fellowship proper is in the service, around the

table, and what happens afterwards is simply the natural extension of it. Where the message has not been understood, the follow-up does *not* seem natural. The priest who finds that, exhort his people as he may, they will not come to coffee, should probably cease such exhortation and concentrate on building up a sense of fellowship *within* the service. The desire for informal fellowship will grow only from that. This is nothing new in Anglicanism. Thomas Cranmer envisaged it in the sixteenth century when he intended communicants to 'draw near' quite literally, not in some spiritual sense, and kneel together around the holy table for a considerable part of the Eucharist.

Other churches have received the message, but at a superficial level. These are characterized by an undue emphasis on the exchange of the Peace and by an inappropriate *bonhomie* at this point in the service. The restoration of both the words and the gesture of the Kiss of Peace is one of the great gains of liturgical renewal and, although its introduction has in many parishes been painful and divisive, for there is a risk and a vulnerability about it from which people shrink, it is now rightly established as an integral part of the liturgy in many churches. But in a minority of parishes there has been an exaggeration of its significance and it has become the expression *par excellence* of the community's fellowship. But it is the sharing of the bread and cup that is at the heart of such fellowship. That is the point of union one with another, just as it is the point of union with God. Brothers and sisters are drawn into fellowship with one another by their fellowship with the Father. It is sad when the Peace has so dominated a service that this truth is lost. A sense of proportion needs to be restored; the Peace is the opening greeting, a sort of identifying of the community, to open the proceedings that will lead to Communion. The Peace becomes the highpoint when it lasts too long, so that the flow of the service is destroyed, or where there is a sort of uninhibited enthusiasm that marks it out as the principal moment of emotional release in the service. For most congregations this has not become a problem. For many the difficulty remains the opposite one, that there is too much inhibition and too formal and stifled a greeting. Nevertheless the Peace has degenerated when it becomes the time of a cheerful five minute walk around, chatting to friends about a great variety of matters.

For the assertion, 'We are the Body of Christ', is, rightly understood, as breathtaking and stupendous a truth as the 'This is my body' of the Eucharistic Prayer. That God is really present in the congregation, that the body of worshippers constitutes the Body of Christ, is as great a wonder as the presence of Christ in the shared bread and wine. It follows that the hand that is stretched out to receive into it the hand of another should reach out with the same joyful reverence as the hand that is stretched out to receive the host. The idea of the Church, including its local expression, as 'a wonderful and sacred mystery', bringing to the Kiss of Peace a reverence and awe that is quite different from a back-slapping *bonhomie*, needs to be understood if this attractive and powerful symbol is to retain its effectiveness.[1]

There is a series of reasons why the element of fellowship has received such emphasis in contemporary worship. In part it has been simply that the liturgists have said that it is good, but congregations often resist very firmly what the experts tell them is good, and this emphasis has met with a significant answering groundswell of support among ordinary church-goers. In part it has been a laudable desire to make people feel welcome, as if such expressions as the Peace were chiefly for visitors. In part, at least in some churches, it has been a conscious desire to give liturgical expression to the 'Body of Christ' theology already discussed. But there are other reasons too – one is to do with the sorts of communities in which we now live. In a settled small rural community in the past, overt expression of fellowship during worship would seem un-natural and unnecessary. For in a community in which every-body knew one another, and met one another all through the week in various situations that formed part of village life, suddenly to greet one another in church in a solemn affirmation of what was self-evidently true was peculiar. But in our strange new world, the Church is very often not reflecting natural community life, but *creating* among rootless people and in

[1] *How* the Peace may be exchanged is discussed in my book *The Eucharist* (2nd edn, pp. 12f). See also *The Kiss of Peace* by Colin Buchanan (Grove Books 1982).

places without tradition or common history a sense of community. The creation of community calls for a more overt expression of it than the mere maintenance of it would do. Additionally, the expression of a warm and reassuring fellowship within the community is a real need for a Church that feels frustrated by an increasingly alien world. Strength is derived from the clinging together of those who feel threatened or a little afraid. As such the language and ritual of fellowship is both a reassurance and a danger, leading to insularity and exclusiveness, in the life of the Church.

None of this seeks to imply that an emphasis on the Church's fellowship is mistaken. It is simply that alongside friendliness and welcome, fellowship in the deep Christian sense also means joyful wonder. Where that has been understood, there is less likely to be the tension between those who emphasize the transcendence and those who emphasize the immanence of God. The contrast has become something of a cliché, but in a more subtle form it goes on worrying many churchgoers. Those who make much of participation – including the active presence of children – and of fellowship sacrifice something of the majesty and dignity of worship which we need if we are to draw close to God, or so the argument runs. The other side rejoins that God is to be found not in the distance – at a high altar way up there, so to speak – but in the fellowship and the mutual concern, sometimes the hubbub, down in the nave. Both have elements of truth about them. But the tension need not be there. Where the fellowship expresses itself in joyful wonder, then, far from detracting from the sense of the numinous, it helps to create it. Indeed a healthier understanding of the nature of the Church emerges where that sense of 'the sacred' is attached to the community more than to the building or the furnishings within it.

For, among the elements and emotions that have their place in worship, there must be a sense of mystery. Awesomeness is quite different from stuffy formality, but the words, actions and silences of worship must lift us up, so to speak, that we may experience a little bit of heaven. The atmosphere must be such that people can wait in quietness and peace upon God with an air of expectancy. This is often said to be missing in much modern worship. The blame is laid upon the allegedly impoverished language of the new services, or upon the music devised to go with it, or upon the rearrangement of the furnishings for a different style of celebration, or upon the presence of children. Where this sense is missing, the cause is often to be found, not in any of these explanations, but in a lack of care in the priest and prayerfulness in the people. Of words, music and furnishings, more will be said later. But there are many churches that have adopted most of the reforms in these areas of worship without any loss of dignity or of the glory of worship, and so a real explanation must be sought elsewhere. Nor is it fruitful to pursue the question of the presence of children as a distraction. For children (not babies, but children from the age of three or four) have an innate sense of reverence and an appreciation of atmosphere. They will often sit entranced by what they see or hear in church. Children brought into a congregation in which there is deep prayerful worship, or the sort of silence in which you can hear a pin drop, will very often (not always, of course) be totally absorbed by it. The church where the children do not seem to behave is often the church where the adults are not totally absorbed in what they are doing. Where there is something wrong, the priest and people must look to themselves, not to the words or the rituals or the children, to find the fault. The fault often lies with the priest who, in the name of informality and making people relaxed, has unconsciously become shoddy in his preparation and presentation of worship. Or perhaps he has simply failed to realize that the new liturgical forms, because they give him and his people far greater freedom, require of him far more work and far greater sensitivity. With the new services, priest and people have more opportunity to make or mar the Church's worship. Or else the people have been content with a superficiality of worship that has not touched them deep down; they have not become a praying community, totally absorbed in the celebration. Liturgy and spirituality have been divorced.

In the Anglican tradition, proclamation is an important mark of liturgy. The public reading of the Scriptures has from the time of the first Prayer Book been a major part of worship in the Church of England. The prominence of the sermon, though it does not have its origin in the Prayer Book, has become so well established that for many, especially of an older generation less enamoured of the new emphasis on eucharistic worship, to go to church is to go to hear a sermon. Whether in teaching the faithful, or preaching to the less committed, it is clear that worship, for all the fact that it is acted out towards God, is used by him as a means of bringing good news, or deeper faith, to those who have come to worship. But it is neither sermon nor lesson, for all their importance, that most effectively preach the gospel in any service. Among the words that are used, it is the oft-repeated words of the liturgy itself that go deepest. It is for this reason that the relationship between theology and liturgy needs to be well understood. The almost instinctive beliefs of the average worshipper are unconsciously assimilated as he hears repeated week by week the words that the liturgists write to express the Church's faith. Where these words are altered by the liturgists, a shift in the Church's theology will inevitably follow within a generation. Where these words are left unaltered, even when theological ideas have moved on, the theology of the worshipper will remain essentially conservative. Among the words that are used in worship, besides the invariable set parts of the service, it is the hymns that probably go the deepest, for their rhythm and rhyme make them memorable. The theology to be found in hymnody is therefore of great influence in the life of the Church. Words aside, it is clear that it is as much in the actions and symbols of the liturgy, and also in the atmosphere that the casual worshipper finds himself drawn into, that either the gospel is proclaimed or else, when the symbols are inappropriate or the atmosphere lacking, some less than Christian message is heard.

Priest and People

If it is true that Christian worship is the celebration of all the people, it follows that all must play their part. So it is that there has been much talk in the Church about the participation of the laity in worship, though what participation involves has sometimes been put in over-simplistic terms. Educational and theological ideas have come together in this renewed emphasis. The educational contribution has been twofold. Increased literacy has meant that a congregation no longer need rely so much on familiar texts. Most people can read and so there is a new freedom to experiment and vary. This is not the same as saying that everybody is familiar with books, for that is not part of everyone's cultural experience, but sufficient familiarity with the written word to be able to cope with variety in worship, and to allow the people to join in rather more of the liturgy, can usually be taken for granted. We have moved a long way from Cranmer's priestly monologue, with very occasional laboured congregational prayers repeated line by line after priest or clerk. Increased education also makes it possible in most parishes for lay people to read lessons and to compose and read prayers. Where there is not the confidence to compose alone, a group may well undertake this task. It is from the educational world also that the Church has learnt lessons about the need to do, not just to hear, if we are to learn and to benefit. The participation of the people means not only their joining in the words, but their involvement in the action and movement of the liturgy. But, however much educational principles and progress may give impetus to this renewed emphasis, in the end it is the theological principle that the worship of the Church should reflect the shape and pattern of the Church's life that is the key.

Lay participation is not chiefly about singling out individuals to do particular tasks, though that is part of it. First and foremost it is about entering fully together into what is happening. It is about being totally absorbed, caught up, in the words and actions. It is the opposite of being a mere onlooker or observer. That does not mean that participation always involves speech. We need to help people to understand how they may worship through what they see or what they hear. There are, for instance, too many places where congregations become frustrated at long choir pieces, even well sung ones, because they have never been helped to *pray* through the words and music that their choir sings. The ability to worship through watching and listening needs to be discussed and taught in every parish.

Nevertheless, speaking together remains the most obvious form of participation. Good congregational spoken responses in worship depend on leadership – the leadership of the offic-iant who by the way he addresses the people elicits the response, and the leadership of the choir who bring to the response a rhythm and a confidence which inspires the remainder of the congregation to join in vigorously. The leadership of the choir in the spoken part of the service is essential. Where there is no choir, occasional congregational practice is desirable.

There has been a tendency in some parishes to imagine that the more the congregation says together the better. This is mistaken. A successful service depends on an alternation between the clear expressive voice of solo speakers and the quite brief, but vigorous, response of the congregation. Long congregational recitations drag. The current liturgical trend to say, rather than sing, the Creed (for the best of reasons: the Creed is an affirmation of faith, not a song of praise) has shown this to be true, and the practice of 'concelebration' by clergy takes much of the power out of the language of the Eucharistic Prayer. The temptation to allocate to the whole congregation parts of the service traditionally reserved to one voice – the opening statement of the Peace, or the set text of the Intercessions, for instance – is usually best resisted.

Lay participation does include calling people out of the congregation to perform particular functions. Who should be so called out? The answer is that preferably all who are willing (even with gentle encouragement) should play a particular part as their turn comes round, whether in presenting the bread or wine, taking the collection, serving at the Eucharist, reading or leading prayers. To these must be added other more 'professional' ministries, such as singing in the choir, ringing the bells or playing an instrument. But very few ministries in church should be undertaken without training and rehearsal. Where the people complain that they cannot hear the reader, the fault often lies with the priest who has not ensured that there has been adequate training and practice. Nevertheless a congregation should be helped to be sensitive enough to accept occasionally a less than adequate reading, providing that it is a labour of love and represents the best efforts of the reader. Every such ministry is an *offering*, and a person's best is a worthy offering, even if another could do it better.

It is important that there does not creep into lay ministry in the liturgy any sense of hierarchy or élitism. It should never, for instance, be a parish policy that only the churchwardens or sidesmen read. It is undesirable that only members of a very

11

small group take it in turn to lead Intercessions. People should undertake such tasks sufficiently often to become relaxed and familiar with the task, but sufficiently rarely that they remember that they have no particular exclusive right to it and that their real place is alongside their brothers and sisters in the congregation. The practice of the Church of England, whereby only lay people licensed by the bishop may assist with the administration of the elements at the Eucharist, was introduced for the best of reasons, to sanction what was then a controversial innovation. Its effect now is unfortunate, for two reasons. In practice it tends to mean that this becomes the prerogative of the few, rather than being shared by a larger, and possibly changing, group. It also means that by making some tasks more 'official' than others, it introduces the sense of a hierarchy of ministries. Neither he or she who administers a chalice, nor he or she who gives out books, does so because he or she is 'worthy' to do so. Every ministry is by sinners for sinners. The Church should resist any move that seems to put a particular task, or the person who does it, on a pedestal.

A distinction is sometimes made, though more often in the Roman Church, between the tasks that lay people do by right, and those that they do simply because of the absence of those to whom they have been historically assigned. It is on this basis that the Roman Church does not permit women to serve at the altar; women were not admitted to the traditional minor orders whose task it was to assist the priest. In the Church of England such minor orders were abolished in the sixteenth century. It is difficult, and undesirable, to employ the Roman argument in Anglicanism. There is a strange imbalance, that has nothing to do with the *ordination* of women, in a church where no women have a place in the sanctuary. There is, for instance, nothing priestly about *administering* the sacramental elements and, where a congregation has called people out for this ministry, it is desirable that some should be women.

A word is needed about the dress of those who assist in different ways in the liturgy and about where they are seated in the church. (This is distinct from the question of the vestments of the clergy which will be discussed later.) Two sides of the question are sometimes in tension. The first is that all should be seemly and that excessive individualism should not draw the attention to, for instance, the reader rather than the reading. Such considerations would sometimes point to the wearing of special robes for such tasks as serving, administering the elements or singing in the choir. In addition, members of choirs sometimes feel a greater loyalty when they have a 'uniform' and young people often 'perform' better if particular dress has helped them get into their part. On the other hand, the 'uniform' that gives solidarity within the choir can also be one of the causes of a false distinction between the choir and the rest of the congregation, while ordinary clothes bring out the truth that the choir is part of that congregation, and not the only part to be exercising a ministry during the service. Those who assist the priest throughout the service are in a slightly different position. Because their ministry is so much a visual one, there is a need for some uniformity of dress, and an alb will often be appropriate. The single server at a said service might, however, quite appropriately serve in his or her ordinary clothes. But those whose sole task at the altar is to administer the elements should not be put in special clothes and assigned special status. They should come out of the congregation, dressed in their ordinary lay clothes, and return to it when their task is done. This is as theologically important as it is practically more straightforward.

The *Reader* (or Lay Reader, as he is often called) sometimes feels threatened by all this talk of lay ministry. He has exercised a lay ministry of great value for many years before such talk became fashionable. There is a need for sensitivity towards him. Nevertheless if his ministry is to be recognized for what it is, the ministry of a *layman* whose training has equipped him to exercise a liturgical and preaching ministry, it is better that he should sit in the congregation when not officiating, that he should wear distinctive dress only when taking the place of the priest at a service, and that all idea of a quasi-priestly figure should be played down. There is no need for a reader to 'dress up' or to have a special stall to read a lesson or administer a chalice, though both are quite appropriate if he is officiating at a service.

In the Church's tradition, the *Deacon* has always had a distinctive role. His principal liturgical task has been the reading of the Gospel at the Eucharist. It is good that, whenever a deacon is present, he should exercise this privilege. Other parts of the Eucharist that may sensibly be delegated to him are the Invitation to Confession, the Preparation of the Bread and Wine, the administration of the elements, the cleansing of the vessels, and the Dismissal. The origin of the greeting 'The Lord be with you' before the Gospel was the deacon's greeting to the people. When repeated by the president, who has already greeted the people only minutes before, it has less meaning. The deacon stands or sits next to the president at the Eucharist. Where a parish has a deacon, it will be well advised to use him in this way. Quite apart from the argument from tradition that this is his role, it is good training for a man soon to be priested to be at the president's side to experience the liturgy as the priest does, and it enables the diaconate to be, at least liturgically, a fulfilling ministry. The curate left idle in his stall through his diaconal year can be very unfulfilled.

Where there is no deacon, his traditional tasks are variously assigned to priest or lay people. If a parish finds it convenient to have at the Eucharist an 'Assistant'² who undertakes these tasks, and probably announces hymns as well, he or she may be priest, deacon or lay person. The Reader may in some parishes be the obvious choice for such a role, but, on the whole, it will probably be better if a variety of people undertake this role in turn, taking their place in the congregation on other Sundays. In many parishes, the reading of the Gospel (as distinct from the other readings) has been the prerogative of the clergyman. In the Roman Church, where there is no deacon the priest alone may read the Gospel in his place. There is no such rule in the Church of England and there is no virtue in having an invariable policy about it in any parish. There are times, especially in informal settings, where lay reading of the Gospel seems wholly appropriate. Nevertheless, the highlighting of the Gospel, both by procession and lights, and also by its proclamation being reserved to an ordained minister, has some effectiveness.

The significant and varied roles of lay people in the liturgy do not detract at all from the role of the priest who presides. The term 'president' has drawn much abuse, though it goes back

² In *The Eucharist* I have set out in greater detail a possible role for the 'Assistant'.

as far as Christian liturgical records go. It is difficult to find a term that is theologically satisfactory and yet which appeals. 'Minister' and 'celebrant' both convey the wrong idea. The priest's task is to preside, to hold together. He is the symbol of unity in the local church, never more so than when he holds together all the different parts of the liturgy with their different ministers. This 'anchor-man' role is essential to worship. Many a service goes sadly wrong where a succession of readers make their contribution, without there being any sense of continuity, no feeling that somebody is 'in charge'. The opening greeting is reserved to the president. It establishes a relationship between him and the people. Thereafter he may delegate, though he reserves to himself parts of the service that belong traditionally to his order or that draw the liturgy or the congregation together. These are the Absolution, the Collect, the Peace, the Eucharistic Prayer and the Fraction. Where he stands or sits is often as important as what he says in creating a sense of unity and of his own presidency.

The task of the priest is a taxing one. He is to bring to worship a constant freshness, so that words and forms never seem stale or simply formal, and yet he is to give to every celebration a consistency that ensures that people are not confused or lost in a mass of unfamiliar words and movements. He is to bring to the worship all the insights that his pastoral work among the people has given him and to share himself at a deep level, and yet he is to have a slight reserve and a strict discipline that will ensure that it is Christ who is proclaimed, never himself. The personality of the priest can help or hinder worship, and he needs to be self-critical and to be willing to invite criticism from others.

There has been a growth in the Church of England of the practice of concelebration, by which a number of priests together say the words of the Eucharistic Prayer and share between them the various parts of the liturgy. There is an appropriateness about priests, with their bishop for instance, or within a team ministry, expressing something about their shared ministry and their relationship with one another, by standing side by side around the altar. But it is doubtful what precisely is supposed to be happening when they chant together the Eucharistic Prayer. Priests tend to like it – at an emotional, rather than a theological level, it strengthens them to act together in this way with their brothers – while the laity find it unattractive, not least because the force and clarity of the Eucharistic Prayer is lost when many voices say it together. The Roman solution, of dividing up much of the prayer between the 'concelebrants', avoids this, but destroys the unity of the prayer. The principal difficulty with concelebration is, however, not a practical one, but a theological one. There is no obvious room, in a view of the Eucharist that sees the people as celebrants gathered around a president, for a series of co-presidents. It will often be right for priests to express their solidarity by gathering together around the altar, but it will not often make theological sense for them to speak the words of the Eucharistic Prayer together. The Church of England has not made provision for concelebration in this fuller sense, and the practice will probably be seen in time to be a transitional practice of the Roman Church, designed to wean clergy away from private daily celebration, and which Anglicans have mistakenly taken over, failing to see the different history in the Roman Church that made it a desirable step there.[3]

Liturgy and Life

The Church's worship is never an escape from the realities of the world. People come to a service weighed down, or sometimes uplifted, by the world's concerns, and the Church must be able to respond to this. The enthusiasm with which the new freedom for intercession in the revised eucharistic rites was taken up illustrated how people responded to the opportunity to spell out their daily concerns within the context of the Church's worship. The enthusiasm for the 'Offertory Procession' illustrates the same point. The idea that in presenting bread and wine, people were offering their daily labour, and that in placing their individual wafer in the ciborium they

[3] This is how the Church of England Liturgical Commission has come to see it (*Concelebration in the Eucharist*, GS (Misc.) 163, 1982). In *The Eucharist* (p. 26) I expressed rather hesitantly the same reservation, but went on to set out a procedure for concelebration. I should now want to write less enthusiastically about such practice. See also *Eucharistic Concelebration* by John Fenwick (Grove Books 1982).

expressed something deeply significant about the offering of their own life, appealed to people in the early years of liturgical renewal. The appeal has remained. Liturgists are right to view this with some suspicion. Some very Pelagian theology has found its way into the Church through such practices, and a very functional element in the service has acquired so much attendant ceremonial that the Offertory Procession has been given a centrality far beyond what it deserves. Nevertheless this exaggeration is a symbol of the desire of ordinary people to see daily life, with its concerns and anxieties, expressed in the liturgy.

But the fundamental point lies in the *transformation* of the gifts. What we bring, God uses, God touches, and we receive back what we have brought, but receive it back transformed. The concern and the anxiety that we bring in our heart, as much as the bread and wine that we symbolically present, is touched by the hand of God and is given back transformed. That is the real point of connection between liturgy and life. It is, as often as not, an argument for time in worship for silence and reflection, as much as for urgent fervent prayer, time for God to touch and thus to heal. The liturgy may be at its most practical – helping the worshipper to self-understanding or to self-acceptance – when it seems most ethereal. People need to be helped to see that it is the *whole* of the experience of worship that can help them to face the realities of life, not any particular part, such as the Intercessions, in which particular anxieties are articulated.

There is a yet deeper level at which liturgy and life are inextricably bound. Liturgy is a bringing into consciousness of deep truths about man's nature. The liturgy of Holy Week and Easter, for instance, is not, in the end, an historical exercise, a glance back into the past to discover what happened to Jesus. It is about a remembrance that makes him present, and that makes his experience present, to the extent that I discover it to be *my* experience; and by entering into the way he lived through his experience, I find the strength to live through mine. If that is rather obviously true of the Holy Week story, it is also true of all liturgy. It reflects life in order that it may inform and transform life. The human being is a being of various emotions, high and low, ecstatic and depressed, excited and

17

relaxed. In order to minister to all these, in order that all these may be unconsciously recognized and responded to in worship, those who order worship must ensure that the same variety of emotion, and the whole cycle of human moods and experiences, have their place in the Church's services. The Christian Year, with its contrasts of restraint and outburst, sorrow and joy, is not principally to bring to mind the past, but to illuminate the present. Liturgy does not simply teach about a life, but is a dramatic acting out of every human life.

Styles of private personal prayer have undergone as much change in our own day as liturgical prayer. The two may even seem to have grown apart, for in personal prayer there has been an encouragement to throw aside set words, such as those found in the more traditional manuals of devotion. People have been encouraged to be more open and free, perhaps more honest, in their private devotion. All this has been for the good. But, now, all the more is it important that people should realize the relationship between personal and liturgical prayer. They should be helped to see that the richness of liturgical worship is a resource, often the principal 'input', for their private devotion. They also need to see that, if there is to be a revival of spirituality in the Church, they need to breathe into the words of the liturgy a deep inner devotion that can only come out of private and silent worship. In the Church of today we have concentrated too much of our attention on the revision of outward forms and too little on the revival of the spirituality that will give life to those forms. The richness of the liturgy, with its message of the fellowship of all Christian people in prayer and praise, must be joined to the deep hunger and longing of individual souls if liturgy, spirituality and life are really to be experienced as the unity they are. Renewal must follow from revision, and, for all the liturgists can do, renewal must start from the individual and the heart.

Structure, Freedom and Tradition

One great benefit of the changes in the law that have allowed the introduction of alternative services in the Church of England is that the revival and renewal of parish life can now be focused where it should be – in worship. The constraints that bound the Church before 1967 meant that, where there was new life, it had to break out elsewhere. In part it did so outside the institutional Church, but within the Church it emerged, for instance, in the house or study group movement. As the Church's life was renewed, yet the worship remained fossilized, worship seemed irrelevant to many. This was a grave misunderstanding of the nature of the Church, but it was almost inevitable in a Church where set forms, of an invariable and rigidly traditional type, were the compulsory weekly diet. Dissatisfied parish clergy tried to use the old rites imaginatively, but there were very severe limits to what they could do.

The Church of England has not found it easy to cope with the new freedom that the Alternative Service Book represents. On the one hand, there has been, in some places, the tendency to use the new rites like the old, to eradicate all options and variety and to stick rigidly to one way of using a service: 'This is the way we do it.' Evidence of this lies in the number of parishes which have printed their own versions of the new rites, excluding, in the name of simplicity, nearly all the variations available. On the other hand, in other places, the new freedom has been abused. The reforms have been seen as a green light to authorize anything and everything. A concern for legality, for order and for the security of the familiar has been thrown overboard, and what has taken its place has been far from satisfying. Extraordinary innovations and local customs, which owe nothing to either theological or liturgical principles, have grown up unchecked. They play into the hands of those who see no virtue at all in liturgical reform and denigrate the careful scholarly work of the revisers.

The familiar gives security. That is as true in liturgy as everywhere else. Liturgy is not always about security. Sometimes it has a duty to disturb and uproot. But, on the whole, it needs to follow a sufficiently familiar pattern for people to be set free from thinking about what to say or do next in order to *pray* the liturgy and allow themselves to be absorbed by it. This does not, in the main, apply to 'special' services, but to the weekly worship of the Church. There needs to be a shape and a structure to provide security. Within that shape and structure, alongside familiar and invariable texts, there is room for much freedom and experiment. Without that shape and structure,

19

the experimentation leaves people lost and bewildered. It is also important that the shape and structure should be *sound*. Both Eucharist and office, for all the difference between the two, have a satisfying balance, development and rhythm. The reason why so many more informal services fail to satisfy is not because the words are inadequate, but because the order is wrong, the content overloaded in a particular way. This is a matter of the utmost subtlety. It may sometimes be no more than the intrusion of one hymn too many, or a long stately hymn where a short sharp one would do, that destroys the development and rhythm of worship. About styles, shapes and structures, more will be said. Sufficient here to note that every exploration and experiment must be within boundaries, not for some legalist reason, but because, without it, there is an insecurity and unfamiliarity that leads to failure.

The change in our thinking about liturgical freedom has been revolutionary. For it has not simply been a matter of allowing us to exercise options and introduce variations at certain points in our worship. The effect of fifteen or so years of experiment has been to change the fundamental questions we ask. We no longer ask, 'What are we supposed or allowed to do?' We now ask, 'What does it seem right or appropriate to do?' The question, 'Is it authorized?', hardly concerns us. This can go too far, for we become congregational sects if we deviate too far from the norms laid down by the Church. Legalism is not a virtue, but church order has its place. The best liturgy is produced where there is a constant dialogue, so to speak, between tradition and church order on the one side, and the creative imagination of the parish on the other.

The Church of today is ambivalent in its attitude to the tradition, especially in worship. It is by no means consistent in what it retains and what it abandons. The Roman Church has rediscovered the liturgical principles of early centuries and reformed its worship thoroughly in line with them. Anglicans have followed a similar course, sometimes denigrating in the process their own liturgical revolution of the sixteenth century. All too often they have failed to appreciate that Cranmer is an ally, though not in every detail, and they have committed a grave error in allowing him to become a hero of the opponents of liturgical reform. Cranmer would have had no time for the defenders of 'Cranmer's incomparable prose'! The Church does well to take seriously both the creative era of the early centuries, from which emerge principles that have withstood the test of time, and also the Reformation insights (its *insights*, more than its texts) and to bring both into play in the creative debate out of which liturgy for today should emerge.

It does well to take them seriously, not only because it may learn from them, but because elements of the past, whether words or rituals, should have a place in our worship for deep spiritual reasons. Contemporary worship that excludes the rich heritage of two thousand years is an arrogant impoverishment of liturgy. There is within us a valuable need to identify with the Church of the ages, and to derive encouragement from that entering into a tradition that the use of the riches of the past allows. Where words have become obscure, or where rituals have lost their power, new words and new rituals that speak to us afresh must take their place. But it is at our peril that we sit light to the tradition. Liturgy must always be a conservative enterprise. It is not the place of the liturgist to enshrine in the service books of the Church the latest theological idea or experimental ritual. They have their place in the total worshipping life of a congregation, but before word or action finds its way into regular forms of worship it must pass the test of time. There has been an inevitable iconoclasm in the first frenzy of liturgical reform. But, for the future, creative imagination must constantly check itself against the wisdom of a rich and diverse tradition.

2
Word and Action

The Language of Liturgy

Worship is more than simply the words we employ to express it. Nevertheless the language of worship is an area in which great care needs to be exercised. Now that there is a freedom to compose words for worship, what criteria should be applied to test the value of what is written? First and foremost, the language of worship must convey, as accurately as possible, the *truth* as we perceive it. Because the language of liturgy influences the hearer, since it is often repeated, more than the sermon or even the lesson, it is important that it should be theologically sound. 'Is this what the Church believes?' is a question that should be posed by all who presume to write words for worship. The 'Thou–You' controversy about the manner in which God is addressed illustrates this. It is not so much that one form is right, and the other wrong, but that they indicate different views of the nature of God. One who wants to address God in a special language, to make him separate and, by implication, 'above' all others, is saying something about his theology. His view of God is different from the one who wants to address God more intimately, to regard him as a readily approachable being. It is clear that the latter view accords more with the pattern that Jesus gave, and was, paradoxically, what Cranmer was trying to achieve, for the 'thou' form had a different sound to it in the sixteenth century. This does not mean that the 'thou' form is unacceptable, but that those who use it should recognize that it implies something about *doctrine*.

Linked with theological integrity is the need to ensure that the words of worship express what is really in our heart, that we say what we most *want* to say. This implies a balanced theology in a service, and sufficient, but not undue, emphasis on the areas of Christian experience and doctrine that most seem to grip Christians today. Thus, what is wrong with the 1662

Communion rite is not, in the end, to do with the antiquity of its language or even its independent liturgical shape, nor with any defect in its theology of the cross, but in its theological *omissions*. It says next to nothing about the doctrines of creation, of the resurrection and of the Holy Spirit, all of which play a major part in theological reflection today. The 1662 rite, not unreasonably, represents the theological emphases of another age. The Wedding Service provides another sort of example. The 1662 Preface to the service, with its talk of 'brute beasts', represents the beliefs of its day about the nature of sex and marriage. The 1928 Preface modified this, because the 1662 words could no longer be used with integrity. Since 1928, there has been a revolution in thinking about human and sexual relationships. The Preface in the ASB reflects a careful contemporary Christian understanding of marriage. Those who opt for 'the old service' choose attractive time-honoured words, but are they able with total integrity to assent to its assumptions about marriage? We do the Church a disservice when we allow people to believe that the meaning of the words does not in the end matter too much.

The language of worship must also be intelligible. That does not mean that it must be conversational or in the style of the average tabloid newspaper (and, despite ill-founded attacks, the modern rites of the Church of England are not in any such style), for formal language for public recitation will never be identical with either a conversational style or a written style. But it does mean that it should not contain confusing anachronisms or unnecessarily technical theological concepts. Not all 'technical' language needs to be removed. Every institution or discipline has to have its own terms, understood by the initiated, but these are best kept to a minimum.

A further mark of liturgical language should be its beauty. It need not be the florid style of the sixteenth century. If its critics would only allow it to speak, they would discover in the ASB a distinctive style, crisp and clear, as attractive and compelling as any. It has its unhappy phrases, and most of them are the result of instant amendments by revision committees and on the floor of the Synod, sometimes destroying the painstakingly creative work of the authors. But a style and a rhythm liturgy must have, and where parishes write their own material for anything but occasional use, they should be prepared to draft, redraft and maybe several times start again, though such a process is not of course necessary or desirable for a 'once-off', possibly informal, act of worship, where spontaneity has an attractive freshness and appropriateness. There is, of course, a danger in always laying emphasis on the beauty of the language of worship. Beauty can sometimes obscure the impact of hard sayings and, since the role of liturgy is sometimes to challenge and disturb, there is a place for the phrase that jars. Unravelled from its King James' English, the message of the Old Testament prophets is often stark and shocking. ·

Liturgical language should also mean what it says. 'Draw near with faith' should mean that the people get up and come to the altar rail, not remain in their places while the clergy communicate as if they were some privileged group. 'Go forth in peace' means 'go forth' and becomes nonsense when it turns out to be an introductory formula for a further hymn. 'O Lord, open our lips; and our mouths shall proclaim your praise' is an equal nonsense after a rousing and spirited first hymn (though both Prayer Book and ASB recognize a validity in some words, but of penitence, before we stand to open our lips in praise). 'The Lord be with you' is obviously a greeting when it is the first sentence the president addresses to the people, but, when he has already given out notices, and possibly said 'Good morning' as well, it appears as another meaningless ritual. We have grown used to a sort of 'spiritualizing' of liturgical language, so that the plain sense and meaning seem irrelevant. Even 'Let us pray' has simply become a spoken rubric about posture, rather than a call to prayerfulness. We do liturgy an injustice when we allow people to think that its words are simply pleasing phrases without exact meaning.

Body and Senses

To turn from words to movement, we find that liturgy is more than the words we say. Indeed a frequent criticism of Anglican worship is that it is too cerebral. We worship not only, not chiefly, with our mind. Every sense is employed: we see, we hear, we touch, we smell. Light, colour, music, movement and, in some traditions, incense, aid our worship. It is the whole self that is offered to God, and those who plan worship should see that all senses are effectively employed. But it is more than the use of the senses. It is the whole body that is involved. It is part of our human make-up to express worth and value in a bodily, as much as a spiritual, way. Indeed Christianity wisely declines to separate the two. We often express the deepest feeling of love in physical touch and union, for words alone have failed us. So, as we approach God, our human nature bids us express our adoration with our whole selves. We need, in ordering worship, to be prepared to take the body seriously, whether by incorporating gestures that express love or wonder or petition (and such traditional gestures as the bending of the knee or the making of the sign of the cross are of this sort), or by recognizing that *variety* of posture (but not too much of it) is desirable for the congregation to be relaxed, and that there are *appropriate* postures for different parts of worship. In the Roman Church, kneeling has been reduced to a minimum. There is no merit in a slavish following of this in Anglicanism, and to kneel to confess or to intercede seems to be the usual appropriate posture. But Anglicans could learn more of the suitability of standing for words of thanksgiving and praise, as in the Eucharistic Prayer. Still, quite extraordinarily, some churches retain the kneeling position for the Peace and the *Gloria*. Of every part of the liturgy, priest and people need to ask, 'What kind of emotion is being expressed here? What posture is appropriate for that?'

The use of body and of senses implies a significant place for *ritual*. The word is an emotive one, but it is simply the name we give to the actions of the liturgy. Sometimes, rarely, these movements are simply ceremonial to please the eye. There is no purpose in them except to provide stimulation to worship. There is nothing wrong in that. It is the equivalent in movement for the eye of what music is for the ear. But, more often, ritual has a symbolic significance, a sort of sacramental meaning. Just as the best music is combined with words that inspire, so the best ritual conveys something important about the nature of God or of the Church. Where the meaning of the ritual has become obscure, or has lost its application, the practice needs to be challenged. In some churches, following an ancient tradition, the reader faces north for the Gospel. Most people do not know why – the symbolism is lost on them. A few know that it is because the gospel must be taken to the north where the heathen are – and realize the symbolism is outdated and meaningless. At the Royal Maundy Service, the sovereign and those with her carry posies and the almoner wears a towel. Again most people do not know why – the symbolism is lost on them. A few know that it is because, once upon a time, the sovereign washed the feet of his or her subjects, the towel was to wipe the feet, the posies were a protection from the smell – and for them the symbolism is a striking reminder that the sovereign today does not undertake this act of humility. The symbolism is exceedingly unhelpful. Those who order the worship of a church need to ask sometimes, 'Why do we do this? Is this symbolism saying what we want said?' Ritual becomes dangerous, and a religion of its own, when the meaning is lost, and it becomes an end in itself.

Furnishings

With the movements of the liturgy may be considered the furnishings of the church. Here something ought to be said of altar, lectern and pulpit, chair and font.

History has given us in many churches more than one, often several, altars, and we have sometimes added to them in the present generation a 'nave' altar for celebrations where the president faces the people. A multiplicity of altars is not a helpful symbol and we may wish that history had given us just one, with possibly a second in a small chapel for weekday use. But, unlike the Romans on the continent, we should not abandon and leave unused the side-altars. Such neglect is a sad sight in many of the churches on the continent. But there are some simple principles on which to work. Where the existing 'high' altar can be moved forward, whether a little, or a long distance in a major re-ordering, this is preferable to the erection of an additional main altar in front of it, for the two then compete as the focal point of worship. However, against that principle must be put the need to consider the design and line of the chancel. In many churches there is *room* to re-order, but such re-ordering does violence to the architecture of the building, or the furnishings, so re-ordered, are not pleasing to the eye. Where that is the case, there is a choice. One possibility is the placing of a second main altar in front of the other, but unless there is a fair distance between them this will appear untidy. The other is to accept the need for an eastward-facing celebration, but to order the liturgy in such a way that the whole of the Eucharist, save that part from the Offertory to the Communion, is conducted from the chancel step at a chair or lectern. It is simplistic to maintain that the building must *fit* the liturgy, even though it would be foolish to maintain that the building must *dictate* the liturgy. There must be adaptability both in the use of the building and in the manner of the celebration. There is no 'right way' to celebrate the Eucharist, only a way found to be most appropriate for any particular building.

There are four further principles, all of them quite small points, that make for a more intelligent celebration. The first is that it is the altar at which the Eucharist is being celebrated that is the focus for any reverence that is made. For clergy, servers or choir to turn their back on the altar at which the Eucharist is being, or has been, celebrated to reverence some distant altar unconnected with the celebration is nonsense, for the reverence is shown to the altar because it is the focus of Christ's presence in the Eucharist and has itself become a sort of sacrament of Christ and his presence in the Church. Similarly, it is nonsense to turn one's back on the altar of the celebration to face another in the distance for, for example, the *Gloria*.

The second principle is that reverence to the altar should never become so fussy that it delays the action of the liturgy. Most obviously this means that, where the members of a long procession, whether of choir or clergy, are going to their places or leaving them, they should not all stop, two by two, to reverence the altar, but when all are in their places should reverence the altar together when the president does so. It also means that a reverence to the altar at the beginning and end of the service is sufficient. Bowing within the sanctuary can easily be overdone. At the end of the service it is often appropriate for the ministers in the sanctuary to reverence the altar from their seats behind it, rather than after forming up especially to do this in front of the altar.

Thirdly, those who stand behind the altar should be aware of the fact that it is always a mistake to *kneel* behind it. From the congregation it looks ridiculous. In the Roman Church, the celebrant alone is instructed to genuflect when behind the altar, but a profound bow is undoubtedly preferable.

A final point concerns receiving Communion at a celebration at a nave altar. In some churches a custom has grown up of 'celebrating' at a nave altar, but then transferring the elements to a distant sanctuary to administer at the altar rails that enclose it. This is a most unfortunate practice. The Eucharist should be so ordered that, to as great an extent as possible, the celebration has the feel of the people of God gathered around the table to celebrate together. Numbers will usually dictate that they cannot 'gather round' until the moment of the administration, and 'gather round' may in practice mean kneeling in a row, but at least it is at the table of the celebration. If there is no room to stand or kneel around a nave altar to receive, it would be better to administer from a 'station' before that altar than to go off to some distant point to administer. (Such an argument relates, of course, to the normal Sunday celebration, and does not apply to the use of several Communion points at a vast eucharistic gathering.)

If the altar is the focus for the action of the Eucharist, so it is desirable that there should be a focus for the Ministry of the Word. All too often, where reverence is shown to the one focal point, the reading and exposition of the Scriptures has no such focus. Lessons are read from lectern, pulpit, the body of the church, the chancel step, without any sense at all of the unity of the Liturgy of the Word. The ideal will normally be to read all the lessons and to preach the sermon from one place, at a lectern in a prominent position. It becomes for the first half of the Eucharist the focus that the altar provides for the second. The Gospel, the high point of the Ministry of the Word, may be given special emphasis by bringing to the lectern at that point lighted candles.

However there is a long and attractive custom of a 'gospel procession', with the proclamation of the Gospel in the midst of the people, all turning to face the book. In a small church this is not particularly effective and the Gospel is probably best read at the lectern. But, in a large church where such a procession makes much sense, the unity of the Ministry of the Word may be maintained by another symbol – the Bible, or Book of

Readings, becomes the focus, rather than the lectern. The book is brought into the church in the procession at the beginning and is taken to the various points from which the Scriptures are to be read. It is desirable that one or other of these symbols of unity should be employed.

The pulpit, as a furnishing distinct from the lectern, is not necessary. The unity of the Word read and expounded argues for one setting for both. Churches will rightly be unhappy to abandon the use of the pulpit, often a fine furnishing of the church, even though many clergy find the elevated position of the pulpit unsuited to modern preaching styles. In some places the answer will be to use the pulpit, rather than the lectern, for the whole Ministry of the Word. The reader will usually be better seen than from the lectern. In other places, the abandonment of the pulpit at the Eucharist will be accepted happily enough, provided that it continues to be used at other services. In yet others, it will be considered that, desirable as this principle of unity may be, it cannot be said to be so important that the traditional design and balance of the church and its worship should be lost.

It is less easy to see whether arguments about the unity of the Word should influence the use of lectern and pulpit at services other than the Eucharist. Where, as at Morning and Evening Prayer, the whole service is a Ministry of the Word, some variation and movement, rather than a uniformity, may be called for. What always remains undesirable is for the reader, clutching his small-print Bible, to be positioned vaguely on a step. The priest would not stand at the credence table to preside at the Eucharist: he stands at the altar. The reader should stand at lectern or pulpit.

Mention has been made of the president's chair. This has symbolic value, as well as meeting a practical need in a liturgy where the priest should be seated during readings and silences. Ideally it is placed behind the altar, and raised a little above it, and in new churches and in re-orderings this is becoming the norm. But it can be placed elsewhere in the sanctuary or, in a church where most of the liturgy is at the chancel step before moving to the altar at the Offertory, at that step. Without dominating the assembly, it should nevertheless be placed in such a way that the president can *preside*. He should be visible, as the chairman of a meeting would be visible even when others were speaking. It is possible to use the clergy stall in the chancel in this way, but it will not always seem appropriate. *Presiding* at a celebration and *officiating* at an office are different activities, and have a different feel to them. At the 'office' the priest does well to merge with the people. At the Eucharist he has a symbolic role as the point of unity. A chair in or near the centre, where he may sit with his assistants, is ideal. If not too grand, the chair often referred to as 'the bishop's chair', possibly moved to a new position, will often meet this need. There never has been a tradition of a chair for the bishop alone in any church except his cathedral, but there is in any case an appropriateness in the priest using it to preside at the Eucharist, for he presides only as the bishop's deputy and local representative.

The font is the focus of the liturgical action in Baptism. The contemporary Church has taken very seriously the importance of this sacrament of initiation and has sought to express this by ensuring prominence for the font. Sometimes this has meant a special area of the church known as the baptistry, but quite apart from the space wastage in modern buildings where such space is valuable, a special area tends to be far from the altar and lectern, and often hidden from the mass of the people. It is important that the font should be seemly. It is also desirable that it should have a permanent place in the church. It is a symbol and a reminder, even when not in use, as much as the altar is. But the principal need is that it should be clearly visible to the people during the liturgy, in order that Baptism may be administered in their presence and view. In many modern designs the font takes the place of the pulpit as the third focal point of the sanctuary – Word, Baptism and Eucharist are seen as a unity. That has a lot to commend it. But, equally, the old custom of the font near the door, the symbol of entry into the Church, is a valuable one, but only provided that the font is in such a prominent position at the end of the nave that all may turn and face it to *see* the sacrament administered.

It would be a mistake to deny the importance of altar, lectern or font and to maintain that it is only the *action* of the liturgy that matters. The focuses that these furnishings provide are genuine helps and teaching aids, and a God working through sacramental forms can reach people through the wood or stone of which they are made as through bread and wine and water. But they do have equal value in a balanced theology. If the altar is treated with exceptional respect, enclosed within the 'sanctuary', but the font is used as a depository for books, messages or casual flower arrangements, that equality has been lost.

Music

Music, of various types, will play an important part in the liturgy. A book such as this can mention no more than the briefest principles. It is unfortunate that many church musicians are opposed to liturgical reform because for them it often seems to mean a lowering of standards. The priest who introduces a new rite is often also the one who brings in second-rate guitarists to accompany folk songs. It cannot be said too strongly that co-operation between priest and musician is almost a precondition to liturgical renewal. The priest must find a way of sharing with the musician the *principles* of liturgical reform; the musician must be helped to *understand* what it is all about. (In such a task the Royal School of Church Music can be an ally, and sometimes the musician will listen more openly if the help comes from that source.) The priest must acknowledge that the choirmaster, or organist, is the church's Director of Music. Only ill-feeling and distrust can emerge where the priest, anxious to by-pass the organist or choir, introduces an independent parish orchestra or folk group. The choirmaster may well be willing to give his blessing to such enterprises and leave their organization to others more in tune with the priest's hopes. Or he may accept responsibility for training them and develop in that a flexibility and freshness he had lost over the years with the choir. The priest should also try to ensure that the musician is involved in the parish's Worship Committee, or its equivalent. Encountering, and perhaps being converted by, the enthusiasm of lay people for new forms, the musician will no longer see these as the priest's personal whims and can no longer think in terms of the all too frequent vicar-organist battleground.

Both priest and choir should know their limitations. The priest should ask for honest assessment of how well he sings and should remember that as he grows older that ability declines. The fact that he sung a long Preface beautifully when a curate does not mean that he can still do so at sixty, but few will have the courage to tell him; he needs to ask! Where he has a poor singing voice, he should delegate to a member of the choir appropriate parts of the service. The versicles and responses at Morning and Evening Prayer, for instance, may quite reasonably be sung by a layman. There are just a few parts of the liturgy that are not suitable for delegation. The opening dialogue of the Eucharistic Prayer is an example. This is essentially a dialogue between president and people in the build up of the drama of that prayer. Here the priest must retain the words to himself and should *say* them, rather than attempt to sing, the congregational response also being said.

But the choir also needs to recognize its limitations. There is a tendency in many small parish churches to imitate the cathedral style. In particular such a tendency often means the attempt to sing anthems or settings, written for professionals, and for voices of greater range and ability. For priest and musicians, the rule should be the pursuit of excellence. But excellence here means doing what you can do exceedingly well. It means striving after a high standard of performance, but it should not mean an attempt at music beyond the capability of the performers. Excellence will, more often than not, mean simplicity.

For some clergy, however, the problem often seems to be, not the choir's limitations, but its ability. A 'choral tradition' can be a great joy, and an enrichment of liturgy, but it brings its own challenges. One of the problems is the frustration of those who do not appreciate the amount of non-participatory music in the service. This frustration is not something that can be ever swept under the carpet, so to speak. In the right way the priest must help the congregation to talk it through, to try to reach some agreement on the amount of purely choral music desirable. But he can also help people to learn to pray through the music they hear. People need help to enable them to understand that worship employs every sense and to listen and hear can lead into a deep reflection in which there is true worship.

Another problem, quite easily resolved once it has been identified, is that a congregation used to leaving the singing to a choir becomes lazy in its habits; it also leaves the choir to respond to all the said parts of the liturgy. Lack of audible participation in the singing leads to weak unconvincing responses in the spoken part of the service. A congregation will usually mend its ways, if this is gently pointed out and an occasional practice given.

A third problem for the musician is the disappearance from the modern rites of the texts of the liturgy for which most church music has been composed. This need not cause great problems, for the rubrics permit the use of the traditional texts for the sung parts of a service, and this is in no way different from the frequent use, in churches of a great choral tradition, of Latin words with traditional English liturgy. There is no need for the introduction of, for instance, Rite A Holy Communion, to mean the abandonment of traditional settings. That said, it is very desirable that churches with fine choirs should sometimes persevere with the new texts in order to find good music for them and to encourage the composition of this. Such music is more likely to appear in response to a genuine need. As it is, there is a far greater choice of music for the new texts than most parishes, which seem only to have discovered the most 'popular' three or four settings, realize.

One of the characteristics of the new rites, and not only in the Eucharist, is the Acclamation, the short, sharp outburst of welcome, praise or glory. On the whole, these do not lend themselves to musical arrangement. But, when said, they can often be limp and unexciting. To *acclaim* is more than to say. Choirs may lead in these liturgical shouts, but congregations need to practise. People need encouragement to let themselves go. It may be the parish priest, or it may be the choirmaster, who will rehearse them. But, for acclamations, for other choral speaking, for new hymns and new settings, the congregational practice – perhaps just five minutes before or after the service quite regularly, or for a whole hour once or twice a year – is vital. There is always a place for spontaneity in worship, but there is a place for careful preparation too, not only for priest, but for all the people.

A brief word is needed about psalmody. Many congregations dislike the psalms, because they associate them with the difficulty of singing, with an unpointed Prayer Book, Anglican chant. Yet the liturgists, recognizing that the

Eucharist is the only Sunday service most people attend, have increased considerably the provision for psalmody in that service. There is a host of ways of using the psalms. It is sad that this rich treasury of spirituality is so neglected, and there would have been an argument for making a few verses of psalms, in some form or other, a mandatory part of the liturgy. The congregation could remain seated while the choir sings Anglican chant – a beautiful form of singing with those who are skilled to use it. Or they could join in, singing plainsong, so easy once they have been taught, or with a responsorial psalm, such as the Romans usually employ. There is a loss with this latter style, for some of the rhythm is lost; and rhythm, almost more than the meaning of the words, is what gives the psalms their power.[1] Or the psalms may be said – slowly, rhythmically, antiphonally, seated – and that needs a great deal of practice. But, once mastered, it is found to be a marvellous aid to worship. The spirituality of the monastic life is, after all, based on the recitation of the psalter. The spirituality of ordinary parochial congregations can also be enriched by it.

In trying to avoid the division represented by the screen, the 'us' and 'them' of choir and the rest of the congregation, it is worth being careful not to present 'choir' and 'congregation' as distinct bodies. It is *'the remainder of* the congregation' that sits for the anthem, not 'the congregation'. The choir is part of the congregation, the assembly. So are the servers. So is the priest.

---

[1] The use of psalmody, especially a responsorial psalm, of which an example is given, is found on pp. 23ff of *The Eucharist*. Pp. 29ff discuss further some of the musical issues raised here.

3
Sunday

Possible Patterns

The traditional Church of England pattern of three Sunday services, an eight o'clock Communion, a main service mid-morning, and Evensong at 6.30 has collapsed in the majority of parishes. The collapse has sometimes been due to the need to devise a pattern that allows the priest to minister in more than one church, or sometimes to the need to conserve energy resources by heating the church for shorter periods, or sometimes to an emphasis on the Family Eucharist to the exclusion of all other services, or sometimes to a desire to be flexible that has abandoned all sense of any pattern at all. For some parishes, one service a day, at whatever time, has proved satisfactory. The whole church community *meets* for worship and there is no sense of different types of people gathering at different hours for their own sort of service. Where this pattern emerges naturally, it has much to commend it; the unity of the Body of Christ is visibly demonstrated. Particular demands are, of course, placed on those who prepare the worship: where there are no alternatives, there is a special responsibility to ensure that the service can meet genuinely the needs of a great variety of people who bring very different expectations with them to church. But in most churches, the one service Sunday is neither feasible nor desirable, and there needs to be a pattern, though a more flexible one than in the past.

It is very important, however, in such parishes that the whole worshipping community occasionally comes together. A real sense of unity can be maintained through the weeks when the parish worships as a series of smaller units, provided that the whole body sometimes meets. This is a major problem only in parishes where the principal reason for dividing the congregation is the size of the building, and in most churches it is some other factor that divides. Two possibilities suggest themselves for the unifying great occasion. One is the use of a fifth Sunday in the month. Where such occurs, four times a year, the usual Sunday pattern might be suspended, and just one service, for the whole church community, be held at an acceptable compromise time. In the summer it might be in the open air. Wherever it is, an opportunity for less formal fellowship might also be incorporated into the time together – a parish lunch or a picnic, for instance. The other possibility is to make much of the great feast days that fall on weekdays – Epiphany, Ascension, Patronal Festival, for instance – and try to gather the whole community together for the celebration on these occasions, though it is difficult in commuter areas to find a time early enough for children, but late enough for workers.

In many churches the early said celebration still has an important place. It is over-simplistic to believe that those who come to this service are always those trying to avoid the later celebration, whether because of the rite used or because of the presence of children. Some come for that reason, but others come, for instance, because the time is more convenient in relation to their work or child-minding, or because the 'eight o'clock tradition' is a long and deep part of their spirituality. Automatic provision of nothing but the Book of Common Prayer is not desirable. If there is a broad cross-section of worshippers present, there may be a case for alternating that rite with one from the ASB. Or, in some parishes, the provision of Rite B may be best every Sunday, for in some places the pressure is to provide a traditional *language* rite, rather than to provide the Prayer Book structure. It is unfortunate where an eight o'clock congregation, using nothing but the Prayer Book within a non-participatory atmosphere, grows further and further remote from main-stream church life. There needs to be a point of contact between old and new, at the same time as sensitivity to the spiritual needs of what may be a most conservative element. This may be achieved simply by following the Prayer Book instruction to have a *sermon* at every celebration. It need not be, indeed should not be, more than a very short homily, normally an exposition of one of the lections, but it has its place and is an opportunity for the priest to ensure in a quiet way that those who come only to that celebration have their faith and church life challenged and deepened.

There can be no general rule for the timing of the mid-morning service. Local conditions or history will often dictate a particular time, and what is appropriate in a farming community, where there is work to be done before going to church, may be very different from what is ideal in suburbia. But, where possible, there is much to be said for an early start, at 9.30 or 9.45, for this opens up two useful possibilities. The first is that, either regularly once a month, or occasionally as need arises, a second, probably non-eucharistic service, can be fitted into the morning at 11.15 or 11.30, without interfering with the social gathering that follows the main celebration. The second is that, after that gathering, there can be parish meetings of various sorts, whether the PCC and its committees, or groups for study or discussion. In many parishes this time could well prove more suitable for such activities than the traditional evening meetings. Many people would willingly give, at least monthly, the whole of Sunday morning, in return for less pressure on a weekday night, quite apart from the desirability of linking the Church's business and study so closely with its worship and fellowship. The earlier time is also necessary if some of the ideas to be mentioned in the following section are to be possible. A time as late as eleven o'clock will nearly always discourage not only these possibilities, but even the presence of the majority of the congregation at tea or coffee after the service.

There has been some reaction in the last few years to the movement, loosely called 'The Parish Communion Movement', that has made it a fundamental principle that the Eucharist should be the main service of every Sunday. The principle does not need restating. At a whole series of levels, from theology through to the power to fascinate and maintain interest, the Eucharist is the best expression of the Church's nature and the most fulfilling form of worship for the committed Christian. The fact that some good churchpeople, whose pattern of spirituality was shaped before the movement for liturgical renewal, have not found this to be so does not challenge the basic truth of the principle. And, indeed the chief need in this area of the Church's life is not a retraction of that principle, but a more thorough application of it, so that people become genuinely *eucharistic* men and women, their whole life and spirituality strengthened by their weekly experience of eucharistic worship of word and sacrament in all its richness.

That stated, and stated with strong conviction, the recent reaction needs to be taken seriously. Sometimes the protest is because of a fear that there has been real loss in the area of preaching, teaching and training. The biblical and didactic element is smaller in the average Parish Eucharist than in the traditional Morning Prayer. The fault lies not so much with the Eucharist, but with the inflexibility of the form in which we celebrate it, and in our own limited expectations of what can be done within it on a Sunday morning. Ideas in this area are set out in the following section. They, and ideas like them, could meet very adequately the need of the Church to rediscover the power of the Word, as we had to rediscover the power of the sacrament, without a sort of 'pendulum swinging', so to speak, that would undermine the achievements of the Parish Communion movement by making the Eucharist one of a series of options, rather than the setting for a variety of experiences related to worship.

But there is a more difficult and challenging side to the reaction. It is that, ideal as the Eucharist is for the committed, it is not (as it *was* not in the early centuries) a suitable vehicle for mission. Yet preaching to the fringers and the half-committed is a vital part of the Church's life, and worship ought to be a vehicle of it. The Church must meet people where they are, not where it wishes they were! It is possible to overstate this argument. The Eucharist can convey a great deal about the Church and its Lord to the most casual of worshippers simply by the atmosphere of worship and fellowship within the community, and now that non-communicant adults, as much as children, are encouraged to come to the altar rail for a blessing, there need be no sense of exclusion. But this is not enough, and every church needs to provide worship that requires no previous knowledge of the Church and its ways and employs no technicalities of language or ritual to baffle the un-initiated. Yet to simplify the Eucharist to make it fit that need, as some clergy do, is to deprive it of all the rich associations and symbolism that give it its power. The moment it becomes a wholly satisfactory 'missionary' service, it ceases to fulfil the weekly communicant. The monthly 'Parade Service' of uni-formed young people provides a particular example of this problem.[1]

[1] But see Chapter 7 for a discussion of liturgy for young people.

There are two principles here and both are valid: the weekly Eucharist is the heart of the Church's life, but the proclamation of the gospel is at the heart of the Church's mission. Some church communities are large enough to sustain a second major service in the day. If this is so, a Family Service of some sort, whether weekly or monthly, may be held later in the morning, as suggested above. Such a service should, rarely but occasionally, be eucharistic, but very simply so, in order that it may always be a *bridge* across to full sacramental participation in the Church, rather than a different sort of experience. Or, the main Sunday morning service should once a month be non-eucharistic; but on that day a sung Eucharist could take the place of Evensong, so that there is still a major opportunity for family eucharistic worship. In parishes where numbers or manpower dictate that there should be only one sung Sunday service, judgements will vary on how, if at all, to fulfil both principles, but it is possible to devise, for monthly use, a form of the Eucharist that is sufficiently simple to be suitable for use with those on the fringe or with children, that has ample time for teaching, but which does incorporate the sharing of bread and wine.

For some country parishes, there are very real problems in maintaining any sort of pattern at all and, unless the Church responds very speedily to the opportunities presented by the movement for Local Ordained Ministry, weekly eucharistic worship will be impossible.[2] Perhaps the most important principle is that, where times of services, or the form of service or, in multi-parish benefices, the place where it is held, have to vary, care should be taken to ensure stability or predictability as far as possible. Variations in time are less unsettling if there is continuity of form and content. Conversely variation in form and content are manageable if the time of the service doesn't change. Some element must be fixed, else the sense of security that rightly forms part of worship is lost.

The Parish Eucharist

The weekly Parish Eucharist at the heart of the parish's worship is the norm assumed throughout this book. That does not mean

---

[2] Provision for non-eucharistic worship, in the absence of the priest, is discussed in the following chapter.

that other forms do not have a valid place, whether the Family services mentioned above, or Morning and Evening Prayer, to be discussed in the next chapter. But the Eucharist is the most satisfactory and enriching experience for the committed Christian, and there is a place within it for much of the familiar and valued material (psalms, canticles and responses) from the office.

The Eucharist is *the* family worship and is often advertised as *Family* Eucharist or *Family* Communion. The term can be misunderstood and can also betray an insensitivity in the way the service is organized. It can be misunderstood because people think it is *for families* and can be insensitive when it seems to be catering for them alone. Many loyal churchgoers are single people, some are widows, quite a number come only with difficulty, leaving behind other members of the family less than enthusiastic about their church commitment. It is important that, when they come, they do not in any sense feel, 'This is not for me'. There are churches that seem geared to nothing but parents with youngsters, or to young people only if they are in couples. Such styles can actually foster loneliness. If the word 'family' is to be used about the Eucharist, it must only be as part of a constant education about the fact that it is the Eucharist *of the family*, that is, of the church congregation, itself a family to which all may belong, rather than the Eucharist *for families*.

That said, it is important that careful thought be given to adequate provision for children in the liturgy, not because they constitute the Church of *tomorrow*, as people sometimes say, but because they are part of the Church of *today*, with rights and needs as great as those of everyone else. Children of pre-confirmation age will need provision for worshipping and learning at their own levels, and it will not usually be appropriate for them to share the Ministry of the Word at the adults' level. But it is important that they should feel genuinely part of the worshipping congregation, not an alternative to it. Sunday School, Junior Church, or whatever it is called, is always a part, never an alternative. Ideally this means the children coming into the church in time for the Peace and all that follows from it. Where the rooms in which the children work at their own level are conveniently at hand, it may also have been possible for them to be present for the opening hymn, greeting and preparatory prayers before going to their rooms for the Word at their own level. But all this assumes a convenient modern church complex of rooms, or at very least a church hall within a couple of hundred yards. Not every parish has this. Sometimes the youngsters have to meet too far away to be able to come into the service, or sometimes they have to meet in the church but at a different time. Where this cannot be overcome, some sense of being involved in the Church's worship can be maintained if some parts of the liturgy are used, some of the same hymns, readings and prayers, even elements of the same structure. 'We sang such and such a hymn this morning', says Jimmy at lunch. 'So did we', replies Dad, and the sense that what Jimmy is doing is 'kid's stuff', out of which he will grow, is lost. It would also be good if the parish priest could, just occasionally, leave the adult service in the hands of others and spend the time in the hall with the youngsters. His presence there makes much the same point.

The principles by which the Parish Eucharist may be a lively celebration of the whole congregation have been discussed fully in the previous two chapters (and I have written elsewhere about the precise details of the text of the new rites and styles of presentation).[3] It is important for a congregation to have devised and understood 'our way of doing things', and to know where it is. It is equally important not to be too enslaved by this! People are set free for occasional variety by the familiarity of the established structure. To give one example, a congregation will cope with a deviation, for a particular good reason, from the norm it has established, for instance, that it has the penitential material in Rite A at the earlier of the two points permitted. But it will not take kindly to there being no norm at all, the priest making his own judgement as the mood takes him.

There is occasionally good reason for a more fundamental departure from the basic structure. There is no harm in this, providing that it does not happen too often and that it is not sprung upon the congregation. On a particular Sunday, for instance, there might be a plan to present the gospel story in

[3] *The Eucharist* (2nd edn) discusses, section by section, the text, and appropriate ceremonial, for Rite A, Rite B and Series 3.

drama or dance. Sometimes the acting out of the Gospel, rather than its simple reading, would fit easily into the usual shape and structure of the service, the actors taking up their positions during the 'Gradual' hymn, and the priest preaching on what they had done when the sermon followed the gospel-drama. But, on another occasion, the drama might seem to dictate a switch around of the service order. It might need, not a sermon after it, but a short spoken introduction to it, not an Epistle reading before it, but a few words of St Paul as a reflection on it in a time of silence after it. Or, if the story was one of those where Jesus forgave sin and brought healing, prayers of Confession and of Intercession might be incorporated into it, the action of the drama being 'frozen' while these happened. Or *Gloria in excelsis* might fit best as the response of the people to the whole drama, the congregation's equivalent of the praising of God by participants or onlookers in several gospel stories.

In other words, the ingredients of liturgy are themselves present in the story and the shape and structure of the story provides, on this occasion, a better order for the Ministry of the Word than the usual one. It must be said that none of the Church of England's eucharistic rites gives sanction to such rearrangement, but such careful and occasional deviation seems to be in the spirit of the new liturgical forms, provided that a series of important questions are always asked: Does this still look like the eucharistic assembly? Is there a role for president and people? Is the Word both read and expounded in some way? Is prayer offered and are the elements of confession and intercession present within it? Is the move back into the familiar pattern for the second part of the service a natural or a clumsy one?

The need to tackle the teaching element in the service in some way other than a sermon will sometimes dictate other changes. Though only an exceptional preacher will hold a congregation for more than about fifteen minutes, some forms of study and discussion could reasonably need more time. Again, what a parish can do will depend on the flexibility of its building, but, where it is possible, it would be advantageous sometimes to divide the congregation up into groups for well-prepared and carefully led Bible study, or discussion, on the readings for the day. The congregation could divide after the preliminary greeting and prayers and reassemble either to say the Creed, or for the Peace if the Intercessions are better done informally in the smaller groups. When anything like this is undertaken, the careful planning involved must include a sensitivity to those who will find participation in a small group quite threatening.

The rubrics of the ASB permit the integration of Morning or Evening Prayer with the Eucharist and, though the same provision is not made for the Prayer Book services, it would be within the spirit of the reforms to use Prayer Book Mattins, perhaps with the address after the second reading as the ASB allows, in place of the first part of the Eucharist, which would begin with the Peace in Rite B. The marrying of the two is not ideal, and there would need to be a very strong pastoral argument to justify it on all but the rarest of occasions. Normally it would be better to employ the eucharistic order with the generous use of psalms and canticles from Morning or Evening Prayer, for the rhythm and shape of an office is different from that of a celebration, and the respective roles of priest and people are different too. In a parish where only one sung service on a Sunday is possible, the Ministry of the Word might sometimes be replaced by the 'Family Service', provided that the structure of that service had been carefully thought out.

There is not a great deal of opportunity for variation or rearrangement in the second part of the service, the Ministry of the Sacrament, apart from the alternative Eucharistic Prayers in both Rite A and Rite B. The pattern is basic and innovation, for innovation's sake, pointless. But in many churches the time taken for the administration of the elements makes for an imbalance in the service. It is right that all should come forward, communicants or not, but in large congregations the administration takes so long that the shape and atmosphere of the service is lost, and children become restless. The obvious answer lies in the use of Communion 'stations' and all receiving Communion standing but, though people accept this in cathedrals and at open air celebrations, they often resent it in their own parish church. It needs talking through within the congregation. A possible compromise is to use the Communion stations when there are the largest numbers, at festivals or, perhaps, at a monthly parade service, but to use the slower procedure of receiving kneeling at rails at other times.

Sunday Evening Worship

Although Evening Prayer has remained popular in a number of churches, often those where there has not been the strong emphasis on the Eucharist that has undermined all other forms of worship, in most churches attendance has become low and, in some parishes, Sunday night can very profitably become the occasion for house groups and study circles. Their meetings can be timed to coincide with television or radio religious broadcasts, avoiding all problems of taping suitable material. Such groups might consider ending their meeting with a short office said together, so that Evensong will after all find its place in the parish's Sunday.

Some parishes, finding it a struggle, are undecided whether to persevere with Sunday evening worship. There is something to be said for retaining an evening service, however small the number who come, in order to have a nucleus on which to build for special occasions, but the attempt to maintain a fully sung service, in the body of the church, and with a sermon preached as if to a great crowd, is often mistaken. There are a number of alternatives to the conventional Evensong, some of which could be part of a regular programme, and some of which would feature less frequently.

The Eucharist might be celebrated, to meet two needs. In a parish where, once a month, the main morning service is a non-eucharistic service, the evening service on this day could be the Parish Eucharist. The other need is for provision, in some places, for the elderly of a celebration at an hour later than 9.30 in the morning. Old people sometimes take a very long time to get up in the morning and to expect them to reach church by 9.30 (or eight o'clock if they want the Prayer Book) is asking too much. An evening celebration meets such a need. The evening service, once a month or once a quarter, might also provide the opportunity for the choir to sing a great choral service, whether Evensong or a specially devised festival service, of the sort published by the Royal School of Church Music. Choirs are usually patient about the restrictions put on them, provided that occasionally they are permitted to burst forth into their own choice of songs. Or the evening service could be an occasion to meet in the church for the office, and then move to the hall for a filmstrip or to the vicarage for a discussion. Or, perhaps, once a month, an evening service might be replaced by an afternoon service at which baptisms were administered, such a service being a necessary provision in some parishes.[4] The evening may also be a time for regular united services.

Many examples will readily come to mind of special services that can fit into such a pattern during the course of a year – a service for those to be married, a service with the laying on of hands for healing, a 'Songs of Praise', and many more. House groups, or parish organizations, or all the church people in one street, might take on responsibility for an evening service of their own devising and draw to it, through their personal contacts, those who would not normally be in church. In a small minority of Anglican parishes, Sunday night has always meant Benediction of the Blessed Sacrament, and, though that is not part of the tradition of most churches, and raises for most Anglicans some real theological difficulties, an occasional evening service that was a reflection on the morning's Eucharist, a chance to express together the thankfulness for it that the individual keeps to himself, in song, silence and prayer, without the rituals associated with Benediction, would meet a real need for those who do not find enough tranquillity in our modern celebrations.

But all these suggestions point to a carefully devised annual, or quarterly, programme for the evening. Whereas stability, continuity and predictability are all virtues for the main act of worship of the week, balanced variety and experiment, suit- ably set out in a programme and well advertised, could well be the mark of evening worship. The pattern could even include the monthly Sunday night when everybody (even the vicar) agreed to stay at home with the family. Sunday evenings in many parishes provide far greater possibilities than are often realized.

A word may be said about the office of Compline. In some places, Sunday evening meetings or discussions might well

---

[4] The need for such services and suggestions for their form are discussed in Chapter 6.

end with this quiet prayer for the end of the day, beloved of many Anglicans, although it has no official place in our liturgy. The 1928 Prayer Book rite is usable, though structurally it is unnecessarily complicated, and the language is of course traditional. Unofficial modern forms have now appeared. A parish might happily use one of these, or adapt the new Roman rite, which is now called Night Prayer, or else use the ASB Shorter Form of Evening Prayer. If this is used with one of the traditional evening psalms, and with a very short lesson, it provides a very satisfactory form of late night office. But where, whether on Sunday or weekday, one of these forms is used with an address, the office should usually follow, rather than precede, the address, for it is a liturgical form of 'good night' prayer – 'I will lay me down in peace.' More talk after the words of Compline strikes the wrong note.

4
Morning and Evening Prayer

The Office as a Sunday Celebration

Despite the re-emergence of the Eucharist as the principal Sunday service, in many parishes Morning or Evening Prayer still attracts good numbers, either as an alternative to the Eucharist on some Sundays or as an additional choral service. It was one of Cranmer's strokes of genius to devise, unwittingly, a form of service that, for many generations, seemed to serve equally well the needs of both Sunday congregation and also parish priest in his daily office. In only a very small number of parishes has the ASB succeeded in the same way. Its form of the office has not had great appeal, in the main because those who prefer an office form to the Eucharist are not, in general, those who respond most readily to the modern language of the ASB order.

To use Morning or Evening Prayer as the main service of a Sunday is to change it from being an *office* to being *the celebration*. Such a comment does not apply to a parish where Evensong supplements a Parish Eucharist, for there the evening service may well have the quiet reflectiveness of an office in intentional contrast to the morning celebration. But where Morning or Evening Prayer is the principal service, and the only service for the majority present, it takes on a celebratory, quasi-sacramental form. This involves a subtle change in style and a slightly different role for the officiant. At a straightforward office, the officiant, whether priest or layman, is not prominent, sits 'in choir' and gives only sufficient leadership to allow the service to continue smoothly. Where the office has become *the* celebration, he becomes rather more 'the president', acting as a focus and 'anchorman', ensuring that parts of the service are delegated to others, but that a unity is maintained, as at the Eucharist, by the way he presides. Whereas the office proper has a gentle rhythm and no sense of climax (it has *development*, but that is not the same thing as a build up to a high point), the celebration often needs this. Where imagination is used in relation to movement and ritual, as well as to words, a gospel reading, for instance, can serve this purpose, or some communal prayer or expression of fellowship at the end of the service may achieve it. Purists of a certain sort will maintain that this is a misuse of the office. But it cannot be entirely wrong, when, used in this way, it has given spiritual sustenance to many generations of Anglicans. Nothing is more ridiculous than that strange Anglican custom of extinguishing the candles after 'the third collect' to indicate that the office proper is over and what follows is not a real part of the liturgy.

The opening of the service needs special care. The Prayer Book begins it with a penitential preface, after which is said or sung, 'O Lord, open thou our lips; and our mouths shall show forth thy praise', and the lips then express that praise in psalmody (at Mattins always *Venite* before the psalms of the day). Where, as in the ASB but common practice for generations, a hymn (often a great hymn of praise) has preceded the penitential section and the call to 'open our lips', the power of the penitential preface is lost and the words of the responses become futile. An opening hymn must *follow* these and, at Morning Prayer, follow *Venite* (to which, in the ASB, *Jubilate* and the Easter Anthems are alternatives).

In parishes where the form of service varies from Sunday to Sunday, it is desirable to be consistent about a lectionary. Where Mattins and the Eucharist alternate, for instance, as the main Sunday morning service, it is wise to follow every Sunday the eucharistic lectionary (which in the ASB always provides an Old Testament reading) whichever form of service is in use. The ASB makes provision for silence after the readings and there is no reason why this should not happen when the Prayer Book offices are being used. About 45 seconds is right in most settings. Another provision of the ASB that might be employed with the older services is the option of preaching the sermon after the second lesson. The development of the service from 'Word' to 'Prayers' is clearer this way.

The structure of the office calls for sensitive choice of canticles. At Evening Prayer, psalmody leads into Old Testament lesson, followed by an incarnation canticle that acts as a bridge between Old and New, then the New Testament lesson and a canticle that reflects life in the new age – 'For mine eyes have seen thy salvation'. The ASB (like the interim revisions) reverses the Prayer Book order of *Te Deum* and *Benedictus*, so that *Benedictus* becomes the morning equivalent of *Magnificat*, and *Te Deum* of *Nunc Dimittis*. This revision is a helpful one and parishes that use Prayer Book Mattins would do well to reverse the canticles in this way. The singing of hymns (whether called 'office' hymns or not) at any point between psalmody and second lesson destroys the shape and development of the office. As has already been said, it is immediately before the psalm, and thus before this development has begun, as part of the opening praise, that a hymn is better sung.

The ASB makes wide provision of alternative canticles. This will be welcome, especially in penitential seasons where *Benedicite* never seemed to sound the right note as an alternative to *Te Deum*. Parishes following the Prayer Book service would do well to make use, nevertheless, of the canticle 'Saviour of the World' from the new order as an alternative to *Te Deum*. It would, however, be a pity if the norm of *Benedictus* or *Magnificat* as the 'bridging' canticle were lost in an enthusiasm for regular alternatives, partly because no other canticles can perform this 'bridging' function as satisfactorily, but also because the unchanging 'gospel canticle' at the heart of the office has a value simply in its unbroken use through the centuries and its universal use today. *Benedictus* and *Magnificat* are used daily in the offices of the Roman Church. Variety of canticles after the second lesson is wholly desirable.

The Prayers at Mattins and Evensong have traditionally followed the collects and preceded the sermon, though with hymns intervening. But the increasingly popular practice of leaving the prayers until after the sermon, and relating the two, has obvious merit. The leading of such prayers is discussed later in this chapter.

In some parishes, particular feast days have been marked by a 'Festal' or 'Solemn' Evensong. This may involve special music and often a degree of ritual not usually associated with the office. Where the office is being regarded as a *celebration*, and on a feast day this may well be appropriate even where there has been a great eucharistic celebration, it seems right to give it a special festal flavour by, for instance, making the officiant more obviously the *president,* attended by acolytes, who might highlight the second reading as a liturgical gospel, and by omitting the penitential preface and, where there is a choral tradition, singing the opening *preces* and responses at the door before a solemn processional entrance during a hymn preceding the psalm. There is also a tradition of a procession of choir and clergy towards the end of the service, but this has its difficulties and is discussed below (in Chapter 17).

In parishes where incense is used, Solemn Evensong has often meant the censing of the altar during the *Magnificat.* This has been in imitation of the Roman Solemn Vespers, but in that service prayer immediately follows the canticle and the censing of the altar is seen as preparing the sanctuary for the offering of prayer. But, in the Anglican rite, the congregation next sits down for the second lesson and the point is lost. But, in any case, the altar is not really a focus at the office. If there is a focus, it is, at least in the Anglican emphasis, on the Word, and it would be better to cense the gospel book before reading the second lesson as a liturgical gospel in the way suggested above.

The Family Service

In some parishes, there can be a weekly Family Service, in addition to the Eucharist, in others a monthly Family Service, sometimes as a substitute for the Eucharist. In others the Family Service will be for special occasions, such as Mothering Sunday or Harvest. In yet others it is in the form of a Parade Service for uniformed youngsters (but see Chapter 7 for more on this form).

Some very practical considerations connected with any service become all the more important when dealing with Family Services: judgement about the length of the service, for instance, or the different postures during the service, or the provision of books and service sheets, or the visibility to the congregation of the leaders of the worship. Family Services, especially where there is no set printed parish order for regular use on such occasions, require greater preparation than formal liturgy and more, not less, attention to detail. The less 'churchy' the congregation, the more it needs to be given confidence by somebody who knows where the service is going and how to communicate to all the people their role in it. It is also important that, in the right way, families are put at ease about the place of the children in the worship. The parents must be helped to relax and not to be anxious about whether children are doing the right thing. But, equally, both parents and children must be helped to understand and enter into a simple *reverence*. Making everybody feel at home does not mean encouraging children to run wild in a way that they would *not* do at home! In a gradual and unstuffy way people must be drawn into a sense of worship.

Those who lead such services need to be clear about their *general* aim. Above all they are seeking to give people this sense of worship. But in a Family Service the aim of *teaching* the faith will often be dominant and the need to create a sense of the Church's *fellowship* will also be strong. They need to know for whom the service is provided. Is it for the regular churchgoers who, on other Sundays, would be at the Eucharist, or for those on the 'fringe'? Is it genuinely for *families*, or just for children? There is a world of difference between a Family Service and a Children's Service. The style will in part be dictated by the answers to these questions. They will also need to be clear about their *specific* aim. What precisely are they seeking to celebrate and teach on this particular occasion? A Family Service needs a theme.

Alongside aims, the leaders will also need to keep in mind those principles of creative worship that they will have learnt in more formal liturgical settings: the need for shape, development, balance, climax, for genuine participation and for the engagement of all the senses. So often these disappear in the Family Service, even when they have been carefully followed in other settings. There is a *right* order to assemble the material in the Family Service as much as elsewhere. There is a need to have a balanced content in terms of prayer, praise, Scripture, teaching, music, etc., as well as the incorporation of 'high points' such as drama, Peace, or procession. Quite often in the service where congregational participation is most important, it is most lacking because the congregation have no service book or leaflet. A Family Service for which only a hymn book has been issued is bound to be leader dominated.

If family worship is not to be divorced from the Eucharist, and is to lead people on to the communicant life, it is important that the Family Service incorporates material from the Eucharist. *Gloria, Sanctus* and *Agnus Dei,* for instance, can happily find a place in the Family Service, and the music for them learnt, so that they are familiar when later encountered in the Eucharist itself. For a similar reason, it is often good that, where there is a regular Family Service, its form should occasionally (perhaps one time in six) be the Eucharist, celebrated with simplicity and careful explanation as it goes through. The Eucharist with commentary is a useful exercise occasionally. Even when the Eucharist is not celebrated, the first half of it (especially in Rite A where the penitential material comes at the beginning) could often form the basic shape for the Family Service, with the exchange of the Peace leading into Lord's Prayer and Blessing, though in this case the Prayers of Intercession need to have a strong flavour of thanksgiving, to compensate for the omission of the Eucharistic Prayer. When the Family Service is not eucharistic, it must nevertheless be an occasion of *sharing.* Something shared or something taken away, something tangible and, in a sense, sacramental, needs to have a place alongside the verbal.[1]

Where there is no Priest

In some parishes, especially in the rural areas, a priest is not available every Sunday for the main service. The conduct of worship is therefore in the hands of lay people, whether licensed readers or others to whom permission has been given to exercise such a ministry. There is no need for one lay person to dominate the service any more than the priest need do so, and there should be a sharing of the leadership of the service. Nevertheless it is desirable that there should be one officiant to maintain its cohesion. What will be best is if he or she can meet in the previous week with those to share the leadership in order to decide on its content together.

There is more than one possibility for the order of service they

---

[1] Dr Kenneth Stevenson's booklet, *Family Services,* published by SPCK for the Alcuin Club in 1981, provides an excellent guide to the compilation of such services.

may employ. In some places Morning Prayer or Evening Prayer will be suitable, in either its Prayer Book or ASB form. In others a Family Service, along the lines discussed above, will be appropriate, at least occasionally. But there are some places where *eucharistic* worship has so much become the norm that to return to a form of service abandoned some years before seems retrograde and unappealing. Such parishes may find the use of the first part of the Eucharist a happier solution. This is what in former days was called 'The Ante-Communion', but in this setting is better called 'The Ministry of the Word'. The service is used, with the penitential section at the beginning (in its later position at the end of the service it would strike the wrong note) and the 'us', rather than 'you', form at the Absolution, up to and including the Intercession. The rubric instructs the minister to add the Lord's Prayer, the General Thanksgiving and/or other prayers, ending with the Grace. The addition of the General Thanksgiving, or an equivalent, is important for the balance of the service. It takes the place of the Eucharistic Prayer, the first part of which could itself be adapted into a fine seasonal non-sacramental thanksgiving. It will sometimes be adequate to lay greater emphasis on the thanksgiving element of the Intercession, but, in general, a confident congregational act of thanksgiving will form a good climax to the service. A parish that expects to use this form of service regularly would do well to provide itself with a series of such thanksgivings available for congregational use.

The other major element that will be missing when the service ends prematurely is the experience of fellowship that the sharing of the bread and wine brings. It is this sense of loss that parishes sometimes seek to meet by administering bread and wine consecrated on a previous occasion, 'the reserved sacrament' as it has been traditionally called. But the House of Bishops, acting on the advice of its Doctrine Commission, has issued guidelines about the use of the consecrated elements outside the celebration itself, 'extended Communion' as it is coming to be called, in which, as a general rule, it deprecates the use of the reserved sacrament to provide for an ordinary Sunday congregation in church. The Eucharist is, after all, much more than the sharing of bread and wine. It is, in fact, more than 'Holy Communion', using that term in its narrower sense. It is the total action of the Eucharist that constitutes the body and, in general, it is theologically healthier, when there can be no full celebration, to abstain from Communion. This cannot be made an absolute rule, and it may sometimes be the judgement of the parish priest that the pastoral value of such Communion from the elements, either reserved at a previous celebration by the same community, or brought from a celebration at the same time in another church of the parish or group of parishes, outweighs the theological problems incurred. But, if he does so decide, careful teaching must precede such practice and the sense that what the congregation is doing is an *extension* of the Eucharist, either from another Sunday or from another place, must be understood. A congregation must also recognize that as a permanent, or semi-permanent, provision for the spiritual life of a parish, such a service is unsatisfactory. If weekly eucharistic participation is thought important, the parish must come forward with proposals in line with current thinking about local ordained ministry.

But, if the sharing of the consecrated elements will usually be inappropriate, in some other way the sense of fellowship must find a place in the Sunday service. One possible solution is to include the Peace, even though the rubric does not encourage it and, technically, it is part of the eucharistic action. To meditate on the theme 'We are the Body', when the bread cannot be shared, is both to build in the sense of fellowship and also to point to that eucharistic fellowship that the community is perhaps only able to express monthly. Even where the 'Ministry of the Word' order is not followed, where there is Mattins or some other form, it is important to build into the service this element of fellowship in some appropriate way.

The idea of self-offering also needs to find a place because, again, this is an important theological and psychological part of eucharistic worship which will otherwise be lost within these non-sacramental orders. It is a real need, as Anglican ritual over the offering of the collection illustrates, even if it has Pelagian dangers. Whether a grand elevation of collection bags is the best way of expressing it is doubtful, but in some way, in word or ritual, this element needs to be present. Section 7 on page 105, and Section 86 on page 173, of the ASB provide suitable words in which to express it at the climax of the service.

Leading Prayer

Too often the Prayers at the Sunday services are a painful mixture of styles, a use of inappropriate forms and an attempt to employ far too many words. Whether at a formal Mattins or Evensong, or at a less formal Family Service, whether led by priest or layman, there are simple principles that can make a good deal of difference.

Unlike the Prayers of Intercession at the Eucharist, these prayers do not have to be chiefly prayers of *petition*. There is a place for adoration, for silence, for thanksgiving. All too often clergy who preach that there is more to prayer than asking for things betray the same imbalance in themselves when prayers are turned into a stream of requests to the Almighty. Nor are these prayers, unlike those at the Eucharist, intended to bring before God the whole range of the Church's concern – prayer for the Church itself, for the world, the local community, the suffering, the departed. The Eucharist tries to encompass all these because it is the offering of the whole man and the totality of creation to God. But, at other times, a more restricted aim is more helpful. On occasions, the theme of the service will be sufficiently dominant and wide-ranging to give the subject matter for the whole of the Prayers. At other times distinct but related themes will emerge. It is only on a rare occasion that a congregation will cope with more than four separate themes and prayers. Often four will be too many.

The most common form of prayer is the *collect*. This disciplined form of prayer has always appealed to Anglicans, who have based many thousands of prayers on the model provided in the Book of Common Prayer. Frank Colquhoun's *Parish Prayers*, published in 1967, exemplifies the best in this tradition. But collects are not by themselves enough, nor are they best used one after another. They are brief, almost terse, summings up in a simple and general thought of a series of more specific biddings. Thus they are best used in the Prayers preceded in each case by biddings, by silence and, perhaps, by a familiar congregational response. It will often be that only one collect, at the end of the Prayers, will sum up a whole series of biddings, to each of which there has been a silent and spoken congregational response. Where set prayers, whether collects or others, are to be read without such introduction, the briefest 'Let us pray for . . .', or 'Let us thank God for . . .', is necessary if the congregation is not to spend the whole prayer wondering for what they are supposed to be praying.

It is only a short step from extemporized biddings to extempore prayer itself, replacing the collect. Sometimes this is appropriate, for all too often the set prayer is not precisely what one is praying for, but verbosity, cliché and the sort of informality of language that would be appropriate in a less formal setting, but jars quite horribly in church, have to be carefully avoided. The danger of the extempore prayer is the monologue. Even if only at the level of an occasional response and an *Amen*, the more traditional type of prayer gives the congregation its part. Those praying in their own words need to build this in as effectively. In much the same category is the meditation type of prayer, made popular by Michel Quoist's *Prayers of Life*. This has to be used with great sensitivity. The man or woman leading prayer will nearly always find his or her *own* words more effective than the calculated chattiness of some written meditations in this informal style. They are very effective for personal reading and as a springboard to personal devotion, but they can sound hollow and false read out in church. Michel Quoist's own writings, though they are not as commonly used as ten years ago, have not worn thin, but his are an exception. Where the immediacy of colloquial language is lost by being committed to paper and read out by one other than its author, the effect is often anything but helpful.

Whatever style is used, there needs to be about the Prayers on any occasion a consistency of style. From week to week variety is good, but within the five minutes or so of prayer on a particular occasion, it is unhelpful to mix styles, from Cranmer to Quoist via the ASB and an extempore prayer. One week let it be bidding, silence, response and traditional collect, another week an extempore meditation, another a litany, another a few sentences of Scripture and a prolonged silence. But the mixture of these on a single occasion is confusing.

A word more may be said about the use of a litany. The ASB provides a fine Litany, and a shorter version of it in the appendix to Rite A Holy Communion. This, or litanies from other sources, may be used happily for the Prayers, as part of a varied pattern. But care should be taken in three respects. Firstly, a litany needs to be said slowly and reflectively, for it is so packed full of ideas that, if at all rushed, much is lost. Secondly, a litany must not suffer from interpolations that destroy its rhythm. 'Especially we pray for . . .' at the end of a delicately balanced petition is unfortunate. But the litany may be preceded by specific biddings in order that its flow may not be interrupted once it has started. Thirdly, a litany must be such that the congregation can easily respond. Either all present must have the text, or else both the response itself must be simple and also the cue for it clear every time it occurs.

If a litany sometimes provides suitable words for the Prayers, it is equally important to make times for silence. As people kneel for prayer, having heard the word of God, they are open to God. It is he who must be given the opportunity to speak. He will do so as likely in the silence as in the words of oral prayer. Every occasion of prayer should *include* a time of silence, but sometimes the prayer *is* silence, preceded perhaps simply by one thought, a sentence of Scripture, or a poem, and followed by just one prayer to bring it to completion and catch up individual devotion in a corporate expression.[2]

The Daily Office

A number of the clergy have expressed frustration about the daily office in the Church of England. Its revision has not been as thorough as many parts of the liturgy. It appears to envisage the office said publicly and corporately, whereas it more frequently has to stimulate the spiritual life of a solitary priest. It has little about it to mark the season of the year and makes less than adequate provision for holy days. It is often compared unfavourably with the new Roman offices, which seem to be strong at all the points at which the Anglican ones are weak, and which are widely used by Anglican clergy. Ever since

---

[2] There are many books of suitable prayers for use at Sunday services. In the modern style Frank Colquhoun's *Contemporary Parish Prayers* (Hodder & Stoughton 1975) and David Silk's *Prayers for use at the Alternative Services* (Mowbray 1980) are the most useful. I have written about extempore intercessory prayer in the Appendix of *The Eucharist*. See also *Intercessions in Worship* by Michael Vasey (Grove Books 1981).

Cranmer's First Prayer Book, Anglicanism has seen the offices differently from Rome. The distinct structure has already been discussed. But principally the change was in a move to a lection-centred office. The reading of the Scriptures took over as the heart of the office, and so it came to fulfil an almost didactic function. In our own day, the reduction of the psalmody, in response to many complaints from the clergy that the monthly cycle provided too much to say at each service, has robbed the office of that slow rhythmical relaxing experience of the recitation of the psalter. Already some clergy are returning to the old monthly cycle, in preference to the present ten-weekly cycle, as they realize that the rhythm and resonance of the psalms, especially when said antiphonally, are often more important than the precise content of them. It may well be that a more fundamental revision of the office should be undertaken and the attempt to provide a single form suitable both for congregational use on Sunday and private use on weekdays abandoned. Meanwhile, because the office is given to help the priest in his spiritual growth, he must so adapt and use the forms available that he finds the office a strength, not a burdensome obligation. For some this will mean an emphasis on psalmody, for some on lection, for some on silence within a framework of words.

There is also the need for each person to find the times of day most suitable for the office. There is no right or wrong time, but there is a time which feels like a natural time for prayer, or the moment when to turn aside from the cares of the day is most pressing. The time will vary from person to person, though it should not vary too much from day to day, for a regular cycle of prayer is part of the rhythm of the office. Adjustments to the text to accommodate realistic practice is desirable. There is nothing wrong with the 'evening' office being at three o'clock, if that is the point in the day that is most helpful, but it is in reality the 'afternoon' office and to pray the Evensong collect is a little absurd. That said, there is an argument for a real *evening* office, after dark, or at least at dusk. Many clergy will find the shorter form of Evening Prayer in the ASB, used at the end of the day's work, a satisfying way of commending it to God. It is, thus used, an equivalent to Compline (but see the end of the previous chapter).

The saying of the daily office is not restricted, however, to the clergy. Some lay people do say a daily office in the privacy of their homes, and many more might be encouraged to do so, using the quite brief and simple shorter forms in the ASB. The advantage of building up this practice is twofold. It is a strength to the individual parishioner to feel part of the daily worship of the universal Church. It is also a strength to the priest to know that he is not alone in his parish in saying the office, and the fellowship of those who pray with him, even if not in the same building, will be an encouragement to him. But there are, in any case, opportunities in every parish for the priest to say the office with his parishioners. Not everywhere is it possible for there to be a fixed daily time when a faithful few come to worship with the priest, but almost everywhere there are special occasions, such as at the beginning or end of a meeting, when a few might come into the church if they were invited, or when, in the room in which they were meeting, they might lay aside files and diaries, and take up Bible and office book together. If the people cannot come to the office, let the priest take the office to them.

The ASB makes provision for the integration of office and Eucharist. There are occasions when this is convenient and when what amounts to two 'Ministries of the Word' in quick succession seems unnecessary to say the least. But there is room for caution, for office and Eucharist both have their own distinct shape and rhythm. The Eucharist is at its best with a thematic approach, but the office is based on *continuous* recitation of psalmody and reading of Scripture. In parishes with regular weekday celebrations, the priest with time to do so may well find it more satisfying to keep the old pattern of office, followed by a time of silence before the Eucharist.[3]

---

[3] Discussion of the daily Eucharist, especially in relation to the office, is to be found in Section 16 of *The Eucharist*.

5
Devising Liturgy Together

Making Decisions in the Parish

Clergy and people need to work together in the preparation and presentation of the liturgy. The battle to involve lay people in the leading of worship has been fought and, in most places, won (and, where it has not, the resistance has as often come from laity as from clergy). But there is a further stage, that of involving the people genuinely in the ordering of worship, both in the pattern and content of the parish's regular round of services and also in some special events. To involve the laity in the planning and preparation of worship is not a threat to the parish priest. Rather, well handled, it is the opportunity for him both to gain freshness and insight in an area where he may have grown stale or blinkered, and also for him to share with others an expertise and to communicate to them spiritual truths that have sustained him through the years, to talk of the things of *God*, when all too often in his ministry he is expected to talk of anything else but that.

But how is this sharing to be brought about? A small group, which can grow in its perception, knowledge and mutual trust, is vital. In some parishes, this will naturally be a committee of the Parochial Church Council, and, where there is a parish committee structure, one committee should be charged with responsibility for the parish's worship, often linked with concern also for its educational and training work. In other parishes, where there is no such structure or where such a committee would have no opportunity to develop usefully, the priest must constitute a less formal group. If it is not to be just a group of those likely to agree with him, it must be *representative* of the parish and those concerned with its worship – the organist, a member of the choir, a server, a sidesman, one of the leaders of the Sunday school. More could be added to the list, unless the size of the committee needs to be kept small – a flower arranger, a bell-ringer, for instance. It must also include a few with particular gifts or expertise. If there is an English teacher in the parish, he or she would bring a knowledge of literature and also a sense of the rhythm and poetry of liturgical language. But, above all, there must be articulate representation of those who sit in the nave and sometimes feel that liturgy is something done to or for them, rather than something in which they are involved. Young people and their organizations should have representation, but so should the elderly, whose needs are often neglected in liturgical reform.

When such a group has been brought together, its first task is not to *decide* anything. There is an important process to be gone through before ever a decision is made. The members of the group will need to share with one another their own understanding and expectations of worship in such a way that there is trust and understanding before practical parish matters are discussed. The group will also need to *learn*, partly by the sharing of the knowledge and expertise of its members (including the priest) and partly by straightforward teaching of the Church's liturgical tradition and of the principles of liturgical reform. It may also be beneficial for the members of the group to worship together in a church quite different from their own in order to broaden their vision and to open up discussion about different ways, whether they like them or not. The group should then devise a simple act of worship. This may be no more than choosing hymns, readings and prayers for a Eucharist. But the very process of, for instance, deciding what hymns are suitable for a specific service and for the particular points in it, will be an educational experience and the opening up for many of a quite new world. Preparing intercessions is an intimidating experience for many. For a group to talk through together a set of intercessions will be a good first stage before individuals tackle the task alone. The first service that the group devises should perhaps be simply for its own use. It may devise a service and then use it and later discuss it. There is a lot to be said for starting people at a very simple level. To devise a whole experimental service, when one has had no experience of choosing hymns or writing prayers, is a baffling exercise. The priest might well, for several months, ask the group to help him choose the Sunday hymns, so that they may acquire confidence in the skills of selection involved. Later they can move on to more creative and challenging tasks. Ultimately they may work together at a whole service, perhaps for a Sunday evening, but a whole year might pass before the group felt itself ready to attempt this.

Meanwhile, if the group is a legally-constituted body, a committee of the Parochial Church Council, it will have the task of advising the PCC on some formal liturgical decisions that lie within its power. The priest seeking some change in the parish's custom, or willing to go along with such a change if the initiative has come from elsewhere, does well to have ensured, not only the support, but the *understanding*, of a committee before proposals are presented to the PCC. Indeed understanding, which will normally involve both teaching and discussion, is vital at every stage of liturgical change. Where a parish makes a change only because, for some obscure reason, it will please the vicar, something has gone very wrong. There must be teaching and discussion before the PCC is asked to approve an experimental change. Once the PCC has made its decision, there must be teaching and discussion in the congregation before it is implemented and during the period of experiment. Most changes are not self-evidently good, but with explanation most congregations respond quite openly.

Experiment can, of course, be overdone, and there is sometimes a cry to stop experimenting and settle to something, and many clergy will themselves sympathize with the desire for stability. But where a fundamental change is to be made in the practice of a parish – the pattern of services, the eucharistic rites, the furnishings of the church and therefore the ceremonial to match it – opportunity for experiment, discussion and improvement is important. But there are *misguided* experiments. One is when two issues are confused. To introduce a new rite at the same time as a new position for the celebrant is mistaken. They are two issues, best kept separate, else, when it comes to a vote, those who dislike one will vote down both. Many people, who have been through a similar confused reform, imagine the *exchange* of the Peace to be a 'Series 3' innovation, compulsory with that rite, but inappropriate with older rites. One step at a time will usually be the intelligent policy. Another mistaken experiment is the one that is too short. People need time to adjust to change, however good the reform. Some parishes have had a one month or six week experiment ('We'll turn the altar round for Lent'!). Very few changes can make their impact in less than three months, and for most six months is desirable. Nor is the 'open-ended' experiment helpful. A date should be set for the end of the experiment, with a PCC meeting two or three weeks before it. The experiment that involves constant alternation is also almost bound to end in disaster. Using a new rite, or a new ritual, every other week, or once a month, will never give it a chance, and meanwhile a parish's sense of worship may well be destroyed. To make its impact, a reform must be allowed to go uninterrupted through the experimental period. Where, at the end of an experiment, a parish wishes to hold a referendum of the congregation, it must be an intelligent questionnaire. To ask simply, 'Do you or do you not approve the change?' does nothing but polarize. But to ask, 'What do you find helpful? Unhelpful? Refreshing? What amendments would you suggest?', is a way both of helping people to analyse their own reactions rationally and of building up a complete picture on which the Parochial Church Council can base its decision.

The PCC committee, or the group convened by the priest, are not the only groups to which can in time be entrusted the preparation and presentation of worship in the church. In a similar way, existing parish organizations or groups might undertake a special service, first going through at least some of the preparatory processes described. But there is also an occasional way of involving a far larger number of the congregation in the process. This is through what might be called a Parish Worship Workshop.

Such a term could cover a variety of activities, some quite advanced and complicated. At a simple level, however, it need be no more than an hour and a half on a Sunday evening, in place perhaps of Evensong, when, first of all, a brief service of 15–20 minutes would take place. This would be specially devised by priest, or worship group, to include, without over-crowding it, a mixture of the familiar and the new – a traditional hymn but also a 'folk' song, a reading from Scripture but also a poem, a collect but also extempore prayer, a psalm said or sung in a different way from usual, a time of silence, the exchange of the Peace. Then follows half an hour of discussion, preferably in groups. 'What did you like? What didn't you like? When is it appropriate to use poetry in church? Can one mix musical styles? Could we have had more silence? Would the psalm have been better antiphonally? Or sitting down? Why don't you like the Peace? Should we have passed it less formally? What about the movements within it?' There would be many more questions like these. Bringing the whole group back together, the draft text of a concluding service is distributed. This has the same structure as the opening service and the same range of contents, though different texts. The congregation, with help from a chairman (not necessarily the priest), proceeds, in the light of the discussion, to revise it, amend it, and to add rubrics to it, and then, after twenty minutes or so, to *use* it to conclude the evening. A series of such workshops, perhaps one evening every six months, would over a couple of years transform the attitudes to worship within a congregation.

Style, Shape and Balance

A number of important principles have emerged in these early chapters that need to be borne in mind by those who devise special services. The principles are much the same, whether it be the priest and the parish Worship Committee devising a great service for a centenary, or the priest with the Guides and Brownies devising the annual Thinking Day Service. The 'hymn-sandwich', with the congregational involvement restricted to the hymns, is hardly ever satisfying.

The cluster of questions with which any discussion of the service should begin include

> For whom is this service principally intended?
> What is its theme?
> What should be its length?
> What style of service would be appropriate?

The question of style is an important preliminary. There are no right or wrong styles, though there is an appropriate style to a particular occasion. Styles may range from a formal, choral service, highly rehearsed, with solemn words and dignified ritual, to an informal and more spontaneous service, with lighter music, words closer to everyday speech and a minimum of ceremonial (though possibly a good deal of *congregational* movement). Both have their place. Both ought to have their place in the same church. There is a whole range of styles between the two extremes. It is good to have some idea of which to follow before turning to the more detailed content of the service. Not that the style adopted must be followed slavishly. A service can include, to its enrichment, some variety, but no sense of style at all will make for a hotch-potch of irreconcilables that will please no one.

The planning group must next turn to the shape and content of the service. Too often the importance of shape or structure is neglected. The Eucharist has its shape, as does the office. Retain the same content, but jumble around the order, and much is lost. One section of the service must lead naturally to another, for a service is never a series of individual items, but always a total and unified experience. Shape and content must be considered together. Talk may begin with content, because there may be particular ideas that the participants want included, but the shape and structure into which these can naturally be fitted must then be worked out, before the remaining details of the content can be decided. There is a wide variety of shapes and structures that make sense, and people soon discover what works and what does not. But, usually, the shape that is most satisfying is the one that has development and climax, the service that seems to be going somewhere, though that high point might come nearer the middle than the end. It should be possible to draw a sort of graph of the development of the service; an upward curve should be clearly discernible.

With the shape and contents provisionally decided, the planning group needs to ask a series of questions that will check the balance of the service. Special services sometimes exaggerate out of proportion some aspect of worship at the expense of others. At this point, some alterations will sometimes need to be made to restore a balance. The group has to ask, among other questions:

Does this service feel like a joyful celebration of the people of God?
What participation is possible for the congregation?

Will the service retain and enhance a sense of wonder and reverence?

Are the elements of thanksgiving, praise, confession and intercession all present in some form?

Is the gospel of Christ being proclaimed?

What is the teaching element of the service?

What expression is there of the Church's fellowship?

Are there too many words? Is there too little silence?

With style, shape and balance established, the group turns finally to practical details. There are 'stage directions' for those taking a leading part and instructions for the congregation on standing, kneeling, turning, etc. There are decisions on personnel and the rehearsal of them. There are sometimes questions about furnishing, staging, lighting and microphones. (So many beautifully rehearsed services involving children are spoilt because nobody can see and nobody can hear.) There is also the need to produce a simple but attractive service sheet, allowing for congregational response and for useful instructions that save too many of the sort of interruptions to the service that destroy the continuity and momentum.

The service is now ready and what emerges will be the product of loving care and hard thinking. Even if little things go wrong, through lack of experience, it will not have been slipshod or hastily thrown together, and the quality will show.

6

Christian Initiation

Initiation and Easter

The relationship between Christian initiation – Baptism, Confirmation and First Communion – and the Easter season is a profound one and it is sad that, for most Christians, it has been lost. The symbolism of water in Baptism goes far beyond the idea of the washing away of sin. The prayer over the water in the ASB rite expresses it thus:

We thank you for the gift of water
    to cleanse us and revive us;
we thank you that through the waters of the Red Sea, you led your
    people out of slavery to freedom in the promised land;
we thank you that through the deep waters of death you brought
    your Son, and raised him to life in triumph.

To go through the waters of Baptism is to go through the Exodus experience, from slavery to freedom, from death to life. The Exodus dimension of Baptism is hardly ever developed, and even the more straightforward relationship between resurrection and Baptism is often neglected. The question that Paul poses in the Epistle to the Romans (6.3), 'Have you forgotten that when we were baptized into union with Christ Jesus we were baptized into his death?', could often be addressed to the Church of today in its baptismal teaching and practice. Yet, to quote Paul again,

By baptism we were buried with him, and lay dead, in order that, as Christ was raised from the dead in the splendour of the Father, so also we might set our feet upon the path of life. For if we have become incorporate with him in a death like his, we shall also be one with him in a resurrection like his. (Romans 6.4–5)

Where this relationship between Baptism and resurrection is brought out, the power and the joy of Easter takes hold of the sacrament and gives it the ethos and excitement that belong to it. For the early Christians this was dramatically brought home by their Baptism and admission to the Eucharist at the great service of the Easter Vigil, in which the contrast between slavery and freedom, dark and light, death and life, was seen to be, not only the experience of Israelites at the Red Sea and of the Risen Christ on Easter morning, but their experience too. This expression of theology in liturgy – the restriction of Baptism in the early centuries to Easter night – gives added weight from the tradition to associating Christian initiation with the celebration of Easter. The point is all the clearer where the Feast of Pentecost, with its emphasis on the giving of the Spirit, is seen as part of the paschal mystery and of the Easter season (but for an explanation of this return to earlier thinking, see Chapter 15).

Theologically and liturgically, there is good reason for the principal occasion of Christian initiation in the parish being during Easter night or Easter morning. Pastorally and practically this is hardly ever possible. The presence of godparents on such a day, or of babies in the middle of the night, or of the bishop in more places than one at a given time, all provide major difficulties. Some churches do manage to have their main Baptism/Confirmation/First Communion celebration at Easter itself, but only for a few will this be possible. It will however be quite possible for most parishes to have a Baptism within the main service of Easter Day, and there is a strong argument for the annual Baptism/ Confirmation/First Communion celebration being within the fifty days from Easter to Pentecost in as many parishes as the bishop's diary will allow. Quite apart from its theological and liturgical suitability, it is a convenient time, towards the end of the school year but before examinations, for the preparation to reach its climax.

Where initiation has to take place outside the Easter season, and, in most parishes, the majority of Baptisms, if not the annual Confirmation, will be in this category, the occasion should nevertheless be regarded as an extension of Eastertide. This can be reflected in the choice of hymns, in the use of the Easter greeting and dismissal and above all in the placing in a prominent position of the lighted paschal candle. It is from this candle, with all its rich associations, rather than from any other, that the candidate's candle is lit in Baptism. That is why it is appropriate that at the end of Eastertide, the paschal candle should be moved to the font, to stand there, ready for Baptisms and also as a permanent sign of the connection between Easter and Baptism, throughout the year.

In the traditional Easter Vigil the unity of the initiation process was clear. Subsequent history, with its division of initiation into three distinct rites – Baptism, Confirmation and First Communion – has obscured this truth and introduced theological problems, especially with regard to the meaning of Confirmation. It is outside the compass of this book to consider all the questions involved, but it is good liturgical practice and sound pastoral common sense to make the *norm* the administration of all three parts of initiation in one rite. The principal celebration of Christian initiation in the parish will therefore be the occasion when the bishop comes to confirm, to baptize all those of the Confirmation candidates who have not been baptized at some earlier stage in their life, and to preside at the Eucharist at which all among them who are not already communicants make their First Communion. Pastoral necessity will sometimes dictate other practices (especially with children), but this is the normal practice that the ASB assumes. It also assumes that *adult* Baptism, rather than *infant* Baptism, is the norm. That does not mean that the Baptism of infants is inappropriate, but, rather, that it is regarded as a modification of the usual discipline, rather than the basic rite on which the variations, including adult Baptism, are based.

Oils for Initiation

Before examining the initiation rites in detail, a word needs to be said about the use of oil at Baptism and Confirmation. In the Church of England, the use of such oil is never mandatory, but provision for the blessing of oils by the bishop and for its use in initiation is made in the ASB. The annual service in which oil may be blessed will be discussed in Chapter 10.

There are two distinct oils for use at initiation. The first is the oil for the signing with the cross, provided that that ceremony *precedes* Baptism. Used at that point in the service, in relation to the rejection of sin, and the signing with the cross, it is the oil of protection. In the old terminology and in the Roman rite, it would be regarded as an oil of exorcism. Olive oil, usually blessed by the bishop on Maundy Thursday, but if necessary by the priest, is used. Words of blessing are not provided in the ASB. Quite apart from the symbolism of the oil itself, the fact that it provides a substance with which to make the sign of the cross commends its use.

The second oil is the Oil of Chrism. This is usually olive oil, mixed with balsam or other perfumes. The blessing or consecration of Chrism is reserved to the bishop. It has two ordinary uses (among its special uses is, of course, the anointing of the sovereign at the Coronation), at the same time as the laying on of hands at Confirmation and (more properly *or*) *after* Baptism. Its use at Baptism is caught up with the question of the giving of the Spirit in initiation and the meaning of the Confirmation rite. To use the signing with the cross *after* Baptism (as the ASB permits) and to anoint with the Chrism at that point is, at least by one interpretation, to 'seal' the Baptism with the gift of the Spirit. It seems illogical to use Chrism at both Baptism and Confirmation and, where oil is to be used at all, it is more straightforward to use only the oil of protection (exorcism) at Baptism, and to reserve the Chrism for Confirmation. The Oil of Chrism is traditionally seen as a life-giving, spirit-giving, sign, and the usual prayers for its consecration by the bishop speak of the coming of the Spirit upon Christ at his baptism and of the Spirit resting upon those anointed with it. It is also associated with the anointing of priests and kings and is therefore a sign of entry into the royal priesthood. As such it can be understood as a commissioning to lay ministry in the Church.

There is another view of the use of oil that rejects the distinctions between different sorts of oil, each with its own symbolism. Such a view recognizes just one oil and one meaning. Oil is, most obviously, about healing and wholeness. As such its use at any key moment of growing in the Christian life, whether at one of the sacraments or at some other significant time, is always a sign of that process of healing and growth towards wholeness, which is part of God's constant plan for all his children. Such a view would call for one form of blessing of oil for use at initiation, with the sick and at other times.

Perhaps the best argument for the use of oil at Baptism is that, because it has been blessed by the bishop, it stands for him, and through him for the involvement of the whole Church in what, in other ways, seems a local, parochial or even family occasion. The oil blessed by the bishop becomes for Baptism what his presence is for Confirmation. Where the parish priest explains its use in these terms, it acquires this additional valuable symbolism.

Baptism at the Parish Eucharist

Not every parish is happy with the present trend towards a strict insistence that all Baptisms should take place at the main public service on the Sunday. But there can be little doubt that this represents more clearly than any other procedure both the responsibility of the congregation for those baptized and also the implication for the family concerned of the membership of the Church that Baptism bestows. In most churches the principle is conceded, but pastoral necessity seems to dictate a different approach, especially where there are vast numbers of Baptisms in the course of the year. But in every church at least a proportion of those baptized should receive this sacrament within the main Sunday service.

Adults and children who are also to be confirmed should normally be baptized at the Confirmation. To baptize Confirmation candidates, whether publicly or privately, within weeks or days of the Confirmation is a nonsense, and a lost opportunity of showing the unity of Christian initiation. Just occasionally the priest will decide to baptize an adult outside the context of Confirmation. However theologically inadequate it may seem, he may, on pastoral grounds, sometimes agree to baptize an adult who does not feel able to be confirmed. The priest has to accept people 'where they are', even when they seem confused or misguided in their view of the sacraments. Or he may agree to baptize a candidate, who needs that Baptism to qualify to marry in church. Where he has grasped the pastoral opportunity that such a case provides, and is sure enough in his own mind that the candidate, after instruction, is genuine in his faith and wanting to go on to Confirmation and communicant membership, he may, even within the Prayer

Book rubrics, baptize him *and admit him to Communion*, delaying the Confirmation until after the wedding, if circumstances make this necessary or desirable.

But, in general, Baptism within the Parish Eucharist will mean the Baptism of children and babies. Once a month is probably as often as the regular congregation can cope with such an occasion. Since it must have a Baptism/resurrection flavour to it, and because it involves the omission of parts of the service, it is not desirable to make it part of the main service more often than this. It is also undesirable as a general rule to have more than four or five candidates at a time. If there are more it is difficult to avoid completely the sense of the conveyor belt.

Using Rite A Holy Communion, the Baptism of Children (on page 243 of the ASB) is easily integrated with the Eucharist. The penitential material of the Eucharist must come at its earlier point, at the beginning of the service. The Baptism follows the Sermon. The Creed, Intercessions and Prayer of Humble Access are omitted and the Eucharist is resumed at the Peace. Precise details of what parts of the Baptism service are omitted when it is integrated with the Eucharist are given on page 250 of the ASB. The priest must decide whether to retain the propers of the Sunday or to use ones particularly suitable to Baptism. (The ASB provides sentences, readings and a proper preface.) On some Sundays he will judge that the regular collect and lections accord sufficiently well with the Baptism theme that they may happily be retained. On others he will opt for some of those given in the ASB on pages 262 to 274. But, whether the Sunday or baptismal readings are used, the liturgical colour should be white. The same procedures apply with Rite B, except that, less satisfactorily, there is not the opportunity to use the penitential material at the beginning of the Eucharist, and the rubrics assume its omission entirely.

The position of the font has already been discussed in Chapter 2. The most important consideration is that the whole action should be clearly visible to the congregation, though, where there is room, there is no reason why the entire congregation should not move to the font. Traditionally the church door has also had a place in the Baptism ritual and in just a few places it may seem appropriate to put the questions of the

Decision and to make the sign of the cross at the door before a procession to the font for Baptism. The symbolism of reception and entry is not then lost as it can be when the font is near the altar. Renouncing the world on entering, the candidate is brought to the place of word and sacrament to be incorporated into the life of the Church.

Particular care needs to be taken, especially when Baptism at the Eucharist is a rare occurrence, to prepare the congregation for its role. Its support, encouragement and welcome is expressed in fine words in which it responds to the signing and the giving of the candle and extends its welcome. But very often the congregation, watching the *action* of the sacrament intently, fails to be ready with the *words*. Practice before the service will sometimes be needed. Some clergy encourage the entire congregation to join the parents and godparents in responding to the questions, making it an act of renewal of vows. This is often a mistaken policy, partly because constant renewing of vows makes what should be a solemn undertaking casual, but also because, for all the support of the Church, Baptism is about standing alone. It is a deeply personal moment and the voices, whether confident, trembling or shy, of those who promise should be heard alone. 'I turn, I believe' is singular, and significantly so. The Church's endorsement and expression of solidarity is in the congregational response, 'This is our faith'.

The priest responds to the Decision with the signing with the cross on the forehead of the child. He may use oil for this, but he should not use water. To do so confuses people about what constitutes Baptism. At the signing, we are still at the stage of preparatory ceremonies before the water is even blessed. The signing is a symbol that the child belongs to Christ, to whom, in the Decision, his sponsors have turned. In the Roman rite the priest may invite the parents and godparents to make the sign of the cross on the child after he has done so, and Anglicans may happily adopt this custom. It need not be in oil, but simply with the thumb, either in silence or repeating the formula, 'I sign you with the cross, the sign of Christ', before the priest continues 'Do not be ashamed . . .' and the congregation responds 'Fight valiantly . . .' The signing represents the Church's acceptance of responsibility for the child and, since it is through parents and godparents that this responsibility will principally be exercised, the symbolism of their taking part in the signing is totally appropriate.

The Prayer over the Water is an important part of the rite. It is more effective if water (and lots of it) is poured into the font immediately before this prayer, or even, by an assistant, during it. It is more than simply the *blessing* of the water, though that is part of it. It also recalls the significance of water as a natural and religious symbol and seeks the Holy Spirit for those to be baptized. In its recollection of the past, its prayer over the element of water and in its calling upon the Spirit, it is a baptismal parallel to the Eucharistic Prayer in the Holy Communion. The priest says it with arms outstretched.

The Baptism itself, which follows, should be *wet* and the font should be *full* of water. However symbolic the action, the water symbolism requires that there be more than a sprinkling. If the child's head can be partly in the water, all the better. The rubric directs, 'He dips him in the water or pours water on him.' Where the water is to be poured, it should be poured generously. In some small measure, the priest is trying to create the sense of immersion in the Jordan and, quite apart from that, the power of the sacrament is best represented by the dramatic gesture, and, though a towel must be available to dry off the worst of the drips, to wipe completely dry the head of the child is inadequate symbolism. The parents and godparents should be rehearsed in making the 'Amen' response to this central moment of the Baptism liturgy.

The child is now handed a lighted candle. It should be lit at this moment from the paschal candle and the priest may briefly explain the significance of that. The rubric does not dictate who shall light it and give it. The priest may do so. Or a member of the congregation may do so. In practice, if the child is a baby, it is to the child's father or one of the godparents that the candle is given. Where the child is a little older and may receive the candle himself, it would be suitable for one of his parents to light the candle and give it to him. It is unfortunate when the candle is then put out for the rest of the service. A candlestick should be ready to receive it, so that it may remain alight until the end.

The Baptism is completed by the Welcome said by priest and congregation. At this point a baptismal card or a gift from the church may be presented when the words are said. The final 'We welcome you' should be a great climax and may be followed by clapping to express congratulation and welcome. Still standing at the font, the priest begins the Eucharist with the words of the Peace. At Baptism, he should always use the 'We are the Body . . .' form with its mention of 'We were all baptized into one Body'. In the exchange of greetings that follows, he first greets the newly baptized, with a kiss when appropriate. The Eucharist continues with the Offertory. It is suitable for the parents or godparents of the newly baptized to present the gifts.

After Communion, one of the prayers from the Baptism service may be used as a first post-Communion collect, or the prayer at section 60 may be turned into a blessing for the family. The present text is weak, but in the form

> May the Heavenly Father bless you, A and B, in your care of C; may he give you the spirit of wisdom and love, that your home may reflect the joy of his eternal kingdom

it is a fine blessing of the couple, who with the child may stand or kneel before the priest to receive it, before the blessing of the whole congregation.

Baptism preparation should always include a rehearsal, partly to put the parents at ease, but partly because the service is itself such a marvellous teaching aid. Where possible, the priest may involve the parents in more than rehearsal. They may take a genuine part in the planning, helping choose hymns and readings (and one of the readings should preferably be read by a member of the family) and considering some of the options discussed here. A service that they have helped to put together will make a far deeper impression upon them.

Page 251 of the ASB makes provision for the incorporation of Baptism within Morning or Evening Prayer. The Baptism follows the Second Lesson, and most of the suggestions in this section apply equally within that context. When, using the provisions of the ASB, the sermon follows the Second Lesson, the Baptism would follow that and thus the Welcome would be, very suitably, the climax of the whole service.

A Special Baptismal Service

In some parishes, afternoon Baptisms will be necessary, simply because of the large number of candidates. It is desirable that the number at a single Baptism should not exceed four, but that there should always be at least two, so that the families may realize that the Baptism of their child is never a private ritual, but always incorporation into something bigger. For the same reason, every effort should be made to ensure the presence of at least a representative gathering of the congregation. In many places it is possible to hold a monthly Baptism service in the later afternoon in place of Evensong. The regular evening congregation are asked to support it and, if possible, the choir may be present to lead it. But where the Baptism cannot be *in place of* another service, and has to be *additional to it*, at least there should be present sidesmen (a welcome at the door and help in being seated and given books are vital on such occasions), servers (to assist the priest and perhaps to 'lift' the service with simple ceremonial) and members of the congregation involved in Baptism preparation or follow up. Many parishes now have some sort of 'Baptism Visitors' scheme. The presence of the visitors at the Baptism, possibly with a special part in it (at the signing or the giving of the candle), is important.

The service for The Baptism of Children provides a quite satisfactory form for such an afternoon service. With or without a choir, hymns may be sung, where there are sufficient numbers present. The ASB suggests a hymn before the Prayer over the Water and allows hymns at other points. At the beginning and before the concluding prayers, hymns may sensibly be inserted. The priest will usually want to give a simple address. This could be before the Decision, but it will often be right to have it at the very beginning of the service to put people at their ease and to lead them into an atmosphere of reverence. Quite apart from the address, the priest will always need to be ready to introduce each stage of the service with a simple explanation. 'Now we are going to . . . This represents . . .'

Details of how the rite may be used are set out in the previous section. Among its provisions suitable for use at an afternoon baptismal service is the blessing of parents. Here the priest may invite the parents and their children to come to the altar rail and kneel to be blessed as families. Quite apart from the value of this for itself, it will introduce people to coming to the altar for a blessing and may be the beginning of a process that leads eventually to the parents' Confirmation. The priest may even say, 'This is something you can repeat each week, seeking again and again God's blessing in the keeping of these vows and the bringing up of these children.'

Many clergy forbid photographs in the church. The taking of photographs during the service does need discouraging, for it can be a distraction at a key moment, but the priest would do well to *invite* photographs at the font after the service and to be willing to do a 'mock up' of the Baptism. It is much better that people should have pictures of the sacrament being administered than of the party afterwards. The growing child, seeing photographs of his or her Baptism, learns a little of what it was all about.

The Confirmation Liturgy

The occasion when the bishop comes to baptize, confirm and preside at the Eucharist during which the newly confirmed make their First Communion is the principal rite of initiation of the year, and every other Baptism should be seen as an extension of it. It should take place ideally in the Easter-Pentecost period, but in any case should have a resurrection/Spirit ethos to it.

It should be, for candidates and for congregation, a great and memorable day. Several important factors will help to make it so. The first is the attitude of the bishop. In a sense, the parish priest can do little about this and certainly the bishop has it in his power to ruin the best laid plans. There are bishops who, ignoring or ignorant of both the principles and the rubrics of the new liturgy, insist on confirming in a style quite out of keeping with them. Nevertheless, a Confirmation is an episcopal service and the bishop's wishes must be respected. Consultation with him well in advance is desirable, especially if any deviation from the strict form in the book or from his own known preferred procedure is envisaged. Many bishops are willing to come to a rehearsal and to meet the candidates before the day itself, and others, usually unable to do so, have chaplains who will come to discuss the service and share the rehearsal with the parish priest.

A second factor is the preparedness of the candidates. All too often in Confirmation preparation, the full significance of the rite itself is not brought out. Yet it is, in itself, a fine source for good teaching. The build up to the great day, so that there is genuine *excitement* about the Confirmation, heightens the whole experience. So does the involvement of the candidates as far as possible in the preparation of the liturgy (and this is discussed in the following chapter).

But the most vital factor, and the one that is often neglected, is the involvement and overcrowding presence of the whole church community. Desirable as the presence of family and friends of the candidates is, it is the presence of the local church that is required if the celebration is really to take off and, indeed, if it is to make theological sense. Whether on a Sunday or a weekday evening, the entire congregation should be helped to see its solemn duty to be present, and if the consequent squash in the church means standing room only, so much the better. What happier memory of one's Confirmation than that so many people came in support that there wasn't room for them all to sit down!

None of these factors, however, will make for a lively and thrilling liturgy where the priest has been slack in his preparations. For an hour or so, his parish church, the worship of which may usually be quite simple and informal, becomes a cathedral, and the same careful, imaginative and detailed liturgical preparations are required of him as would be found in the ordering of a great cathedral liturgy. This is one occasion when it is desirable for everything to work 'like clockwork' and for the candidates to know that it will, in order that they may be relaxed.

The liturgy may begin with the Easter greeting. This may be at the door where representatives of the congregation may welcome the bishop before the processional hymn. (For discussion of such a welcome, see Chapter 17.) This hymn, and those later in the service, should be chosen to reflect the themes that run through the service – resurrection, the giving of the Spirit, personal commitment, incorporation into the Body, participation in the Eucharist. The new rite allows for the penitential material before the Collect, but in a service where there is to be a renewal of vows this will often serve to give the service that element. At least the first two of the lessons should be read by candidates.

After the bishop's Sermon, the candidates will come forward. It is better that until this point they should be seated with family or friends rather than in a place specially reserved at the front for them. It is also better that they should later be able to take their ordinary place within the congregation once they have been confirmed. One of the weaknesses of the new rite (as indeed of the old) is that it makes little provision for the congregation to indicate its support of the candidates, both by presenting them and by upholding them. With the bishop's permission, an adaptation of the form used at Ordination would be appropriate. The candidates come forward to stand around the bishop. The priest, or a lay person involved in their preparation, says

> Reverend Father, I present these persons to be (baptized and) confirmed within the Church of God.

He then gives their names. The bishop presents the candidates to the people, and says

> Those of your congregation whose ministry it has been to prepare these persons for (Baptism and) Confirmation believe them to be ready to receive God's sacramental gift. Is it therefore your will that they should be (baptized and) confirmed?
>
> People: It is.
>
> Bishop: Will you support and strengthen them in their Christian discipleship and receive them as your brothers and sisters in Christ?
>
> People: We will.

In addition to words such as these, or as an alternative to them, each candidate may receive the support of a sponsor (whether a godparent or a representative of the Church) who stands behind the candidate and, at the moment of Confirmation, places his right hand on the candidate's shoulder. This is the practice of the Roman Church.

The bishop addresses the candidates who stand before or around him. The questions of the Decision are put at once to candidates for Baptism and also to candidates who are only to be confirmed. But only those to be baptized are marked with the cross. Since the Prayer over the Water now follows, there may need to be a procession to the font. This becomes unnecessary if a temporary font has been made ready at the front. But if there is a procession it is necessary for *all* the candidates, not only those to be baptized, to precede the bishop to the font, possibly during the singing of a hymn such as 'Guide me, O thou great redeemer'. There the bishop says the Prayer over the Water and puts the threefold question about belief to all the candidates. He then baptizes those who are unbaptized. He should not delegate this to a priest, though he may delegate the giving of the candle to either a priest or the candidate's sponsor. When candles are given to the newly baptized, it is wholly appropriate to give them also to those candidates previously baptized as a reminder of their own baptism.

What happens next will depend on *where* the Confirmation is to take place. If it is to be at the chancel step or before the altar, the candidates, carrying their lighted candles, precede the bishop back to the front of the church. They then place their lighted candles on a table near the altar (a box of sand will serve as well as individual candlesticks to receive them) and stand before or around the bishop. Alternatively, if the number of candidates and the visibility in the church allow it, the bishop may conveniently and properly confirm at the font, the congregation remaining standing, in which case the table for the lighted candles is placed near the font, rather than the altar.

Local custom will vary about the ritual of the Confirmation itself. The bishop may prefer the candidates to stand or kneel in the circle around him. It is probably better that for the laying on of hands each candidate steps forward alone to stand or kneel before the bishop, because for all its corporate setting this is a personal moment. There is certainly nothing to commend the 'two by two' tradition. Nor is there any particular virtue in the bishop *sitting* to administer the sacrament. Better that he should stand, holding his pastoral staff. Before the laying on of hands, the bishop prays, with arms outstretched, for the gift of the Spirit. The priests who have shared in the preparation of the candidates should gather around him and may extend their right hand also as the bishop alone says the words. As each candidate individually comes forward, a card may be held up giving his or her name, but it is far better that the candidate should look the bishop in the eye (in itself infinitely preferable to the traditional bowed head) and say, 'I am N'. In response, the bishop lays his hand (the rubric is clear that it is just one hand; the other hand may be holding the pastoral staff) on the candidate's head and confirms, using the name he has just been given. If Oil of Chrism is being used, though additional words *may* be used, it is better that the bishop makes the sign of the cross in oil on the forehead in silence after laying his hand on the candidate's head.

After the congregation has joined in the prayer, 'Defend, O Lord, your servants . . .', the people welcome those newly admitted to communicant membership and this leads naturally into the Peace, with the newly confirmed still grouped around the bishop. The bishop first greets each of them and they then give and receive the Peace in the congregation. The Peace has a particular significance in the Confirmation rite where it becomes a welcome into full eucharistic membership. But it is important not to overplay it, as if it were the third element in initiation. That third element is First Communion and the service must continue to build up to that climax, and not lose its impetus when the candidates go back into the congregation.

The rubrics allow a congregational Renewal of Baptismal Vows between the Welcome and the Peace. The suggested position is unfortunate, for it divides two elements that belong very much together. But there is good point in a Renewal of Vows by the whole congregation, especially since many whose own commitment will have grown slack over the years will be moved by the occasion to want to make a fresh affirmation. It is better to place the Renewal of Vows by the congregation before the candidates say the same words, in order that the candidates may experience the encouragement of the whole congregation's solidarity. This means that the congregational renewal follows the bishop's Sermon. A rubric on page 275 of the ASB permits this position.

The Offertory Procession could well, on this occasion, be on a larger scale, in order that all the candidates may express their

new communicant status by bringing to the altar the orna-
ments, vessels and elements needed for the celebration. Only
at a very large Confirmation would this be impossible. A great
procession with the fair linen cloth, the candles, the chalices,
ciboria, paten, cruets, lavabo bowl, book, cushion, etc., would
over-emphasize the Offertory at a normal Eucharist, but on this
occasion it is very suitable.

The Eucharist then proceeds as usual. The newly confirmed
may come up to receive Communion first, but it is probably
better that they receive with their families. Because of the
number of visitors in the church, this is one of the occasions
when the priest will do well to have made a point of inviting all
non-communicants to come to the altar for a blessing. During
the last hymn, the newly-confirmed collect their lighted
candles. They are then ready, after the Easter Dismissal, to
precede the bishop out of the church. The congregation might
happily greet such a procession with applause, for clapping at
any earlier point might have destroyed the continuity of the
liturgy, and, where there are bells, they should be ringing
overhead as the bishop and the newly-confirmed with their
candles emerge from the church.

White is the liturgical colour where Baptism and Confirmation are administered together; where Confirmation alone, red
may be used.

The Renewal of Baptismal Vows

The ASB provides a form for the Renewal of Baptismal Vows for
use 'at Easter, at New Year, and on other suitable occasions'.
Easter is the principal occasion in the year for its use, whether at
the Easter Vigil or on Easter Day itself (see Chapter 15). There is
also a good case for such a renewal at the principal celebration of
Christian initiation during the year – usually the bishop's visit
to baptize, confirm and admit to Communion. The whole congregation is put in mind of its own promises by the affirmation
of those being baptized and confirmed. The use of the Renewal
of Vows at such a service is discussed above.

But there is a compelling argument against extending the
practice to every Baptism or to every occasion in parish life that
has an element of rededication about it. To renew baptismal

vows is best undertaken as a solemn act, of which notice should be given and for which preparation should be made. It is to cheapen both the vows and renewal to spring it upon people or to do it too often. Twice in the year will be quite enough. The Renewal of Vows should be a solemn, sacred moment, parallel to the practice in an increasing number of dioceses to the renewal for clergy of commitment to priestly ministry on Maundy Thursday.

There is another occasion when *individuals*, rather than congregations, may profitably renew their vows. It is when a confirmed Christian either has drifted away from the Church and has then returned or has later undergone a deeper religious experience that leaves him or her dissatisfied with his or her Baptism or Confirmation. Theologically the Church cannot accede to the request for re-baptism. Unfortunately very often it offers nothing in its place. But there is a real spiritual and psychological need that must be met. One possible way of doing this is by the renewal of vows, within the Eucharist, to which the Church is able to respond in anointing with Chrism. Whereas Baptism cannot be repeated, there is nothing once-for-all about anointing. To offer a sacramental rite such as this will often satisfy the need, though it will not of course be sufficient for those who, on strict doctrinal grounds, have come to reject infant Baptism.

First Communion

The norm assumed by the Alternative Service Book is that First Communion takes place within the same rite as Confirmation. But there are two sorts of occasion when a different practice needs to be followed. One is where candidates have been confirmed, not in their own church, but at some central church of the area at a service which has not included the Eucharist precisely in order that the newly confirmed may receive Communion for the first time within the congregation where they usually worship. There is something to be said for omitting the Eucharist at such group Confirmations, even though the unity of the initiation rite is lost. In any case, the whole rite *in* the parish *for* the parish is preferable, whenever a bishop is available. But where First Communion is so separated from Confirmation, some form of reception and welcome in the local church at the Eucharist on the next Sunday is desirable. At a suitable point, probably before the Peace, the newly confirmed come to stand with the priest in front of the congregation. The priest may adapt the form of presentation suggested above (on page 79) in order to present them to the congregation and seek its support. The Welcome from the Baptism and Confirmation order follows and, at the Peace, the priest, in the name of the congregation, first greets the newly confirmed. At the Offertory, they may all join in the preparation of the altar and presenting the elements in the way described above.

The other occasion of First Communion apart from Confirmation is where permission has been given to admit children to Communion before Confirmation. The increase of this practice, whereby children from the age of 7 upwards may become communicants, with Confirmation delayed for some years, necessitates some guidelines on the occasion when they are first admitted. In order that their admission to Communion may not be confused with Confirmation, the presence of the bishop is unhelpful. Their admission should be at a Eucharist at which their own parish priest is the president. For the same reason, it is undesirable to include the Renewal of Baptismal Vows. Indeed any formal promises are best avoided; part of the *rationale* of admission to Communion before Confirmation is that the candidates are not yet at an age to make the sort of act of commitment that formal promises entail. But, within the service, the priest may question both candidates and sponsors informally as he seeks to impress upon them, as he will have done in the weeks of preparation, the need for faithfulness in the candidates and support from the sponsors.

There is no need for (indeed there is reason to avoid) any rite of admission by laying on of hands, anointing or blessing. The receiving of the consecrated bread and wine is itself the admission. But to signal the congregation's welcome of the candidates into eucharistic participation, they may appropriately gather with their sponsors around the priest for the Peace. He greets each of them, they then move among the people in the exchange of greetings, and then they are all involved in the preparation of the altar and the presentation of the elements.

A word may be said about sponsors. Normally these would be parents, for a precondition of admission to Communion before Confirmation is often that the children have the support of a churchgoing family, the members of which will continue the process of Christian nurture that will lead eventually to Confirmation. But sometimes quite young people do become attracted to the Church, often through parochial organizations, although there is no parental connection. To deny them admission to Communion when their friends are admitted would be unfortunately divisive. The Church must therefore provide from among its members, preferably among those who have frequent contact with the children concerned, sponsors who will stand with them at their admission and stand by them in the years that follow until they come to Confirmation. It is also important that the sponsors, whether parents or not, are involved as much as the children in the preparation for First Communion.

There is no *right* day for First Communion. Easter is probably better avoided, because of the confusion with Baptism and Confirmation. Maundy Thursday or *Corpus Christi* would both provide suitable occasions, but any Sunday of the year would meet the need and, if it were not a particular feast day, the propers for the Thanksgiving for the Institution of Holy Communion, and white as the liturgical colour, could be used.

Services of Thanksgiving

The ASB provides two services of Thanksgiving, one after the birth of a child, one after the adoption of a child. Although there is within these services a blessing of those present, the rites are careful to avoid the title 'Services of Blessing', because of the consequent confusion with Baptism. They may be used as a substitute for infant Baptism, to meet a pastoral need in a parish where the policy is not to administer Baptism to the children of the uncommitted, or in a situation where the parents cannot with integrity make the baptismal promises. The desirability of eventual Baptism is stressed in both rites. But these services are much more the equivalent, not of infant Baptism, but of the Prayer Book's Churching of Women. They are best used, in anticipation of Baptism, as a family thanksgiving for the gift of a child. Although provision is made for this to be in a public service, it will normally be private, for it is not the whole congregation's concern in the way that Baptism is, and may even be used by the priest when he visits the home soon after the birth or adoption. Both services are an excellent source of prayers for homes, family life and children, which may be used happily outside the context of these services.

7

Young People and the Liturgy

Principles and Guidelines

Young people do not have a place in the Church's worship on sufferance because, without them, there will be no Church tomorrow. They have a place because, as baptized Christians, they are part of the Church today. The Sunday School movement, for all its virtues, did a great disservice to the Church when it allowed it to think of children as a separate unit, a sort of Church-in-embryo. The norm from which the parish needs to begin is that children should be present by right at the worship of the parochial family. With that right firmly entrenched, one can begin to talk about 'taking them out', appropriately, for instance, for the Ministry of the Word at the Eucharist, in order to approach it at their own level. But it is always a 'taking out' from where they belong, rather than a 'taking in' to a place that is not really for them. It is also important to bear in mind that children, just as much as adults, come to *worship*, to experience a whole range of emotions in relation to God and to one another, not just to be *taught*. Learning about the faith is always a part of worship, for all age groups. But, in work with young people, it is sometimes emphasized almost to the exclusion of all else.

Resistance to a sense of the unity of the whole congregation may come from more than one source. It may come from adults (especially those without children) who find the presence of the young people, or the concessions in the service to their presence, irritating. But it may come from the young people themselves who complain that the parish's normal worship is 'boring' (a much over-used word among the young, when more specific complaints do not seem to articulate themselves!) and who prefer their own young people's services. It would be very easy for the parish to give in to these complaints and allow each age group or culture group to have its

87

own style. In the Roman Church this happens to a great extent in a large parish where a series of different Masses on Sunday each has a different ethos. But as a regular Sunday pattern it raises more difficulties than it solves. The problem with the 'Children's Eucharist' is that children grow out of it and, where it has not been part of a commitment to the Church's worship in some broader sense, they believe that they have also grown out of church altogether. But, more fundamentally, if the Church's Sunday worship is an expression of the pattern of its life, it must have about it the give and take, the accommodation to the spiritual needs of others – young, old or middle-aged – that the whole of church life needs. Every age group needs to be prepared to worship with every other group on Sunday, to recognize that the liturgy will not therefore be exactly what it would have been if there had been less of a range to cater for, and that, to meet its own specific need, it may *additionally* have an act of worship with a different emphasis, whether on a monthly basis on a Sunday, or on a regular weekday.

Such 'group' services must be seen as *additional*, rather than alternative. Whether it be the members of the Youth Club or of the Mothers' Union, they need to be helped to see that their commitment to the worship of the whole body comes first, and their sectional interests second. For this reason Sunday provision for particular groups should not normally be more than monthly, but there is nothing to stop a weekly such service on a weekday. The old idea of the 'Corporate Communion' of particular organizations has gone rather out of fashion, but, where it is an *additional* service, it has much to commend it. A weekday morning Eucharist followed by breakfast together in school holidays is often popular with young people, and, in some parishes where Sunday activities for children integrated with the Parish Eucharist are impossible, either because of staffing or of inadequate plant, a late afternoon act of worship with 'church teaching' may be a viable alternative.

Children are often less inhibited than adults about the roles they will play in the liturgy. There will be no shortage of volunteers at a young people's service to read, take the collection, present the elements and assist in various ways. But it is also important that at the *Parish* Eucharist, young people have a place in the rotas for lesson readers, leaders of prayers

88

and other tasks that are shared. Any idea that, three Sundays out of four, it is an *adult* service needs to be dispersed. In many parishes it is possible, at the time of Confirmation, if not before, to ensure that all children have their own distinctive liturgical ministry. It may be to ring bells, to sing in the choir, to play musical instruments, to be on a rota of readers, to give out books, or it may be to serve at the altar. This last ministry has great potential in helping young people to develop their sense of reverence and worship. Even the smallest parish church, that has not the resources to 'dress up' its servers, will do well to have this form of ministry. But, where there are servers, there should always be sufficient of them for a rota. It is not a good thing for young people to serve *every* Sunday and so to grow unused to the experience of being in the congregation! As has already been said, there is no good reason why girls should not be altar servers, but for pastoral reasons the priest will often find it best to keep a balance between the two sexes. Once girls are in the majority, boys will sometimes think it a 'girlish' thing and give up. This would be a severe loss for a church prone to have more women than men in its member-ship. It is also a good policy, while making serving predomi-nantly a young people's activity, to have one or two older servers, in order to dispel the idea that serving is necessarily something one grows out of.

There is a need to be clear in work with young people of the age group with which one is dealing. Too often 'young people' are classified as one group, whereas the needs of primary and secondary school children are quite different, and the attempt to cater for both in one service disastrous. For instance, for children of primary school age, participation is a necessity. For many teenagers, however, at a certain self-conscious stage, to be allowed to sit quietly and reflectively in the back row is often far more appealing. Some sermon illustrations or visual aids, ideal for the younger group, are met with scorn by the adolescent anxious to appear sophisticated. 'What age are we aiming at?' is a vital question in work with youngsters.

The very young also have special needs. Not many clergy feel able to cope with the needs of the under-fives, but quite a few hold special weekday services for 'mums and tots', sometimes calling them 'Pram Services'. The priest needs to be clear for whom this service is devised. If it is a chance for the mothers to come to church at a time when they need not be worried about the behaviour of their children, one form is appropriate, for it is the mothers for whom he is principally catering. If, however, it is the child he has in mind, something very different is needed – simple songs and stories and prayer. He will do well very often to invite the mothers to lead such a service. It becomes then a natural extension of the 'nursery' atmosphere. The priest is present, and takes some small part, simply in order that he may be a natural part of the child's world as he or she grows up. When such a service is in the church, the children should be encouraged to explore, with some supervision and explanation, and to discover gradually what a fascinating and exciting place it is. But there is a need to exercise from the start sufficient control that the child begins to learn that this is a special place, where the needs of others have to be considered. It is more like a 'family room' than a 'nursery'. The child who, at a very young age, is allowed to do anything he wants in church, will be confused when, a little later, he is expected not to run around or to shout, for the sake of the rest of the congregation.

In other words, from the very start, children need to have developed in them that natural sense of awe and reverence that they have. And, indeed, in children's worship, it is important to remember that young people do have a capacity to be spellbound, to be transfixed, to be silent and deeply reverent. They will often also have a sense of what is shoddy and second rate and must be given superficialities no more than adults. They develop a sense of what is appropriate that is suspicious of the simply 'trendy' and are not necessarily helped by a relaxation of all formality. There is a place for the informal in worship, just as there is a place for the carefully structured, rehearsed act of worship that unfolds like a great drama. Children and adults equally need and respond to both. Where the only experience of worship children are given is the first, they miss out on a great treasury to which they are quite capable of responding.

In the realm of music, young people like the songs that belong to their own culture and they may, for a while, have time for nothing else. But they do develop a discernment that is not for long satisfied with something less than the best. They will learn the difference between the good and the indifferent among modern songs, and they will begin to appreciate some of the riches of the past. Sometimes they must be allowed to make these discoveries only by going through phases of trying out, and for a time liking, the second rate. Only the gentlest help by priest or youth leader is needed to lead them through this natural process of discovery. But where a style of young people's worship has not changed in a parish for years, something is wrong. This applies as much to prayers, and to the general 'feel' of worship, as to the music. Young people grow up; their worship should grow up with them.

In planning worship for young people, the priest needs to be very aware of the influence of school on the young people's thinking. On the one side, school (though not necessarily school *religion*) employs a whole series of modern insights, techniques and equipment to gain and retain the attention of the child. Where children's worship in church is less interesting, less carefully and attractively presented, it will fail to engage, and will be shown up for the inferior thing it is. The priest who feels out of his depth in the modern educational world will often be able to enrol for some training but, more important than this, he will need to have the humility to share his confusion with, for instance, teachers in his congregation, or even in his local school, and invite their assistance.

But the influence of school has another aspect to it. Church is not the same as school, and should not be so. Churchgoing is not primarily a didactic exercise, and, in any case, most young people, however much they enjoy school (and not all do!), do not want church worship to be a Sunday *school*. At the same time as taking seriously all educational insights, the priest must be aware of the need for church to be *different*. Never is this more so than when the members of a school come to church together, probably compulsorily. There has to be sufficient familiarity with what the children are used to, in the way of music and presentation, but enough difference for the church to be experienced as something new and refreshing.

One word more needs to be said about music. Over the last decade or so, there has been a great change in the hymns and songs used in school worship. This change has been far more sweeping than the development in the majority of our churches. The virtual exclusion of many of the old hymns, and the concentration on new songs (only some of which have found a place in the new hymn books in church) in school worship presents the priest with a real problem. He must include in most services material familiar to young people from their school experience, and in any case much of it is lively, refreshing and good. But he must also broaden their repertoire by introducing them to traditional hymnody. He needs to be aware that much of it is unfamiliar and therefore needs to be taught and rehearsed. He cannot take for granted now that his hundred favourite hymns will be familiar to his younger congregation.

The parade service of uniformed organizations always raises a question about the suitability of the Eucharist for such groups. Various options about the place of the Family Service have already been examined (in Chapter 4), and the parade service is only a particular version of a Family Service – or it should be so, if at all possible, for the priest should seek to reach the parents as well as the children on parade. Where the particular group is closely involved with church life, it will probably be appropriate to have a Eucharist, for, where there is a strong connection, many of the young people and their parents will be a part of the regular weekly communicant congregation. But, with groups less closely tied to the church, one of the other forms of Family Service will be more appropriate, especially perhaps one of those geared to lead people on to eucharistic worship. Many leaders of youth organizations would be very happy to share in a short course on worship, along the lines advocated in Chapter 5. Both because they lead prayers in their own meetings, and also because their organizations are sometimes called upon to devise worship in the church or to contribute to it, they know the need to acquire some knowledge and skills in this area and are only waiting to be invited. A parish will also do well to build up a small library of material for children's worship. There are a great many books of themes, readings, prayers and songs, including good material from the Roman Catholic Church that has, on the whole, given more thought to the needs of children in *eucharistic* worship than have other denominations, and these should be easily available to all who work with youngsters in the parish, leaders of uniformed youth organizations as much as those more obviously 'church' organizations.

The key to the participation of young people in the Church's worship is their participation in its planning, the seeking of their views (which may have to be challenged as well as heard) about the normal Sunday worship, and their involvement in the drawing up and execution of those services that are particularly for them. As with the adults, there should be a group of them who meet regularly enough to develop an expertise that can make them real fellow-workers with the priest in the planning of the liturgy. Where several youth organizations join together in a monthly service, the organizations should take it in turns to 'host' the service, helping with its planning and leading it when the day arrives. The priest will do well to trust his young people and their leaders to devise worship that will help them, without too much direction from him, and even be prepared to tolerate mistakes on the way to a more mature and satisfying standard, but he will also do well to be alongside them, sharing the planning with them, and offering his experience and expertise in a gentle and patient way.

Young People's Eucharists

Where a Eucharist has an emphasis on young people, one of the principal problems will sometimes be length. An hour is an absolute maximum for most young children, and preferably rather less, yet the teaching part of the service, the equivalent of the sermon, will sometimes be quite long where the youngsters are themselves involved in answering questions or where there are audio-visual aids. Rite A can be used, without too many modifications. The optional parts of the service may be omitted and economies of time created by such devices as using the *Gloria* as a hymn between the readings or the *Kyrie* as the Confession. Only the Creed and the Eucharistic Prayer provide particular difficulties, not so much because of their length as because of their difficult theological concepts. The Eucharistic Prayer is discussed below. The solution to the question of the Creed may be the substitution of the Apostles' Creed or a form of the baptismal affirmations:

> We believe and trust in God the Father who made the world, in his Son Jesus Christ who redeemed mankind, in his Holy Spirit who

gives life to the people of God. This is our faith. This is the faith of the Church.

In every other way faithful to the ASB rubrics, the Eucharist could follow this form without becoming too long (ASB Rite A section numbers):

1	Hymn
2	Greeting and Setting of Theme
6	Informal Invitation to Confession
9	*Kyrie Eleison* as Confession
8	Absolution
11	Collect
13 or 15	Reading
16	Hymn or *Gloria* (10)
17	Gospel
18	Address
(19)	Statement of Belief (see above)
20	Intercessions (own words but set response)
30	Peace
32/35	Hymn with Offertory Procession
37	Eucharistic Prayer (see below)
42	Lord's Prayer
43	Breaking of Bread
45/46	Communion
53	Post Communion Prayer
55	Dismissal

But the Eucharistic Prayer does provide a problem. It is both long and also theologically difficult. It is to be hoped that the Church of England will reverse its decision not to provide, as the Roman Church has done, Eucharistic Prayers for use with children. Meanwhile there are a number of possibilities, some of them within the provisions of the ASB. One is to use, as they stand, the 'Eucharistic Prayers for Masses with Children' of the Roman Church. These retain all the traditional elements of the canon, but expressed in very simple language, with brevity and the verbal participation of the people in a series of acclamations. The second possibility is to use these with sufficient amendment to give them a more Anglican 'ring'. For instance, the expression, 'Change them for us into the body and blood of Jesus Christ' would be difficult for many Anglicans and small adjustments of wording would widen their acceptance. Another possibility is to use one of the authorized Rite A Prayers, but to break it up with acclamations drawn from Roman sources. This does not solve many of the problems, but may seem more loyal to the ASB. A final possibility, which meets the objection of length, if not that of intelligibility to the young, is to use the Eucharistic Prayer for the Sick in the Appendix of Rite A (section 84). None of these is ideal. An Anglican approved form is urgently needed.

The length of the service is also affected by the administration, especially where there is a large number of non-communicants to bless. This is an occasion where, whatever the normal weekly custom of the parish, it will often be wise to introduce 'Communion stations' around the church so that the administration does not take too long. When it does children fidget, talk and lose all concentration. This may mean that lay people are administering the consecrated bread, as well as the chalice, and raises the question of lay blessing of the unconfirmed. Parishes will vary in their attitude to this, but it is not difficult to devise words acceptable to all and which may be accompanied by a hand placed on the head. 'May the Lord give you his peace' is one example. But can there be any real objection to a lay person saying, 'May the Lord give you his blessing'?

There are a number of aspects of the Eucharist that are always important, but particularly so with children. One is the need for a clear theme, enunciated at the beginning. Another is care with posture. In the order suggested above, it is doubtful whether it is worth the disturbance, for instance, to kneel briefly for the Confession, whatever the usual parish custom. Children who have disappeared under the pews are not as likely to pray as those who remain standing reverently! A third feature is the Offertory. There is a case for involving lots of children in the presentation of gifts, not only bread, wine and water, but also things they have made or tokens of work they have undertaken in the time since the last such service. Occasionally a complete 'laying of the table' is appropriate. Children love movement and the involvement of some of them in Entrance, Gospel, Offertory and other processions is good.

Why should the Gospel always be read between *two* candles, when on occasions it could be read *surrounded* by children's candles? Silence also needs preparation and inclusion in children's worship. Children are not good at maintaining silence simply because the action has stopped (during a long administration, for instance), but this does not mean that there is no place for silence in their worship. On the contrary, an invitation to keep a corporate silence to think or pray on a particular matter will meet with real response, providing it is not for too long.

Devising the Confirmation Together

The need to make the Confirmation liturgy as memorable and rich an act of worship as the bishop's requirements allow has already been discussed (in the last chapter). The more the candidates themselves can be involved in the process, the more unforgettable the celebration will be. The last part of their preparations should be the consideration of the service itself, examining the text and the meaning of the various symbols, and planning with the priest the appropriate hymns and readings, devising an Offertory procession in which all can take part, choosing the readers, perhaps making banners to adorn the church and reflecting the work done together.

On the day before the Confirmation, they can also be involved, not only in the rehearsal, but in the preparation of the church for the liturgy. They can help move in the extra chairs or alter the furniture as needed, fill the font with water, change the altar frontal to the appropriate colour, and put everything for the Eucharist in the place where it will be needed. This will involve much more work than if priest, wardens or sacristan did it quietly on their own, but it will help to create the sense of a great occasion and of it being *our* celebration. The last preparation is of the candidates. The rehearsal over, the church all ready for the next day, a final few moments is spent in reflection and prayer.

8
Marriage

The Wedding Service

In Marriage, the bride and bridegroom are themselves the ministers of the sacrament. The priest is, in a sense, the chief witness and the master of ceremonies, and, only when the couple is married, does he 'take over', so to speak, to give them God's blessing. More than at any other service, therefore, it is right to allow the participants to have a say in the form that it takes, and the wise priest will not make too many rules about what he will or will not allow to be said, sung or done. Sometimes he must say 'No' to a suggestion that would make a mockery or a nonsense of the service, but, in general, it is his task to help the people to celebrate in the way that to them seems natural and genuine. He is not, on this occasion, an arbiter of good taste. The degree of involvement of the couple in the drawing up of the service will depend a good deal on their understanding of even the most simple idea of worship. Every priest knows the blank faces that can meet his suggestion that the couple might choose even the hymns. But it is not always like that and, where the couple have some church background, to involve them as far as possible in the decisions is good. On the other hand, a liturgical principle, that they should be actively involved in the planning and execution of the service, should not be taken so far that an already nervous couple are made the more so because they feel a degree of responsibility for the smooth running of the service. The chief pastoral need is to help them to relax and to feel assured that the service is in safe hands.

The couple should have a part in the choice of which service they are to use. Most who ask for 'The Prayer Book' really want Series 1. But, in any case, the Marriage Service in the ASB has been welcomed as one of the finest parts of that book and will naturally commend itself to many. The important thing is that, in making their choice, the couple should be helped to understand that it is not principally a choice about language and intelligibility, but about different views of marriage. The picture of married life that each presents in the section of the service where the priest spells out why 'marriage is given' is significantly different from the other and, in various small ways, the ASB service points to a more contemporary and realistic view of marriage. For instance, the older service does not allow for the possibility that the bride has property to share. If anything, she *is* property to be given and received. The new service requires both bride and groom to say, 'All that I have I share with you'. Similarly, in choosing what form of the promises to use – whether the bride shall 'obey' or not – the couple need to see that the choice ought to depend, not on convention, fashion or sentiment, but on what sort of understanding they have of the marriage relationship. Liturgical questions turn out, therefore, to be the way in to some important discussion about the nature of marriage.

That strange custom, the calling of the Banns, provides a pastoral opportunity. The priest will usually encourage the couple to come to hear them read and, even without such exhortation, the couple usually do come. But such encouragement probably does more harm than good if there is not also an exhortation to the regular congregation to make them welcome and to ensure that they can find their way around the service, and also great care taken to see that the Banns are then read as if they matter (for they *do* matter to the couple), rather than hurried through as an irritating formality. Many clergy say a prayer for the couples at the end of the Banns (though even this, with the same prayer week after week, can begin to sound part of the hurried formality), and it may often be better to include the names in the Intercessions.

The couple will need help in the choice of hymns. Having provided them with a list of 'possibles' and an invitation to go outside the list, the priest does well to give them until their next meeting to decide or, if the decision must be taken on that day, at least to leave the room for a while so that they may talk more freely about the choice. They need help not only in choosing so many hymns, but also in the sort of hymn appropriate to different parts of the service. Most ordinary weddings will have three hymns. The first, at the beginning, will often provide better entrance music for the bride than an organ piece. The position of the second is more difficult. Traditionally it comes between the Marriage and the Prayers, but in the new rite this is too far into the service, for in the ASB a reading and an optional address are preferred *before* the Marriage and the prayers are briefer than in the Prayer Book. The second hymn should probably come either after the Sermon or when all the preparatory words have been said and immediately before the Marriage itself (before section 9). In the latter position it brings the congregation on to its feet for the promises, as the ASB directs. The third hymn will, except when a choir is present, replace the psalm, before the final prayers. It is unnecessary to have a hymn between the Lord's Prayer and the Blessing.

The priest greets the bride at the door. If there is a choir, it should not come to the door. The bride does not want to come up the aisle at the back of an ecclesiastical procession. It is quite sufficient for the priest alone to lead her and her attendants. After the hymn, he greets the congregation. This greeting may be expanded beyond the formal liturgical words to make people welcome, to put them at their ease and to invite them to participate fully in the service.

A rubric in the ASB directs that there should be seats for the bride and groom during the readings and sermon. These should be placed together on whichever side of the church is more convenient. Best man, bride's father and attendants should have seats kept for them at the front of the congregation. If there is only one reading and no sermon, it will be unnecessary for them to sit, but a brief address will normally be desirable, and so seating should usually be arranged. The couple should have been encouraged to make the choice of readings, and it is also appropriate that they should suggest readers for them (who should be present at the rehearsal). If the priest gives an address, it is to the whole congregation that he addresses himself in the main, not to the couple, to whom he has already talked in private, and certainly he should not talk to them in a sort of stage whisper, as some clergy have done in the past. The wedding sermon requires great sensitivity, for it has to reiterate the principles on which the marriage of Christians is based, yet with regard to the fact that some present will have experienced the breakdown of marriage. An insensitive word can do much harm.

The 'giving away' of the bride by her father, or another relation, and, indeed, her entry with him, rather than with her future husband, represent a strange and bygone concept of marriage. But they are, on the whole, harmless customs which allow father and daughter to express affection and thanks, and, though the priest may well gently question their appropriateness, he should not be worried if, nine times out of ten, they opt for the traditional custom. But, much more importantly, the ASB instruction that, for their marriage vows, the couple face one another is a fine new rubric that those who employ the older service would do well to incorporate. Let them face one another and let them *look at* one another! The vows may be memorized, read or repeated after the priest. The first is very effective, but nerve-racking for all but the most confident of couples, the second loses the strength of the facing and looking, and the third, traditional, way, for all its clumsiness, is probably the safest and most successful. The Acclamations, with which this section of the service ends, need introduction with a plea that they be vigorous and increasingly loud. A good choir will lead them effectively. If they are likely to be half-hearted, they are better omitted.

The ASB's preferred place for the Signing of the Registers is at this point, after the Marriage and before the Prayers. At whichever point the Registration takes place, it is better that it should be publicly in the body of the church. A procession to the vestry is quite unnecessary and prolongs the service. More seriously, it destroys all sense of build up and the members of the congregation all too often talk. Done decently but speedily in full view of the people, with only those necessary (couple, priest and two witnesses) involved, it maintains their attention and nothing of the atmosphere is lost. It may be done in silence or during music. If it is *not* done publicly, it would be better to keep the congregation occupied singing a hymn than sitting chattering. Placed at the end of the service, the registration destroys a fine conclusion. It is better for prayers, blessing and procession out to follow one another without interruption.

For the Prayers, the ASB permits the couple, with the help of the priest, to choose or compose their own after the set two or three. The Lord's Prayer may of course be said in its traditional form, and a wedding is an occasion when this will often seem sensible. The final blessing is of the whole congregation. The priest sends the newly married couple on their way with words of encouragement and congratulation before they turn to leave the church.

Many clergy have strict rules about photography during weddings. It is sensible to make a restriction on who may take photographs and on where they may stand. But it is a pity to forbid all photographs of the wedding in the church. It is not unreasonable for a couple to want to have preserved for posterity the moment when they make their vows, and good that there should be a record of their kneeling before the priest to be blessed. Obviously the priest will want to guard against flash bulbs, the sound of cine-cameras, etc., and this needs talking through with the couple, who will usually see the need for the service not to be disturbed unnecessarily, but it is possible for the priest to be too rigid. There is much to be said for encouraging a straightforward tape recording of the service. The couple will benefit from the opportunity to listen to the words of the service over again and even to play it each year on their wedding anniversary as a reminder of the vows they have made. The more modern video tapes provide more of a problem unless there is very strict control of the movement of camera men. (There is of course with all recordings the need to have the consent of organist and choir, especially if these are professionals.)

It is also unfortunate when the only words, outside the formal liturgical words, that the priest says to the congregation are to ask for money and to forbid confetti. The image of the Church presented by such clergy is unfortunate. There should be a collection. The ushers may be instructed to hold the plates at the door, the priest may talk to the couple during the preparation about the need to encourage the guests to give generously, and the order of service might include a note to that effect. But an appeal for money by the priest within the service jars, and the financial gain is not worth the harm done to the Church's reputation. Similarly, if confetti is to be banned (and it might be better to allow it, but charge a small sum to pay someone an honorarium for sweeping it up), let it be talked through with the couple, who will tell their families, and written notice be given, but let there be no announcement to spoil the service.

Where a couple intend to have a printed service sheet, not only is it important that the priest check the text (or preferably provide it), but desirable that he include in it, as well as the hymns and the rather vague headings such as 'The Marriage', the parts of the service in which the congregation joins. All too often congregations at weddings are simply left to be spectators. For instance, after the first hymn the text might read:

> The priest greets and welcomes the people and they reply.
>
> Priest: God is love, and those who live in love live in God: and
> God lives in them.
> The Lord be with you.
> All: And also with you.

Where no printed service sheet is envisaged, the priest might, for a small sum, provide a duplicated sheet with the hymns and the congregational parts of the service. It is, of course, preferable to this practice to issue the entire congregation with the whole Wedding Service, whether in the ASB or 'separate'.

When a bishop is present at a wedding within his own diocese, he would normally preside over the service, while delegating parts of it to others. He would usually preside over the exchange of vows and the declaration of the marriage, but this also could be delegated, but he should always retain to himself the blessing of the marriage. For the continuity of the service, it is always desirable for one priest, when the bishop is not present, to preside and to delegate, rather than to have a series of clergymen and no focus of unity.

A Wedding Eucharist

The ASB provides (on page 301) two possible ways of integrating the Marriage Service with Holy Communion. The first is preferable. It is to follow a basically eucharistic shape, with the Marriage following the sermon and the Eucharist being taken up again in the Peace. The second order is more in line with the Series 1 (following 1928) provisions where the

Marriage comes first, and then the Collect, Readings, Sermon, Peace and all that follows. It is a less satisfactory, as well as a less familiar, pattern. There is much to be said for using the Eucharist order precisely (perhaps including Collect for Purity and *Gloria*), partly in order to give the 'feel' of a celebration of the Eucharist from the start, but also because the Eucharist books in use at that point, in preference to the Marriage books, give the text of, for instance, gospel acclamations.

At the Peace it is appropriate for the newly married couple to greet one another and for each then to greet, not only his or her own family, but also the family of his or her new spouse. The couple then follow the priest to the altar step, where they present to him the bread and wine for the Eucharist. They remain standing or kneeling before the altar, but return to seats (whether the ones they used for the Ministry of the Word or others nearer the altar) if there is to be a general Communion. An opportunity for all who are qualified to do so to receive Communion, and an invitation to non-communicants to receive a blessing, should be the norm for a Wedding Eucharist. The old custom of Communion only for the couple is not normally justifiable, though there can be special pastoral reasons. The service declares that the couple 'begin a new life in the community', and it is that life among friends and neighbours that receives expression in a general Communion. Certainly there is no need to restrict the Communion to the couple on the grounds of time. It is possible to celebrate the Wedding, with short address, Eucharist and general Communion, using the new rites, in less than an hour, providing there is sufficient assistance with the administration. But if the priest and couple believe there is an important reason for not having general Communion, they can feel justified in deviating from the norm. For instance, if one of the partners comes from a totally unchurched family, there might be concern at the divisiveness of a general Communion.

Where the wedding is set within the Eucharist, it is all the more important that the idea of presidency be established. It is not ideal for one man to officiate up to the Peace and another to take over at that point. But the president having begun the service and officiated until the Collect might then delegate all until the Peace (or, if he were a bishop, until the Nuptial

Blessing). Nevertheless too many different voices simply in order to give clergy a part in the service is undesirable. The first reading should be by a lay man or woman. It can hardly ever make sense to have more than three clergy with speaking parts in the service.

The Blessing of Civil Marriages

The Blessing of the Civil Marriage of a couple, one of whom has a former spouse still living, is a theological nonsense, but sometimes a pastoral necessity, while the Church's marriage discipline is in such confusion. Theologically, we should have to say that, if a second marriage is possible and valid, the Church should be willing to celebrate it for its members. If it is not possible or valid, the Church has no business blessing it. But clergy who believe the former, but out of respect for Church authority do not marry divorced couples, often find the blessing of the civil marriage the best way pastorally to meet a need. How they understand what they are doing varies widely. Since the principal function of the priest in a marriage is to bless, some would regard the present custom as a parallel with the usual continental practice of Town Hall ceremony followed by church service.

What clergy are allowed to provide in the way of Service of Blessing also varies from diocese to diocese. In some, the priest may not perform such a service without the bishop's permission. In others there are restrictions of when it may be, who may attend and how invitations may be issued. Most dioceses provide their own authorized form, but most pre-date current liturgical reform and also have about them a some-what condescending style. There has been no national attempt to provide such a service because of the uncertainty about its future. The change, accepted in principle but not yet implemented, in the Church's discipline would do away with the necessity for it, except where a couple *preferred* a blessing only to a full celebration of marriage in church.

There are priests who will make the service look as much like a legal wedding ceremony as possible. But most clergy will want to make a distinction between the two. This will be achieved, not so much by petty restrictions on flowers, bells, choir or some of the other outward trappings, but by an insistence that the husband and wife, for so they are, walk up the aisle together and that there is therefore no 'giving away', that vows are not exchanged and, if rings are blessed, they are blessed already on the fingers of the husband and wife. In place of the exchange of vows, the couple may kneel before the priest and, after some introduction from him, say words such as these:

> God our Father, we offer and present to you ourselves, our souls and bodies, our thoughts and deeds, our desires and prayers. Take us as we are, and fashion us according to your will. Keep us faithful to you and to each other, and bring us to the fullness of your eternal kingdom.

The priest may add:

> May Almighty God, who has given you the will to undertake these things, give you also the strength to perform them and to grow together in love; through Jesus Christ our Lord.

He may bless the rings and the husband and wife. Both the beginning of the service up to the Sermon and also the Prayers at the end may follow the ASB Wedding rite. Among the prayers No. 34 in the appendix is particularly suitable for a second marriage.

Where both husband and wife are communicants, and have been restored to communion if that status had lapsed between marriages, the Blessing of the Marriage may be set within the Eucharist. When Rite A is used, the penitential material could be retained at the beginning, for an admission of past failure and a prayer for pardon should form part of the couple's prayer in this sort of case. Where such prayers are not to be part of the wedding service (and, except as part of a general confession by the whole congregation, they are probably best kept private), the priest may invite the couple to pray in these terms with him on some prior and private occasion. It is important that in such prayer the point of failure or sin is located in the breakdown of the previous marriage, not in the divorce or the decision to remarry.[1]

---

[1] A full order of service for the Blessing of a Civil Marriage is given on pp. 136ff of *Prayers for Use at the Alternative Services* by David Silk.

Renewal of Commitment to Marriage

Many parishes have found it a pastoral and evangelistic opportunity to hold occasionally a service variously called 'A Renewal of Marriage Vows' or a 'Marriage Reaffirmation'. To this they invite, where they are able to trace them, all the couples married in the church over the previous few years, who join the regular members of the congregation. Pastorally such services would be far more useful if a method could be devised in the parish of finding out what newly married couples had moved into it over the same period, wherever they had been married, since it is the ones who live locally to whom the Church's ministry can be most helpful.

The tone of such a service needs to be set with some care. It must be a celebration and affirmation of marriage, but at the same time it must minister to a variety of people, not all of whom will have radiantly happy or easy marriages. Superficial reconstruction of the wedding day, with Wagner to begin and Mendelssohn to end, a token bride and groom dressed up at the front or the too easy turning to face one another of each couple to repeat the vows, could be a most dreadful disaster. If the vows are to be used at all, it would probably be best to have them read by a single voice, followed by an invitation to reflect quietly on the good times and the bad, and a form of prayer that all could say giving thanks for all that has gone well, seeking forgiveness where there have been shortcomings and failures, and renewing commitment to one another for the future.

Hymns and biblical readings often used at weddings could be incorporated into the service, as could some parts of the text of the service. That part of the Introduction to the Marriage in the ASB which begins 'Marriage is given . . .' could form another reading or the introduction to prayer. Several of the Additional Prayers in the ASB service are suitable. Since there will be present members of the regular congregation whose spouses have died, a prayer for the departed would be appropriate too. The service should be sufficiently personal for each couple present to feel it is for them, but also sufficiently general, an affirmation of the whole institution of marriage, for single people, widowed people and even divorced people to be able to assent to it and gain from it. It is a difficult undertaking, but one worth the effort, perhaps every three years. It would soon wear thin if over-used.

In his book, *Marriage, Faith and Love*,[2] Dr Jack Dominian argues persuasively for a 'liturgical cycle for marriage'. What is envisaged is not a series of services involving unusual elements, such as some of those discussed above, but a series in which the ordinary theme of the service (Dr Dominian envisages it will be the Eucharist) helps Christian people to reflect on marriage in its various stages. He identifies four such stages – courtship, the early years of marriage, the middle years and the late years – and advocates that all four should find a place within the annual cycle of the Church's year. Readings and psalmody applicable to each are suggested. In helping people to reflect on the changes and developments over the years in marriage, the scheme is probably far more helpful than the sort of renewal of vows that looks *back* to the wedding day. Development of such a liturgical cycle in a parish would greatly enhance the congregation's contribution to the strengthening of marriage.

A different but related question is the wedding anniversaries of the members of the congregation. For ordinary anniversaries, they can be encouraged to shout their joy in a small way by asking for a thankful prayer within the eucharistic Intercessions on the nearest Sunday. For special anniversaries, when there will be a family party, they may be encouraged to come to church first for an anniversary Eucharist, open to other members of the congregation. The Roman Missal provides prayer and readings for such anniversaries.

There are occasions when a couple whose marriage has been 'on the rocks', but who have come through, will want to give thanks and to renew their vows. Here a quiet service is more appropriate, either just themselves or only with those who have shared their troubles and stood by them. In such a case, after the use of penitential material, a renewal of vows would be quite right. Using the ASB vows, for instance, the husband would begin 'I, N, renew my commitment to you, N, my wife, to have and to hold . . .', and the wife would respond

---

[2] Darton, Longman and Todd 1981.

in the similar form. But such a service, which involves such a solemn reaffirmation, should normally only be used after open and honest discussion between the couple and the priest.[3]

[3] An appropriate form for the renewal of vows on such an occasion is given by David Silk on page 135 of *Prayers for Use at the Alternative Services*.

9

Liturgy in the Home

Blessing a House

The priest is often asked to bless a house. Usually this is when the house is new, but it may also be requested when a new family moves into an old house. This is quite appropriate, for it is the family that makes the house a home and the prayers of blessing should be as much a blessing of those who live in it as of the house itself. There is a long-established tradition of going from room to room, saying in each a prayer especially suitable to that room's function.[1] It is also appropriate that, where there are to be any religious symbols in the house, whether crucifix, ikon or other picture, they should be put in place as part of the blessing of the house. But in the majority of cases the most appropriate way of blessing the house will be to celebrate the Eucharist, with the family inviting their Christian neighbours to be present and to stay for a party afterwards. Where possible, the Eucharist would be around the dining table, the readings chosen and read by members of the family, who would also present the bread, wine and water for the Offertory.

A House Eucharist

The term 'House Eucharist' is used to cover a wide variety of sorts of occasion. At one end of the scale there is the celebration that simply *happens to be* in a private home, possibly for a group of old people who cannot easily get to church. At the other end there is the celebration for a particular group who meet for study and fellowship and are probably seeking an informal and unstructured act of worship, somewhat in contrast to what they experience on Sunday. The two occasions

[1] David Silk provides such a series of prayers on pp. 139f of *Prayers for Use at the Alternative Services.*

need quite different handling. In the first case, the conditions of a church will need to be reproduced as far as possible – altar-type table, candles, the priest probably vested in alb and stole, an adherence to a set text. Some of the customs associated with House Eucharists, and commended below, will be unsettling for those for whom the House Eucharist is a necessary *substitute* for worship in church, rather than an optional extra to it. However, two modifications are nearly always necessary for a House Eucharist.

The first concerns posture. A constant getting up and down is undesirable, and difficult in comfortable chairs. Yet to remain seated throughout is an impoverishment, except with the very old and frail. It is usually best if the people *sit* until the Peace, stand for it and remain standing until all have received Communion. All then sit again for silence and the final prayers.

The second modification is in the president's gestures. All too many clergy have 'my way of celebrating', a series of movements, gestures and rituals used unfailingly at every celebration. But what is appropriate in church – a profound bow, for instance – appears out of place in a sitting room. The *setting* of worship must be taken seriously.

There will, however, be House Eucharists where the participants will welcome a more flexible liturgy and the opportunity for greater freedom than the needs of the whole parish congregation or the constraints of the church building will normally allow. Such flexibility and freedom may include the abandonment of vestments, the use of 'real' bread and ordinary table wine, the passing of the consecrated elements from one to another (though this can be clumsy and unhelpful if the 'mechanics' have not been talked through beforehand), discussion of the lections, rather than an address, and Intercessions in which all feel free to make a contribution. In such groups it is not uncommon for unauthorized eucharistic rites to be used. It is unfortunate that the Church of England makes no provision for such experiment or freedom as is found in the Episcopal Church of the United States. In the American Prayer Book a 'skeleton' order is provided, where all may be extemporized except the latter part of the Eucharistic Prayer. The rubrics state, however, that 'it is not intended for use at the principal Sunday or weekday celebration of the Holy Eucharist' and that the rite 'requires careful preparation by the Priest and other participants'. It cannot be over-emphasized how important that second instruction is. Such a celebration should only emerge out of a long and painstaking exploration of what is involved in the Eucharist. The American order is set out as follows:

THE PEOPLE AND PRIEST

Gather in the Lord's Name

Proclaim and Respond to the Word of God

The proclamation and response may include readings, song, talk, dance, instrumental music, other art forms, silence. A reading from the Gospel is always included.

Pray for the World and the Church

Exchange the Peace

Either here or elsewhere in the service, all greet one another in the name of the Lord.

Prepare the Table

Some of those present prepare the table; the bread, the cup of wine, and other offerings, are placed upon it.

Make Eucharist

The Great Thanksgiving is said by the Priest in the name of the gathering, using one of the eucharistic prayers provided. The people respond – Amen!

Break the Bread

Share the Gifts of God

The Body and Blood of the Lord are shared in a reverent manner; after all have received, any of the Sacrament that remains is then consumed.

The order adds a final rubric that 'when a common meal or Agapé is a part of the celebration, it follows here'. It may be noted that this American order is not intended only for use in private houses, though this is probably its principal use. Its framework could be used in an English setting, with loyalty to the Rite A rubrics, provided that a Collect is said, a second scriptural reading is included, confessional material is used and the authorized text of the Absolution used, the Eucharistic Prayer follows one of the approved forms, the Lord's Prayer is said and the set text is used for the Fraction. Many will wish that the shorter Eucharistic Prayer in the ASB (on page 171) 'for use with the sick' had been entitled 'for use at a House Eucharist'. It is entirely suitable for use in such a context, except in its lack of congregational response; *Sanctus, Benedictus* and Acclamations are omitted.

There is a danger in the proliferation of House Eucharists. It is that, just when people have come to realize that the Eucharist is never a private rite, somehow only involving God and themselves, rather than a participation in the life of the whole Church, and more specifically in the life of the local Christian community, a new danger emerges of regarding it as a semi-private rite of a small group. It is a very rare sort of house group that needs regular eucharistic worship. An occasional celebration, perhaps at the end of a series of meetings, is appropriate; and the presence of the parish priest to preside at it will act as a counterbalance to any tendency towards exclusion or sectarianism in the group. But even there the wise priest will sometimes think it right to remind the group that such occasional eucharistic worship is an offshoot of what happens regularly in the parish church. This warning does not apply, of course, where a different pattern of church life has been developed and approved and the 'House Church' has become the basic regular weekly unit for Eucharist, as well as for other church life and activity.

Extended Communion

Extended Communion, or Extended Distribution, is the name now more usually given to that custom, previously termed 'Communion from the Reserved Sacrament', by which the sick or housebound person receives Communion from the consecrated elements set aside at a previous celebration in the church. It has sometimes been regarded as a necessary second best, where the number of such communicants is sufficiently great that it would be impossible for the priest to 'celebrate' in every home. But, in reality, it should be regarded as the norm, and the celebration in the home as the unusual, but sometimes pastorally desirable, variant. For, when the sick or housebound person receives Holy Communion in the home, it is far more than the making of a personal Communion. The Eucharist is not primarily an act of personal piety, but the proclamation and forging of corporate identity. The housebound communicant is therefore joining with the community in its celebration, and is thus being reassured and enabled to say: 'No. I am not cut off and isolated. I am still part of the Church and its worship.'

Such thinking has implications for the manner in which the Church exercises its eucharistic ministry to the housebound. First and foremost, it becomes clear that the practice of the priest visiting the sick to conduct a private celebration in the home is a theological and liturgical nonsense. Yet if a communicant is housebound for a long time, perhaps permanently so, he or she will want occasionally 'to hear the whole service'. In such a case it will be desirable to hold a celebration of the Eucharist within the home. It should, in this case, be made clear that this is in no way a 'private' celebration, nor a substitute for that regular extension of the Parish Eucharist into the home. For such a celebration, the members of the family should be present, and with them, or in place of them if they are not Christians, Christian neighbours and, if possible, other members of the congregation. If the housebound person belongs to a house group or other parochial organization, then let the celebration be part of that group's activity. The Church of England has now authorized an Order for the Eucharist with the sick, where the 'full service' does not seem appropriate.

The change from talk of 'Reserved Sacrament' to 'Extended Communion' marks a shift of theological emphasis which, while perfectly acceptable in intelligent Catholic circles, makes the practice far more acceptable in the Evangelical tradition than in the past. The presence of Christ under the sacramental form of bread and wine in the aumbry has often been presented as almost independent of the sense of eucharistic community in the parish. Thus, in the majority of churches, the consecrated elements have been renewed on a monthly basis, probably at a weekday celebration. There is therefore no obvious sense in which the housebound communicant can say, 'I am participating in the Parish Eucharist'. Where the elements are set aside week by week at that Eucharist, where those who are to be incorporated into the experience by the extended distribution are prayed for in the Intercessions, and where the time gap between Eucharist and distribution is reduced to a minimum, the sense of belonging and participation is enhanced.

The weekly renewal of the consecrated elements at the main Parish Eucharist is fundamental to this fresh understanding. The recent House of Bishops' Guidelines advocate this practice. The ideal is that, during the time of the Eucharist, the housebound communicant will be preparing for Communion, especially by reading the earlier parts of the service, including the lections. At the Breaking of the Bread, or immediately after Communion, or at the end of the service, with as little delay as possible, the consecrated elements are taken to those at home. The distribution is extended beyond the church. Of course, it is not always necessarily right for the distribution in homes to follow immediately. Sometimes the parish priest will want to take the sacrament himself, or to spend a lengthy period of time with the communicant. In such cases, he waits until a convenient weekday, but it is still an extension of the community's Eucharist.

But in cases where individuals who are subsequently to receive Communion are joined in prayer to the Parish Eucharist, it is clearly desirable that the Extended Distribution should take place immediately after the service. Where this is to be done, lay people must be trained and authorized for this ministry. This is nothing novel, for it was part of the liturgical practice of the early centuries for the lay people to take the sacrament to those who could not be present in church. Dioceses will vary in their procedures, but Church of England practice requires that it be *authorized* lay people who share this ministry with priests and deacons. In some instances, it will be sensible to use those same lay people who are authorized to assist with the distribution in church.

Those who are to take Communion to the housebound need to be carefully instructed, not only in the reverent conduct of the service in the home, but also in the need to develop a genuine pastoral relationship with those to whom they take the sacrament. They should go straight from the service and, on arrival, should not delay long in 'chat' before beginning the home liturgy, though sometimes a pastoral conversation with the communicant about his or her condition, fears, anxieties or joys, which can be gathered up in the Intercessions, will be appropriate. How much of the authorized service needs to be used will depend partly on the health of the housebound person and partly on the extent to which he or she will have 'read the service' while the Eucharist has been going on in church.

The Bishops' Guidelines and the authorized services themselves insist that Extended Communion should normally be administered 'in both kinds' (unless the communicant cannot receive solid food), but reception by intinction is an acceptable, convenient and well-established form of Communion in both kinds. In administering the bread on which a spot of wine has been placed, the minister says, 'The Body and Blood . . .' It is desirable that the sacrament should be taken in a pyx. Where a parish does not have sufficient pyxes, other similar and suitable containers may, at least as a temporary measure, be happily used.

There is much to be said for those who take the sacrament leaving the church immediately after the Fraction and themselves receiving Communion with the housebound person, but this procedure need not necessarily be followed. Where other members of the household are communicants, they should be encouraged to receive the sacrament at the same time. The 'minister' should hardly ever leave without a time of informal conversation with the housebound person, and very often with the family, who frequently find the care of the housebound a strain. Before leaving, the 'minister' should consume any of the consecrated bread that may remain, unless it is to be returned immediately to an aumbry in the church.

A word may be said here about the use of the 'Reserved Sacrament' in church, though strictly it is outside the compass of this chapter. There has been some increase in the use of the Reserved Sacrament to give Communion in church when no priest is available. In the Prayer Book of the American Church, a deacon may preside at such a service. In England its use has grown to meet the problem provided by the decline in the number of clergy. In a multi-parish benefice, for instance, the priest might preside at the Eucharist in one church, sending the consecrated elements to the other churches where the people had gathered. It would be wrong to rule this out in all circumstances, for where there is a genuine sense of the unity of all those involved in their different churches it might just be defensible. But, on the whole, it is best avoided (as the Bishops' Guidelines insist). For the total eucharistic action of priest and people, including the consecration of the bread and wine, is a single and indivisible whole. The Eucharist is more than 'taking Communion'. The Church must seek a more satisfactory means of providing full eucharistic worship for all its people, presumably by the development of non-stipendiary and local ministries.

Another theologically indefensible use of the Reserved Sacrament is the practice of reserving in the aumbry what remains after one celebration, normally because numbers have been miscalculated, for use at another celebration. It is little less than ludicrous when bread and wine are brought to the altar, thanks given over them, the bread broken for distribution, and then quite other bread and wine, belonging to some other celebration, and often that of some different group entirely, are brought out for the sharing of the sacrament. It is obviously convenient, when vast quantities remain, to put the remainder in the aumbry, but only in order that it may be more easily and reverently consumed after the service.

Ministry to the Sick and Dying

There is of course much more to the pastoral care of those who are ill than simply a liturgical ministry. But prayer and worship do have an important place and, the more sick the person is, the more likely that familiar liturgical words and actions will help where conversation and counselling fail. The Church's ministry of healing is by no means concerned only with those housebound or in hospital. Its concern for the wholeness of the human being, for psychological and spiritual well-being as much as physical cure, has given it a central place in the Church's life, and ought to lead to acts of worship in the church itself for all those who, while appearing to be physically fit, have come to know their need of divine healing and reconciliation. But there is an important connection between this ministry of healing to the whole Christian body and the more specific ministry to the sick and to the dying. Where talk of healing has been part of the congregation's ordinary experi-

ence, where prayer for wholeness has been real and powerful, and where outward signs have reinforced the prayer –
the laying on of hands or anointing with oil – the sick person,
too ill perhaps to be taught something new and too likely to
be alarmed by new and apparently extreme rites, will nevertheless respond thankfully to the familiar.

When a parishioner is dying, it is a bit too late to commence
a course of sacramental theology. Preparation for ministry in
extreme sickness should have a regular place in the life of the
local church both by careful teaching and by use of these sacramental forms wherever they are appropriate. It is also too late,
when there is extreme illness, to begin to teach that profound
Christian truth that 'cure' and 'healing' are two quite different
things. It is not often granted to the Church to work a 'cure' in
God's name. But it is not unusual for it to be the instrument of
his healing, in terms of acceptance, peace and self-offering in
the face of adversity. Where that has been well taught, prayer,
the laying on of hands and anointing will not be misunderstood, nor consequent disappointment engendered. (Of the
theology of healing and of anointing, see more in Chapter 10.)

Not all the sick to whom the priest may minister are communicants. His judgement here is vital. He may, just occasionally, believe that sickness has brought the person to the point
where Confirmation should be administered. The crisis of
illness can often turn into the moment of faith. Where this is the
case, he should not hesitate to ask the bishop to visit the sick
person to confirm. In another instance, he will judge, not that
Confirmation is needed, but that a baptized person, near
death, should receive Communion for the first time. This can be
left to his own pastoral judgement. But, more often than not,
the life-long non-communicant needs to receive the Church's
ministry at a more familiar level, that of the simple prayer,
psalm and bible reading, and the hand squeezed as much as the
hand laid upon the head.

But, for the communicant, the sacrament of the Eucharist
will be the regular and repeated means of spiritual sustenance
and healing through illness and in the face of death. Whatever
elements find an occasional place, this remains the basic rite
of healing for the sick. On occasions it may be preceded by
Confession, either the rite of Penance in its sacramental form

where that has been previous custom, or something less formal. On other occasions there will be a laying on of hands. This can vary from a solemn liturgical act to a simple gesture when pronouncing the blessing at the end of the Eucharist. On yet other occasions, the sick person will be anointed. Whether the outward sign be the laying on of hands or anointing with oil, it needs to be emphasized that these are *with prayer*, preferably the prayers of those gathered in the home with the priest and, when circumstances allow, the prayers of the sick person as well.

Although there can be no hard and fast rule, it will very often be right to regard the laying on of hands as a regular and frequent ministry to those who are ill, usable when the illness is not extreme, repeatable throughout the illness and not necessarily requiring preparation on the part of the recipient, but to regard anointing as a solemn act, not used for minor illness, to be administered only once except in a protracted illness and, except *in extremis*, preceded by preparation, and maybe teaching, of the recipient. Anointing would normally be within the Eucharist, or within the administration of the Extended Communion, and therefore a priest would be the minister of it. Because of its solemn sacramental nature, it would not *normally* be right for the priest to delegate anointing to the laity, but a particular pastoral circumstance could arise in which it would be appropriate, and there would be no theological objection to this, for the link with the Church and its authority is provided by the fact that the oil has been blessed by the bishop. Reserving anointing for special times must not, however, be taken so far as to reinforce the traditional misunderstanding that unction is solely a preparation for death. It is a solemn act of *healing*, and sound teaching must repeatedly make this point if these powerful ministries of the Church are to be valued, used and understood.

In ministering to those who are ill, special care needs to be taken about the form of service used. The new Church of England rites, authorized since the ASB, provide Rite A and Rite B forms, but it will, with the elderly, often be appropriate to use the language of the Book of Common Prayer. The more ill the person is, the more important that the *familiar* be used. An important question emerges here about the variety of liturgical and biblical texts available in our own day. When we, who are used to so many different rites and translations and who commit so much less to memory, grow old, what liturgical words will those who minister to us be confident we shall find familiar?

It is not very often now that, outside hospitals, clergy have the privilege of ministering to the dying. Where this does happen, where, for instance, a parishioner spends a week or more in gradual decline and, towards the end, is only semi-conscious, a type of ministry becomes desirable that normally would not be so. When fully conscious and not in any immediate danger, most people would prefer the priest to stay long enough to pray with them but also to talk to them. Recognizing the demands on his time, they would rather he came once a fortnight, and made of it a genuine pastoral opportunity, than rushed in and out more frequently, but with no time to talk. With the dying, it is different. When somebody lingers on, it is good if the priest can call at the home, clasp the hand of the dying person and say a few familiar prayers, *every day* until the end comes. In this situation, the five-minute visit, without time to stop and talk, will be appreciated just as, under other circumstances, it would be thought a discourtesy. The priest will never know, of course, how much of what he prays the dying person hears, though the sudden gripping of his hand or the lips parted to express an 'Amen' will suggest to him that, when all else has failed, familiar liturgical words and actions are 'getting through'. Many clergy know of situations where they themselves, or even the dying person's family, have been unrecognized, where the family are saying, 'He doesn't even know who we are', but where, in semi-consciousness, the Our Father or Psalm 23 have produced signs of response.

Even when the priest suspects that the dying person hears or comprehends nothing, his regular 'popping in' will be a great consolation to the family. Ministry to the dying is always also ministry to those whose mourning begins before ever the body has breathed its last. In some cases there will be the need to talk with them as the illness continues, helping them to acceptance and peace. In others, there will be little to say, but great point in drawing them into the prayer at the bedside or even sharing for a while their own silent vigil. When death has come, if he can do so, the priest will want to gather the family together to pray. If they can be persuaded to gather around the body, it will often make coping with the death easier later on. Words to pray are provided in various books, but this, of all occasions, is an obvious time for the personal and the impromptu. But, *whenever* the priest visits a sick or dying person, he needs to bear in mind the spiritual needs of those who are under great strain in giving constant care while watching the deterioration of those they love.

10
Healing and Reconciliation in Church

The Ministry of Healing

In the New Testament, in St Mark's Gospel, for instance, where the twelve are sent out to preach repentance and to anoint the sick, or in the Epistle of James, where the elders of the Church are to be called to anoint and to pray over the sick, there is a *community* setting. People are being put into a right relationship with the community and, through the community, with God. Similarly, repentance, and with it sacramental 'confession', are closely linked with ministry to the sick, not because sickness is a punishment for sin, but because sin itself, offence against God and his people, his community, is a form of dis-ease. In this chapter, therefore, the ministry of healing, 'unction' as it has traditionally been called, and the ministry of reconciliation, 'penance' or, less happily, 'confession' as it has traditionally been called, are considered together, distinctive but inter-related aspects of the Church's ministry of bringing whole-ness. They are also both considered within the context of the Christian community – Healing and Reconciliation *in church* – and public worship is envisaged as their usual setting. In the same way as Communion in the home is an 'extension' of the community's Eucharist, so 'private' laying on of hands, anointing or absolution is an extension of corporate worship.

The English Reformation sought to do away with the super-stitions that had grown up around the ministry of healing. Its first reappearance within the Anglican Communion was in the 1928 Prayer Book of the American Church. But today the ministry of healing is becoming widespread as a regular feature of the Church's ministry. And *regular* it should be; not a last, desperate hope, but an ever-present, ever-available sacrament for use whenever and wherever required, however serious or small the illness.

The symbols used in the ministry of healing are reminders of the corporate nature of our faith and of our belonging to the Body of Christ. Olive oil, an ancient healing and soothing balm, is now reintroduced also to its historic place in the liturgy of *initiation*, as well as of healing, and is suggestive of the wholeness of the new life to be found in being of Christ and his Body. The laying on of hands, an ancient symbol of blessing, commissioning and (as at Confirmation) empowering, evokes, asserts, acknowledges and enables the Holy Spirit at work in us as members of the community of the Spirit. In anointing with the laying on of hands we have, therefore, the symbols and proclamation of belonging to the community: of Christ's presence, sharing in suffering, bringing new life. This sacrament is not a private prescription, a magical potion or a wonder drug, to be used in emergency if all else fails. Rather, behind it lies the belief that wholeness of life requires right relationships with God and each other in the Christian community, that what makes us the individuals we are is, not only our physical bodies and our minds, but the extension of ourselves into relationship with one another, with the community and with the world. Sickness distorts this relationship, puts us at dis-ease. This dis-ease needs more than clinical cures to bring us back to the wholeness. Acknowledgement of this reality is the first step to healing our dis-ease. The ministry of healing enables the Christian to do this, to put himself into a right relationship with God and the community, and to say to his Lord, 'Your will be done'.

It is against this background of thought that the parish priest needs to appreciate, teach and practise the ministry of healing. The healing works that Jesus himself did were signs of the Kingdom already present and growing in the world, signs of the ultimate transformation of man that is our purpose and destiny. In administering the sacraments to the sick, the Church is proclaiming and sharing this corporate faith and vision.

It is a mistake to look for so-called 'results' of the healing ministry in a clinical sense, for that is an attempt to confine God's work to our own immediate horizons. Nevertheless, that being said and that needing to be repeatedly taught, many can testify to the reality of the Church's healing ministry. There are many examples of those enabled to grow through pain and suffering to become people of great spiritual stature, of those given the confidence which enables the doctors to do their work so much more effectively, of those enabled to die well, who could not previously face that step in life, of those patients and relatives whose bitterness with life, with God and with each other has been healed and transformed, of those who, despite handicaps, have received the courage and grace to live life to the full, and of those who come out of the depths of despair and guilt weeping with joy and relief at the assurance of a fresh start. There is no limit to these experiences, and it is not the task of the Church to define too narrowly their bounds.

Nor is it always desirable, or even possible, to define the point where sickness turns into sin or, to put it differently, where what we are not responsible for turns into what we are responsible for. In our fallen world, sin and sickness are inextricably linked. The wisest of confessors or counsellors will often be unable in a particular situation to distinguish the two, and ordinary people will more often than not be uncertain in this area. Some of the psychological and sociological insights of our own day have added to our confusion. But it is too easy simply to attribute all our ills to causes outside our control and to seek, as a consequence, a healing from the outside, so to speak. In our own day just as the ministry of healing – Holy Unction – has become far more readily used, so the ministry of reconciliation – Penance – has been used the less. Here is a danger and a warning. For all its intrinsic goodness, the ministry of healing can be an escape from *responsibility*. It need not be this, for penitence should nearly always form part of the preparation for the laying on of hands or anointing. Without a fairly rigorous opening up of the self, whether privately or to priest or counsellor, the healing power has little chance of impact. Even where the illness seems to be a straightforwardly physical one, the opening of the heart in confession, of some sort or other, before anointing or the laying on of hands is to be recommended.

Services for those who are sick should be part of the usual provision in every parish church. This is no esoteric ministry for those with particular gifts, though there are special forms of healing and reconciliation, such as the ministry of deliverance – exorcism – that are best left to experts (and in many dioceses are restricted to such experts on the bishop's authority). The gift of healing is given, not to clergymen in their ordination, but *to the Church*. The role of the priest in this ministry is one of liturgical and organizational presidency. Where a service is in church, the priest presides. Where a sick person is to receive Communion or the laying on of hands or anointing, it is an extension of that service, and lay people may administer with the goodwill of their priest. Where oil, blessed by the bishop, is used, the ministry is seen more clearly to be the work of the *Church*, not of the individual who administers it. But there are, undoubtedly, among both clergy *and laity*, those who have been given special healing gifts. The priest must not feel intimidated or threatened when one of his people clearly has such a gift. Rather, enthusiastically and thankfully, he should use that person both pastorally and liturgically. Let that person exercise the ministry of laying on of hands or anointing at or from the service at which the priest presides. The Canons are clear that lay people may exercise this ministry on behalf of the Church. There is particular value when a Christian doctor will share this ministry in the parish, a helpful sign that the Church's liturgical healing ministry is not in opposition to, but complementary to, the medical profession's work of healing.

The Church's ministry of healing should be centred upon the Eucharist. If the theological reflections with which this chapter began are accepted, the reason will be obvious. Never is the health of the Body of Christ more in mind than when the Church gathers to celebrate the Eucharist. It could also very reasonably be argued that no words or rituals additional to those that normally form the Eucharist need be used. For every Eucharist is, in a sense, a sacrament of healing, every Communion a service for the sick. The Prayer Book Communion Rite, and particularly Thomas Cranmer's much loved 'We do not presume . . .', taken up in poetry such as George Herbert's 'Love bade me welcome . . .', makes this point tellingly. It would be a loss if, in all the renewed emphasis on the laying on of hands and anointing, that were lost. It is *par excellence* the healing sacrament. When, therefore, there is nevertheless to be a special healing service, with particular words and sacramental actions, it is best contained within a eucharistic framework. The new Church of England services for Ministry to the Sick envisage this, though they make provision also for the context to be Morning or Evening Prayer. This authorized order envisages laying on of hands or anointing after the readings and prayers and before the Peace. Such an order is wise, and preferable to the quite frequent practice of some remaining at the altar rail for such a ministration after Communion. This makes less sense, for the Peace is the symbol of the reconciliation and wholeness of the Body and it should follow the laying on of hands or anointing. And the sharing of the sacramental elements should be seen as the climax and completion of the reconciling, sustaining and healing process, and not as a prelude to something 'more special'.

An important issue lies behind such questions as, 'Who is in need of healing?', or 'Who is to be anointed?'. There is too easy a tendency to categorize people into 'sick' and 'healthy'. Such an attitude (and it can sound painfully condescending) often marks intercession for the sick in church at ordinary services. Those in need of healing are nearly always 'they' and not 'we'. While it would be unhelpful to undermine people by undue emphasis on their own 'sickness', it is important in the Christian life that all recognize their constant need of forgiveness and restoration. Prayers that obscure that truth need to be avoided. So do healing services where people appear to be categorized too easily into healers and needing healing.

Mention must be made of the particular ministry of the Church to the handicapped, whether to the blind, the deaf and dumb, those confined for a variety of reasons to wheelchairs, and those mentally handicapped. The Church of England often seems a good deal too self-conscious in its ministry to handicapped people. It has not been able to free itself of the embarrassment when faced with handicap that many ordinary people feel. Quite apart from special services for groups of handicapped people, there is a need to create as far as possible an easy and relaxed atmosphere in which the handicapped need not feel too singled-out. At a purely practical level churches should ensure that there is provision to allow those in wheelchairs to enter the church, without problem of steps, and to find room to sit in their chairs *as part of the congregation* and not separate from it. Provision should always have been made for giving them Communion and they as much as anybody else should take their part in the various ministries of the liturgy. A blind man or woman can read the lesson. A man or woman confined to a wheelchair can lead intercessions. A deaf person can present the Offertory. Every Christian congregation should try to ensure the *acceptance* of the handicapped as part of its ordinary life. But, in addition (and this must be outside the compass of this book) provision should be made very sensitively for handicapped people to worship sometimes in ways particularly suited to them, and here there is a need for the publication of material to help priest and congregation in this task.

A final word is needed to emphasize one aspect of this ministry mentioned briefly earlier. It is very easy for the Church to fall into the habit of speaking as if *its* pastoral and liturgical work constituted the sum total of God's healing activity. This is false in two ways. It is untrue because the major contribution to the Church's healing work is probably through the skill and devotion of Christian doctors, nurses and others working full time in medicine and allied social work. It is also untrue because God clearly works also through individuals and agencies who do not recognize themselves as part of the Church. Those Christian folk who work in the medical profession need to be assured of the constant prayerful support of the whole Christian community which recognizes its work as part of, perhaps the front line of, the Church's ministry of healing. The words used in healing services and in the regular eucharistic Intercessions should strengthen, rather than undermine, this view.[1]

The Reconciliation of Penitents

The power to absolve sin, like the authority to anoint, is given to the Church, rather than to the ordained ministry. That is the biblical emphasis. In pronouncing absolution, a bishop or priest speaks in the name of the Church, for, as has been said

[1] There is, incidentally, in Christian praying, and books of prayers, a strange bias for *hospital* medicine, at the expense of the general practitioner. The local doctor is a significant agent of God's healing, in quite a broad sense, in the local community.

above, it is from the body of the faithful, as much as from God, that we are estranged by sin. It is the privilege of the bishop or priest to reconcile the sinner with the Church as much as to proclaim his reconciliation with God. Confession and Absolution, therefore, for all the privacy that naturally protects it, is very much an act of the community. In the recently proposed Church of England order, the penitent, for instance, confesses 'to almighty God, and to his whole Church', and the same idea lay behind the more traditional confession to God and the saints.

The sense of the corporate gives an important dimension to our talk of sin and evil that might otherwise be lost. Even though, in the Anglican tradition, our emphasis has chiefly been on corporate confession, in the context of public worship, our teaching has very often been in terms of sin as our very personal and private failures. Our implication in the great social and political evils of our time, the inevitable consequence of our living in a fallen world, is not often what is in our hearts when we confess *our* sins. And, indeed, were it always so, there would be a danger that we would be able to obliterate the memory of our personal and private sin by an undue concentration on the social shared sin in which we are caught up. Nevertheless the wider perspective, and indeed a whole range of levels that includes, for instance, the corporate sin of our local church in its particular blindness, prejudice or harshness, needs to be taught. In previous generations, the words of the liturgy themselves strengthened this understanding. It is strange that a generation that had known about Auschwitz and Hiroshima could so easily reject such phrases as 'the burden of them is intolerable' as unsuitable. It sometimes seems that there *are* times of national or international tension or crisis when only the extraordinary and over-powerful language of a Cranmer will cope with the emotions that are aroused and need expression, even though in times of peace and prosperity those same words and phrases seem remote and unreal.[2] Perhaps it is a false solution to turn to old words because they convey the right mood. Perhaps we should seek new words and accom-

---

[2] These reflections arose, for me, during the shortlived 'Falklands War', when only the language of the Prayer Book seemed to be able to articulate deep emotions of confusion, horror and sadness.

panying rituals to express in contemporary forms that sense of deep confusion, perplexity or even penitence that must sometimes affect communities or even nations. But whether the old or the new, the Church must be able to find the means by which the burden of the intolerable can be worked through liturgically.

None of this is to argue for the return of services week by week that have a strong penitential note. One of the welcome liberations of the liturgical renewal of the last generation has been the freedom to shake that off and to make our worship more joyful and celebratory. But it does argue for the inclusion in the year of occasions when the congregation may gather to reflect on the need for penitence and, expressing that penitence, to be assured of the divine forgiveness. The liturgical year provides occasions in the use of Advent and Lent. Among national celebrations Remembrance Sunday gives another opportunity. At such services there should be opportunity for reflection on both individual and corporate sin, much time of silence, the pronouncement of absolution and an element of praise and thanksgiving. It would also be possible, in some parochial circumstances, to hold such services on weekdays in preparation for some of the great feast days of the year. A corporate service of Penance of such a type as this, built into the regular parish programme, but available also for use if particular national or international circumstances seemed to make it appropriate, would give a sober balance to worship which in our day sometimes gives the impression of treating evil too casually. Such services would be similar to corporate services of Penance in the Roman Catholic Church, and material could well be drawn from these, though in the Roman tradition there is built into this corporate service a private moment when each individual may make his confession to a priest. This would not be appropriate in many Anglican settings. In the Roman Church such services have been introduced partly to emphasize the corporate nature of the sacrament and partly to try to halt the considerable decline in the use of the confessional.

But, when all this has been said, it remains true that the reconciliation of penitents, other than in the sense that this is done at every public service, will more often than not be in a private context. The proposed Church of England 'A Form for the Reconciliation of a Penitent' (which the General Synod failed to authorize) provides a satisfactory shape for this. The rubrics ('The priest welcomes the penitent . . .', 'The penitent should be encouraged to confess his sins in his own words . . .') indicate the desirability of creating a relaxed and informal atmosphere, and in any case the title implies that other forms may be used. This opportunity to mould the service to suit the occasion is welcome. There will also be the opportunity to give different parts of the service greater or lesser weight depending on circumstances. In one instance the occasion may be principally one of counselling. In another that element may be unimportant and the giving of absolution the principal need. Many clergy have found that normally their study is a better place than the church for this ministry, and two arm chairs more appropriate than the old arrangement with the penitent kneeling beside the seated priest. Many have been helped by this 'loosening up' of the style of penance who would never have coped with the formal confession at the advertised time in the parish church.

But there are warnings to be sounded. They are these. First there is the danger that someone who comes for assurance is given a helpful chat and goes away assured of the vicar's sympathy and understanding, but uncertain of the divine forgiveness. The offer of confession and absolution at the end of a pastoral interview may deepen the encounter, make it a meeting between penitent and God, rather than simply penitent and priest, and bring both clarity and resolution. Too many clergy fail to make that offer, which, if it is made sensitively, can always be refused, and so miss an opportunity.

Secondly, there is the danger of confusing too easily the distinct roles of counsellor and confessor. There are those who come seeking advice who must be helped to self-understanding and thus to the sacrament of penance. Equally, there are those who come seeking to make their confession who must be helped to perceive themselves otherwise than their confession indicates. But, on the whole, the priest must not impose his own preferred style of help. There are those who come seeking to make their confession, in a fairly formal setting, the familiarity of which gives them confidence to pour out their souls. Devotional habits such as these are to be respected. There is a sort of liberation which so removes familiar boundaries that it creates fear and confusion, rather than the freedom intended.

Finally, there is the danger – with some people only – of robbing the sacrament of its power by depriving it of its solemn formality. Sometimes deep guilt and keenly-felt sin is taken away, not by a reassuring and casual 'Don't worry!', but by a painful self-exposure in penance and a powerful solemn declaration of forgiveness. The church building, the kneeling position, the wait for one's turn, the purple stole, all *help* (just as, for other people, they all hinder, and even do grave harm). All this argues for an adaptability in the priest who must be ready to provide different sorts of settings for people of varying temperaments, and to be himself relaxed in all of them.

A word has already been said of the interrelationship of healing and reconciliation. Penance is nearly always part of the preparation for anointing or the laying on of hands. The converse is also often true. There will be occasions when a penitent comes full of his sin and guilt. The priest will help him to sort out the areas of his responsibility and the areas where he is a victim of circumstances not totally within his control. The area of his responsibility, his sin, will be met with the grace of absolution. But there will be occasions when the priest will want to meet the sickness with the laying on of hands or anointing. The use of these sacramental acts, with their message that sickness as much as sin is responsible for his condition, will in itself be an act of healing and reconciliation.

The Blessing of Oils

The use of oils in both initiation and healing has been mentioned in both Chapter 6 and in the more recent sections on ministry to the sick. Where it is accompanied by explanatory teaching, this return to biblical and primitive practice can be a great enrichment of the Church's sacramental life. At root its use is about unity and wholeness. Whether it is the concept of protection in pre-baptismal anointing at the signing with the cross, or of joy and gladness at the Spirit's indwelling in the Chrism oil at Confirmation, or of healing in the anointing of the sick, it is always about health, wholeness and fullness in the Christian life. In a sense all these different anointings, though the occasions seem very different, are about the very same thing. God marks us as his own, sets his seal upon us, and therefore places us under his protection.

The sense of unity is indicated by the fact that the oil has been blessed or consecrated by the bishop. The ASB provides propers for the Eucharist on Maundy Thursday when this takes place, and more recently an order of service has been drawn up giving the text for the blessing of the oils and allowing a renewal of priests' vows at the same service. (The General Synod has so far declined to approve this text.)

There is a very respectable school of thought which says that 'oil is oil', so to speak, and that to bless and set aside different oils for different sacramental acts is unnecessary. Indeed – so the argument would run – the point that the same processes are at work in initiation and in healing is lost if there are distinctive oils. Nevertheless the Church of England's proposals have preferred to follow the more ancient tradition of three distinct oils. The oil for the sick is olive oil, is normally blessed by the bishop but may be blessed by the priest using the authorized words, and is blessed that those who are anointed with it may be freed from pain and suffering and given inward peace. The oil for the signing with the cross before baptism is also olive oil, blessed by bishop or priest. The prayer of blessing prays that those who are anointed with it may be strengthened in their fight against sin and brought to share in the victory of Christ. The third oil, the Oil of Chrism for anointing at Confirmation, is traditionally mixed with balsam or other perfumes. The rubrics indicate that the blessing or consecration of Chrism is reserved to the bishop. In addition to its use in Confirmation, it may be used at Baptism, where the signing of the cross is performed after the baptism, and in other rites of blessing and consecration. The prayer of blessing prays:

> Let this chrism be to those who are anointed with it
> a sign of joy and gladness.
> Let your Holy Spirit rest upon them

that they may bear witness to Christ,
and so live in the power of his Gospel
that they may proclaim the coming of his kingdom.

The Eucharist at which the oils are blessed has traditionally been called 'The Mass of the Chrism'. It is normally celebrated on Maundy Thursday morning and is quite different in character from the Eucharist of the Last Supper in the evening. In the Roman Church an annual renewal of priestly vows has been added to it and it has become customary for the bishop to summon his clergy to celebrate this Mass with him. Many Anglican dioceses have taken up this custom and it is now enshrined in the rubrics of the service for the Blessing of Oils (but without the text for the renewal of vows). In some places clergy have protested at the inconvenience of the day chosen for such a service. Its origin of course was the need to consecrate the oils for initiation at the Easter Vigil. But, even though that argument is no longer very significant, it is difficult to think of a better day, for Maundy Thursday is wholly suitable. The day of Christ's 'high priestly prayer' and of the institution of the Eucharist is marvellously appropriate. The renewing of vows, within the atmosphere of Holy Week, where the cost is spelt out, is a moving experience. The chance to turn aside and to experience worship which one has not had to order, before leading the people through the liturgy of the evening, of Good Friday and of Easter, must enrich the experience of Holy Week for the priest and the people to whom he returns.

An objection raised is that it is not sufficient to have in the parish one Eucharist after dark, lovely as that occasion is, because of those who will not go out at night. Where this is a real issue and transport cannot be provided for them, it does not follow that this second Eucharist must be in the morning. It could well be at 5 p.m., thus preserving some sense of the Thursday *evening* gathering of Jesus and his disciples for supper. But, in order that the Eucharist of the Last Supper is not in any way pre-empted by the Chrism Eucharist in the morning, the bishop and those who draw it up with him should try to ensure that its quite distinct ethos is kept and that elements that belong to the atmosphere of the evening do not creep in. The Chrism Eucharist, with its renewal of vows, blessing of oils and expression of priestly solidarity should be a great strength to clergy and a moving experience in the life of a diocese.

11
Funeral Rites

Funeral Rites and Paschal Liturgy

In its ministry to the bereaved, the Church is greatly aided by the potential power of the funeral liturgy to reinforce the message of hope that the priest will try to proclaim in his pastoral dealings with the family. The funeral service that strikes the right note will minister as effectively as any less formal words of consolation, and good teaching about the Church's faith will continue to strengthen and sustain the mourners long after the funeral. What is needed is a service that, at one and the same time, proclaims the Christian gospel in all its richness, speaks to the mourners 'where they are', which will often mean at a level of theological confusion as well as personal grief, and is genuine about the one who has died. Honesty is important at a funeral if the Church is to be respected.

The Christian gospel that must be proclaimed in all its richness is about the resurrection. It is not primarily an occasion for looking back over a life now ended, but looking forward to the adventure that lies ahead. The mood of the service is that of the hesitant dawn breaking through the darkness on Easter morning. The Burial Order of the American Church, in a marvellously pastoral footnote, puts the matter as well as it can be stated:

> The liturgy for the dead is an Easter liturgy. It finds all its meaning in the resurrection. Because Jesus was raised from the dead, we, too, shall be raised.

> The liturgy, therefore, is characterized by joy, in the certainty that 'neither death, nor life, nor angels, nor principalities, nor things present, nor things to come, nor powers, nor height, nor depth, nor anything else in all creation, will be able to separate us from the love of God in Christ Jesus our Lord.'

This joy, however, does not make human grief unchristian. The very love we have for each other in Christ brings deep sorrow when we are parted by death. Jesus himself wept at the grave of his friend. So, while we rejoice that one we loved has entered into the nearer presence of our Lord, we sorrow in sympathy with those who mourn.

The Easter element, however restrained, must always be present. The new rites, in their prayers and readings, give this emphasis. The priest must help the mourners to see this emphasis reflected also in the hymnody. This cannot be taken so far that he refuses to use the 'old favourites', but very often mourners are only too willing to accept his advice about at least one of the hymns. Unfortunately many of the Easter hymns are unfamiliar and difficult to sing. Failed alleluias are worse than no alleluias at all! But 'Jesus lives! thy terrors now can no more, O death, appal us' is well known, and 'Love's redeeming work is done' both suitable and easy to sing. The same Easter spirit shines through two more familiar hymns, 'Praise, my soul, the King of heaven', with its hauntingly beautiful alleluia refrain, and 'All creatures of our God and King', with its moving and deeply appropriate penultimate verse:

> And thou, most kind and gentle death,
> Waiting to hush our latest breath,
>   O praise him, alleluia!
> Thou leadest home the child of God,
> And Christ our Lord the way hath trod,
>   O praise him, alleluia!

It is surprising to find hymns such as these used so rarely at funerals. But the Easter element may also be underlined by the use within the funeral liturgy of the paschal candle. In many churches candles are placed around the bier, but there is far greater significance in one single candle, the paschal light, standing by the coffin, and, in some circumstances, carried into and out of the church in front of the coffin. If, outside Eastertide, the candle stands normally by the font, it will not be difficult to move it for use in the funeral liturgy.

There are the funerals of some Christians that will be marked by a joyfulness that is normally associated with the Easter season at its height. Such will be the funerals of churchgoers who have died at a ripe old age in the fullness of time. Even then, of course, there will be a sadness of a sort, and tears will be shed, but still the service will have about it a sense of celebration, and the Easter Dismissal with its alleluias may be spoken with joyful confidence. But these will be the exceptions. On most occasions, the very real sense of joy will be tempered by a sense of shock, with a sudden death, and especially with a young death, and sometimes bewilderment. On some occasions there will be a sense that the earthly life that has come to an end was not always very Christian or very good. All sorts of elements like these will be part of the mix that gives the service its ethos. Pure unadulterated joy will be rare. There will usually be a restraint that human sorrow imposes, and a realism about the person who has died and his relationships with those who are left that will ensure that there is a note of penitence too. Sensitivity to this restraint and realism will be the mark of the good pastor. At a funeral there is a need for honesty, an assurance of forgiveness and a consequent note of resurrection joy. For it is not a glib or superficial playing down of sin or sorrow that the Church needs to proclaim at a funeral. It must take these elements seriously, and not sweep them under the carpet, so to speak, but lead people beyond them. The paschal candle is often a poor flickering light, but it burns on in the dark. It is in that sense, rather than in the broad daylight of Easter Day, that every funeral is an extension of the paschal liturgy.

Traditionally the liturgical colour for funerals is black. That is not appropriate. Black may be an honest expression of the mourners' sorrow, but the Church is not in mourning, except as a gesture of solidarity with the mourners. The Church's involvement is to proclaim both forgiveness and resurrection. Of the former, violet is the traditional colour. It is appropriate for funerals. But white is the colour of Easter and will nearly always be the most suitable liturgical colour for a funeral. The black scarf gives quite the wrong emphasis.

A Funeral Eucharist

Only a small minority of the funerals that a parish priest takes is of regular communicant members of his congregation. In

most cases therefore the Eucharist is not the appropriate form
for the funeral. But where the person who has died, and the
members of the family, have been communicants, it is a pity not
to have the Eucharist as the funeral service. Theologically it
expresses our faith in the resurrection and in the communion of
saints as no other rite will do. But it is not on those grounds
alone that it commends itself. It says something important
about the relationship of the Church and the individual
Christian if the funeral is not so much a private or family rite,
but a celebration of the Christian community. As such it is of
benefit to the mourners in giving them support and sympathy.
It is also of benefit to the Church as a powerful means by which
its resurrection faith is proclaimed and assimilated.

What is here being recommended is not necessarily the
old practice, common in more Catholic circles, of a Requiem
Eucharist in addition to, normally a few hours before, the
funeral service proper. Though that had something to
commend it, it had the disadvantage that the Eucharist,
essentially a celebration *of the Church* was often turned into
the very private observance of the family alone, while the
mourners in general, including the members of the Church,
came to the later funeral service proper, which in its style and
ethos is a more personal and private rite. The ideal is, not that
the Eucharist should be *additional* to the funeral, but that the
Eucharist should *be* the funeral. But, inevitably, there is a very
real and practical problem in many communities in assembling
the Christian congregation at an hour when undertakers are
at work and crematoria open. In such communities it will
probably be best for the body to be received into the church one
afternoon, the Eucharist for the community to be celebrated in
the evening and a brief funeral service for the family and those
not at work next day. But, whenever it be (and it could be, less
satisfactorily, several days after the interment, or, better, when
the ashes are brought for burial), let there be for every church
person at their death a celebration of the Eucharist to mark their
passing to the company of heaven.

The style of such a Eucharist will vary according to circumstances. It will be, as the previous section urged, an Easter
liturgy, with the paschal candle burning and the Easter greeting and dismissal. How much of it is sung will depend on the

tradition of the parish and the estimated attendance. But, as far as possible, the style needs to reflect the style of the usual *Sunday* Eucharist. For it is not a funeral that happens to have Holy Communion tacked on, so to speak, but it is a gathering of the Christian community, to do what it always does, but on this occasion with a particular person and theme in mind. For this reason, the rubrics on page 328 of the ASB are not ideal. These indicate an order for the service that follows the shape of the non-eucharistic funeral rite, but with eucharistic material placed between the Ministry of the Word and the final prayers. This is quite workable, but better still is the order of the ordinary Parish Eucharist, with minimal changes. The *Gloria* should certainly be said or sung. The first readings should be read by mourners, not necessarily members of the family, if that is asking too much, but by those who, in the impotence of bereavement, will be glad to be able to exercise a small ministry as a way of expressing love or sympathy. If members of the family are willing to present the elements at the Offertory, that is good. There is no *need* for the Creed to be said, but at the funeral of a believer it has a certain appropriateness. Section 60 of the Funeral Services of the ASB provides a suitable form for the Intercession. The American Prayer Book also provides an excellent form. The Eucharistic Prayer will include the proper preface, of which the ASB provides two forms. After Communion the commendation follows, the priest standing at the head of the coffin, before the final prayers and dismissal. Where the interment or cremation is to follow immediately, the priest precedes the coffin from the church. He, or another member of the congregation, may carry the paschal candle before the coffin.

Although this form of service is clearly intended for *communicants* who have died, its use at the funeral of a Christian child, who has been part of the Church's fellowship but unconfirmed, is wholly appropriate. The ASB provides helpful material for such a funeral. The eucharistic form would also be reasonable, even if the person who had died was not a great churchgoer, if the principal mourners were communicants who would value this form. But, of course, something would be lost by the inevitable absence of the church community if the deceased were not of their number.

The Service in Church

Although, at least in the urban areas, the majority of funerals are in crematoria chapels (about which more in the following section), the priest is still called upon to take funeral services that are to be followed by burial, in his own church or in a cemetery chapel. The ASB rite, 'The Funeral Service', provides him with the texts that he needs, but does not go far in the rubrics to help him to lead the people through a difficult experience with sensitivity. In what follows in this section, it is assumed that the priest is dealing with a non-church family with whom his only contact has been before this funeral or at previous weddings or funerals.

He will want to meet them at the door; not just to meet the coffin, but to meet and to greet the mourners, and to spend a moment or two putting them at their ease and reassuring them about what they now have to go through. He may want to say a short informal prayer with them, especially if they have to go in and 'face' a church full of people. He will, of course, have consulted them earlier about whether they are to follow the body into the church or to go to their places first. Except where people have a definite sense of the rightness of following the coffin, there is much to be said for getting them settled into their places before the service begins.

Although the service begins with the Sentences, the custom of reading them as the body is borne into the church has not much to commend it. The visual impact of the placing of the coffin in the chancel is such that people are unlikely to listen to words. At a big funeral, a hymn may be sung; at a smaller occasion, silence or organ music is better. When the coffin is in place and all are settled, then is the moment for the Sentences.

After the Sentences and an opening prayer, there follows the psalm. Psalm 23 is often preferred and may of course be sung in a metrical form. Where the psalm version is used, it is better said than chanted, unless a choir is present. When said, it is better said by all together throughout. Though as a general rule antiphonal psalm saying is preferable, in this setting, where the priest is often the only person speaking with any confidence, his voice is needed to lead throughout.

The scripture reading follows, preferably read by a lay person. The ASB provides texts for this and gives references for various alternatives. In making the choice, the priest will want to bear in mind any request from the family and also the sort of people they are. For some, the *conceptual* will be very difficult and a story form nearly always preferable. The Raising of Lazarus story, for instance, can be abridged sufficiently to be suitable or one of the Easter stories can be used. It is a great pity when a clergyman's way of taking funerals has become so stereotyped that he no longer asks, 'What is suitable for *this* family?', but always reads the same lesson. If he always follows it with the same address, and uses it dozens of times in the year, that mechanical overuse will show.

Clergy seem to disagree about the merit of an address at a funeral. Certainly there are things better left unsaid, and addresses about the deceased that do not ring true bring the Church into disrepute. Nevertheless a marvellous opportunity for preaching the gospel is being presented at every funeral, and the priest who does not seize the opportunity to talk of the faith, simply and sensitively, is failing miserably. It is about the Church's *faith* that he is to talk principally, not about the deceased, so the fact that the person who has died was a stranger to him need not render a sermon inappropriate. Nevertheless the impact will be greater if he has taken the trouble to find out sufficient about the family for his theology to be rooted in their reality. He will need to be honest if he is to make his point – to *idealize* either the Christian commitment or the family life of the deceased does no good, for above all his words must ring true. Where there is a request for a lay person, possibly a family friend, to 'say a few words', the priest will normally be advised to allow this, while suggesting a time limit and urging a prepared text, but he should be ready to add a Christian comment if what is said is somewhat secular, and looks only to the past rather than to the future.

After the address, the ASB orders the *Te Deum* or a hymn. Where neither seems suitable, and a different *said* canticle is required, the Easter Anthems may prove satisfactory. Alternatively the address can lead very naturally and directly into the prayers. The priest will want to invite the congregation 'to sit or kneel for the prayers, whichever you find more natural'. This is not an occasion for urging too strongly 'meekly kneeling upon your knees', but people will value guidance to put them at their ease. The ASB gives the modern text of the Lord's Prayer. Its use at a funeral such as this will hardly ever be appropriate. If the congregation has the text in front of them, they need to be urged to follow it with care or to ignore it and use the familiar, but simply to launch in and use it will never be right. Other prayers may follow and the selection in the ASB (pp.334ff) is a good one. Three major themes suggest themselves. The first is thanksgiving – both for the departed person and for the resurrection faith. A bidding would be well followed by the prayer at section 50. The second is a prayer for the departed. Here the priest might well name also the spouse of the departed, if he or she has already died, or other close departed relatives who will be in the mind of the family. The prayers at sections 51–4 and 56 sum up that theme. The third is prayer for the bereaved. Here the priest may bring into their minds 'those who have not been able to be present, with you, no doubt, in spirit', and invite them to give thanks for the support each is to the others and to pray for courage. He may pray for the closest relatives left behind by name. The prayers at sections 55 and 57 take up this third theme. In these prayers, as at other points in the service, it cannot be stressed too strongly how important it is to get the usual first name of deceased and relatives right. Again, it is part of that 'ringing true' that gives the service its validity. The priest should not be too shy, if necessary, to go through a 'check list' of names with the family.

There are other themes for prayer that will suggest themselves at particular funerals. But when all has been said, a time of *silence* is desirable. People need time for their own private thoughts, prayers and thankfulness. The prayers end with the prayer at section 10. A hymn may be sung before the words of Commendation, which in the ASB form lack the power of some more traditional texts. The priest should stand facing the coffin for this Commendation and may appropriately make the sign of the cross over it.

The Committal will follow in churchyard or cemetery. It is unfortunate that the ASB makes no provision (any more than did the Book of Common Prayer) for the dismissal of the mourners with a blessing. The priest is well advised to add this at the conclusion of the Committal.

The rituals of death and bereavement are deeply important. The priest has, at one and the same time, to try to lead people to a more mature faith and yet to treat them with respect 'where they are'. This may mean his introduction into the service of elements they are not expecting – a sermon, extempore prayer, etc. – but it will, equally, mean his respecting those elements and traditions that, for them, are sacred as part of the mourning process, however sub-Christian or even vulgar they may seem. His task is to build, not to destroy. Even some of the funeral rites of organizations such as freemasons and other orders and lodges are normally better allowed, provided that the Christian gospel is clearly proclaimed as well. Unnecessary negativity does not meet a helpful response in the mourners.

When there is to be Cremation

There is much to be said for the school of thought that maintains that, probably because of its initial opposition to cremation, the Church never thought out, theologically and liturgically, how it understood the burning of the body as part of the 'last rites' at and beyond death. The cremation has become the equivalent of the burial, though it can never be quite that, logically speaking. The real equivalent is *the burial of the cremated remains*. That is the ultimate point of disposal, the moment of real finality. Had the Church always had this more definitely in mind, it would possibly never have attached religious significance and ritual to cremation, but would have regarded it, rather like 'laying out the body', as part of the process of preparing it for burial. The casket of ashes would then have become the focus, the equivalent of the coffin, for the funeral, which could invariably have been in the parish church, followed by local interment of ashes. The advantages are clear. Long and time consuming journeys are avoided. All the undesirable elements of crematoria – rotas, 'canned' music, and the sense of a conveyor belt service, with another funeral every twenty minutes – are rendered unnecessary, and the bereaved are able both to have the funeral within their own community and thereafter to visit the buried remains without making a journey away.

Pressure on clergy time has made it increasingly desirable to find a new pattern. Some progress may be made along these lines. But variations on the usual procedure cannot be sprung on mourners. The bereaved cannot be used as 'guinea pigs' as we try to find a better procedure. No doubt, for the time being, the most common practice will continue to be either simply a service in the crematorium chapel or, where there is a church connection, the service in church with simply the committal at the crematorium. The two variations on this that are worth considering in those rare appropriate cases are, firstly, the funeral in church, concluding with the burial of cremated remains, the cremation having taken place previously without religious ceremony or, secondly, a funeral service in church, followed by a cremation without religious ceremony, but with the burial of the cremated remains at a later date, preferably as soon as possible, the very next day if convenient. What is important is that, in any such rethinking of procedure, the difficult and painful, but absolutely vital, *moment of final parting* should not be lost. Whether it be at the crematorium or in the burying of the ashes, there needs to be a moment, witnessed by the mourners, which is final. To be deprived of that is to lose out on something psychologically very important. The practice of saying the words of committal at the church door and then sending off the coffin to the crematorium, with no provision for the final interring of the ashes, is not therefore to be encouraged.

Mourners do need this moment of finality. Most also need a *place*, to which they can occasionally come, or even simply that they can picture when far away, where the body, or the ashes, of their dead relative has been laid to rest. The priest cannot insist on either of these. If the family want to leave the crematorium chapel without the coffin being lowered or enclosed behind the curtain, the priest cannot insist they stay. But, if they are in any doubt, he can encourage them to go through with it and enable them to see how in the end it may help them. Similarly, he cannot, reasonably, refuse to allow the *scattering* of ashes, but he can encourage their *burial*, and see that his parish church has an attractive area, a 'Garden of Rest' as it is usually called, to make this possible.

Where the whole service is in the crematorium chapel, most of what has been written in the previous section applies. But in order to establish a link between the mourners and himself, and, indeed, between the mourners and their own community, he should make every effort to invite them *to their own church*, either on the Sunday following, when the departed person will be remembered, or for the interment of ashes or for some other occasion with which they would be able to cope. Relating rootless people to a community in which they may find support is an important element in ministry to the bereaved. It is not as individualistic a ministry as it sometimes seems.

The ASB provides a brief form for the Interment of Ashes. It may be used as it stands simply as a churchyard service or become the heart of a full service. In some instances it may be the right time for a Requiem Eucharist. In others, it may be the opportunity for a Memorial Service. But for the sake of the family, this final act of the funeral rites should not be delayed longer than necessary beyond the funeral date.

Memorial Services

Memorial Services are not a common part of the ministry of most clergy, though in certain town churches they can be a regular feature. They are not simply 'repeat funerals'. The fact that they normally come several weeks after the funeral means that the family are at a different stage in the process of mourning. Their greater composure will sometimes encourage the priest, mistakenly, to ignore *their* needs and to concentrate on the community's mourning. For most memorial services are principally not the mourning of the family, nor of the Church, but of a local, or sometimes a national, community. They provide an opportunity for Christian principles to be set before people who do not normally enter the church. The atmosphere, welcome and acceptance that they encounter will influence strongly their future view of the

Church and willingness to accept its ministry. But, important as this is, it should not prevent the priest from ministering again to the family, at the heart of the service, overawed possibly by a bigger occasion than the funeral, and needing the reassurance both of his comfort and of the gospel.

It is right that for a Memorial Service those who arrange it should have greater say than at a funeral about its form and content. It is right also that it should have its eulogies and reflect in a very personal way the one who has died. Favourite hymns, readings and prayers of the deceased can reasonably have their place if they help to recreate the 'flavour' of his or her life, and the priest will be ill-advised to reject too much of what is proposed. As with a funeral, he will do better to let the layman who wants to give the address do so, but make sure that at another point he has the opportunity to preach the Church's Easter faith. He will do well to allow that strange poem to be read or piece of music played, but will ensure that the Scriptures are also read and prayers said. He will also be prepared to work quite hard with the organizers to see that, as far as possible, all the diverse elements are worked into a coherent whole.

As has been suggested above, the Memorial Service may sometimes be the occasion for the Interment of Ashes. For a communicant Christian, the appropriate form of service may be the Eucharist, but if the occasion is principally 'civic' rather than 'ecclesiastical', there will be hesitation about this. Where another form is to be used, the ASB Funeral Service provides a suitable outline, though a special bidding will need to be composed at the beginning and the prayers will normally include intercession for the community.

Remembering the Dead

There are two ways in which the Church remembers those who have died in the community. One is by the annual commemoration usually called 'the year's mind'; the other by a service at All Saints'–All Souls' tide. This remembering is, first and foremost, a spiritual act, part of the Church's ministry of prayer. But it can also be part of its pastoral opportunity and outreach.

It is a simple matter to keep a book in which are recorded for each day of the year those members of the parish (and those friends and relations of parishioners) who on each particular day died or were buried, and a godly custom to remember them at the Eucharist by name. It is the more useful if a card is sent a week or so before to the relatives of those who are to be remembered telling them of the service, not pressing for their attendance, but simply letting them know of the Church's care. It is better still if the card is delivered in person by a member of the congregation, who would indeed offer to come with them to the service.

An annual service at All Saints'–All Souls' tide is another occasion when such cards could be distributed to, say, all those bereaved in the previous three years. But the service to which they are invited must be a well prepared one. If, for instance, they come to a service so specially devised for them that the regular congregation is absent, the Church's mission will not be well served. There must be a warm welcome into a worshipping community. No priest can plan such a service without the enthusiasm of his congregation. Even assuming the presence of the ordinary worshippers, there is an important question about the appropriateness of *the Eucharist* for the vast majority of the parish's bereaved. This could point to the holding of a special, non-eucharistic, annual commemoration, and, in order not to overstretch the congregation with a service additional to the parish's eucharistic keeping of All Saints and All Souls, a Sunday evening date in Eastertide could be considered. (But, for more on All Saints and All Souls, see Chapter 16.)

12
Advent

The Keeping of Advent

The shape of the Christian year in the calendar of the Alternative Service Book is a simple one. The year revolves around two great feast days, Christmas and Easter. Each of these feast days inaugurates a season in which the themes of the feast are proclaimed and developed. The season of celebration ends on a further feast day, which serves both to sum up the season and to end it on a distinctive note. In the case of Christmas, the season is of twelve days and concludes on the Feast of the Epiphany. In the case of Easter, the season is of fifty days and concludes on the Feast of Pentecost.[1] Each of the two feast days is preceded by a period of preparation – weeks 'before Christmas' and 'before Easter'. The other weeks of the year, outside the periods of preparation and celebration, are, however the Sundays are designated, 'ordinary time'. The Roman Church, rather confusingly, actually calls them, and them alone, 'Sundays *of the year*'.

But there is an immediate complication in what otherwise would be very straightforward. There are nine Sundays 'before Christmas', yet Advent lasts only four weeks, and there are nine Sundays 'before Easter', yet Lent lasts only six weeks. The confusion is the product of a tension between the desire to have a longish period of 'build-up' to the two feasts, with a carefully thought out and developing series of themes, and the desire to preserve the traditional length and shape of Advent and Lent, the very familiarity of which is valuable in the Church's life and devotion. Historically, Advent has passed through a number of phases and has sometimes been of longer duration than its present four weeks, and in the East remains a longer season. In the present Anglican calendar, with its nine Sundays before

[1] The fifty days of Eastertide are discussed in Chapter 15.

Christmas, there is a pronounced shift at Advent Sunday, both in the names of the Sundays and in the themes they develop. In theory, the present arrangement is clumsy, and it is certainly untidy, but in practice it seems to work. The new beginning of the Ninth Sunday before Christmas, in mid-October, and the 'change of gear' of Advent Sunday, both contribute to the build-up for the Christmas celebration.

But the new cycle does call severely into question all talk of Advent Sunday as 'the first day of the Church's year'. Liturgically the Ninth Sunday before Christmas fits this role, and it is on that day that the lectionary changes from one annual cycle to the other. There is, in any case, an argument for playing down talk of 'the beginning of the year'. For one thing, part of the value of the liturgical cycle is that, in a sense, it has *no* end or beginning, but simply a continuity, in which there is theological and psychological value. And, in addition, there has been in many parishes a proliferation of 'new years'. With the return from holiday in September, there is talk of 'the year ahead'. It is repeated at Advent and often again on January 1st. Other anniversaries and feasts, of local significance, become other new starts, with inevitable rededication for what lies ahead, and this can be overdone to a ridiculous point. If one is trying to teach the shape of the Christian Year, better to start with the two high points, Christmas and Easter, and develop the picture from there.

The ethos of Advent has also been through various phases. At some points in its history, the emphasis has been more definitely on the concept of the *second* coming of Christ than is usually the case today. There has also often been an element of *penitence*, giving it the same feel as the Lenten season. Most often today we talk of it as a *preparation* for Christmas. All these elements are properly present in Advent, but none is precisely its dominant aim. The purpose of Advent is to 'build up' to Christmas, to develop in Christian people a real sense of anticipation, a longing hopefulness, that will reflect the yearning of Israel for its Messiah, make ready the heart of the Christian for the Christmas festival and arouse a passion for the coming of Christ's Kingdom. Where talk of a second coming helps that aim it is an appropriate Advent theme. Where fasting, self-discipline, prayer and study assist, then they are appropriate in Advent and Lent, together with the penitence they often engender. And the appropriate form of preparation is everything that heightens the awareness and raises the expectation in the build up to Christmas. An increasing hope, excitement and sense of impending occasion should mark the Advent season. Like Lent, it must never be a static season, but one of unfolding and development. In a sense, Advent serves for the Church the same function as the first chapter of Luke's Gospel does for the New Testament. It is an unfolding of distinctive elements in a growing drama, noting the inter-relationship of them and leading them up to a glorious moment when the inevitable and joyful climax will come. *Joy* cannot be excluded from the Advent season, as if it were improper until Christmas Day. But it is a joy of anticipation and excitement, rather than of fulfilment, and it is *hope* that is most truly characteristic of the weeks of Advent.

The Church has been painfully aware of the contrast between its own observance of Christmas and the way the world celebrates it. For the Church, Christmas *begins* on December 25th, for the world of commerce it ends the day before. One way in which the Church has responded to this has been the purist path of denouncing the secular approach and having nothing to do with it. 'Christmas carols must not be sung in church till Christmas Eve, and the annual Carol Service must be on the Sunday after Christmas.' There is a sort of head-in-the-sand defiance about such a policy that is almost admirable! But there is a strong irony in a policy that expounds the truth of the incarnation by refusing to soil itself with the world. To take the incarnation seriously is to take the secular Christmas, with all its half-truths and semi-perception, with deadly serious-ness, and to seek to identify the Christ, as much as the Father Christmas, who is to be found in the exchange and discourse of the department store. How does the Church respond to that without destroying the keeping of Advent?

There is no answer that does not involve a degree of compromise. There *is* merit for churchpeople in holding out for a carol service no earlier than the Fourth Sunday in Advent, for a church free of Christmas decorations until Christmas Eve, and for the blessing of the crib at the Midnight Mass and not before. Provided that these are denied through most of Advent only with the right sort of teaching and with genuinely Advent liturgy that does have the characteristic Advent build up, then their absence will simply add to the almost unbearable sense of expectation that will make Christmas thrilling when it does suddenly burst upon the Church. But alongside this, in the Church's evangelistic enterprise, there needs to be a whole-hearted acceptance of the secular Christmas and a determination to take advantage of it. The eyes of the world are on a Christian tableau and its ears are hearing the Christian story. With its torchlight processions, carol services of varying degrees of formality and its nativity plays, and with its welcoming open door to schools and organizations wanting to hold their own carol services, the Church is presented with marvellous opportunities to deepen the faith of many people whom it cannot reach at other times. Parishes – laity as well as clergy – need to plan quite honestly how best to 'cash in' on Christmas. Liturgy in its widest form – song, drama, procession – will form an important part of the strategy.

A further word should be said about the great Advent theme of hope. It is linked very closely to the concept of the 'coming of the Kingdom', a phrase open to various levels of interpretation. Hoping involves watching and waiting. For Christians that has often meant 'vigil'. Another great Advent theme is that of the move from darkness to light. That is often portrayed through the experience of the night and then of the dawn breaking. There is much to be said in the Advent season for a parish vigil (and not necessarily, despite the fashion, simply for the young), a night of prayer, study and reflection – of watching and waiting – seeking the coming of the Kingdom, understanding that term both spiritually and socially, and ending with the first light of the dawn. In nurturing that sense of expectancy that is the mark of the Advent season, such a vigil, with the use of the appropriate Scriptures associated with Advent, could play an exciting part.

The Prayer Book calendar includes that strange entry, on 16th December, *'O Sapientia'*. This is the Latin title of the first of the seven Great Advent Antiphons.[2] Originally these

---

[2] To be found in David Silk *Prayers for Use at the Alternative Services* or in *The English Hymnal* (No. 734).

beautiful antiphons, in use in the Roman Church since the eighth century, were antiphons for recitation before and after *Magnificat* at Vespers, and they may still be used in this way at Evensong. But their possible use is far wider, as themes for an Advent Carol Service for instance, or as Introit sentences at the Eucharist. In spite of their antiquity there is something time-less about these antiphons and they make their own moving contribution to the developing momentum of the week before Christmas. On 22nd December, for instance, the antiphon, *O Rex Gentium*, runs:

O King of the nations and their desire (Haggai 2.7),
you are the cornerstone which makes both one (Ephesians 2.20).
O come and save man whom you formed from clay (Genesis 2.7).

Many churches, as well as individual Christian families in their homes, have for the four weeks of Advent an 'Advent wreath'. The Advent wreath has four blue or red candles in a ring around a white or gold candle. This latter candle could be the paschal candle, probably now quite short since the year of its use is three-quarters through. The first candle is lit on Advent Sunday. An additional one is lit each Sunday and the central candle on Christmas Day. Each lighting is accom-panied by a prayer reflecting an Advent theme. The traditional themes, together with those of the ASB calendar, are given below.

	Traditional theme	*ASB theme*
Advent 1	The Prophets	The Advent Hope
Advent 2	John the Baptist	The Scriptures
Advent 3	The Blessed Virgin Mary	John the Baptist
Advent 4	God's People	The Annunciation
Christmas	The Nativity	The Nativity

The traditional themes are the more satisfactory, for there is a more obvious development and relationship between them, but it would, nevertheless, be ill advised to use a series of themes out of step with the liturgy of the Sunday.

An Advent Liturgy

The change in mood that Advent Sunday brings is well accentuated by a special service bringing out the Advent themes. Such services have come to be called 'Advent Carol Services', and indeed there are a number of 'carols' that belong more obviously to the Advent than to the Christmas season, but the term is in some ways unfortunate, partly because it can mislead people into expecting something more attuned to Christmas than is planned, and partly because the heart of any truly Advent service will not be carols but the Scriptures that lead up to the coming of the Lord. 'An Advent Liturgy', or 'Words and Music for Advent', would be more accurate. Such a service need not necessarily be held on the First Sunday in Advent, though on that date it inaugurates the season effectively. There may sometimes be good reason for opting for the Second Sunday.

The service, which will be of local devising and will require the careful co-operation of priest and choirmaster at an early stage in its formation, will usually consist of a series of sections, the one developing from the other, each section certainly including a scriptural passage, a hymn and a collect, and often also an anthem, canticle or psalm, non-scriptural readings, and silence, possibly followed by a spoken congregational responsory, before the collect concluding the section. Because the Advent themes so obviously have a sense of movement towards a climax, an Advent liturgy may often be a processional service – whether, depending on size of building and of congregation, it be a procession of all present, or of choir and other ministers, or simply of priest, readers and acolytes. If it is a processional service, each section will constitute a 'station', with the high altar often the setting for a final gospel reading. Very often such an Advent Service will have the journey from darkness to light as an undercurrent of its developing theme, with the careful use of candlelight (and dimmers where available) to mark the movement from dark to light.

A number of different cycles of readings are possible, and a parish will want to 'ring the changes'. Four model outlines follow.

The first is a general Advent service, drawing on both Old and New Testament. It is suitable for use by candlelight (the final gospel reading, for instance, speaking of the light that has come into the world), but is not tied to the dark/light theme and is quite suitable for use without emphasis on this aspect. It has seven sections, but two are dispensable without any important loss of development. The last reading could be read as a liturgical gospel.

1	Zechariah 2.10–end	Silence, all mankind
2	Isaiah 40.1–8	Comfort, my people
(3	Malachi 3.1–4, 12 & 4.1–2	Suddenly the Lord will come)
4	Luke 1.5–25	The Annunciation to Zechariah
5	Luke 1.26–38	The Annunciation to Mary
(6	Matthew 1.18–23	The Annunciation to Joseph)
7	John 3.16–21	Light has come into the world

A second model, which, again, is usable with or without the emphasis on the darkness and light theme, draws, except for a final liturgical gospel, on nothing but the prophecy of Isaiah.

(1	Isaiah 6.1–8	The prophet's call)
2	Isaiah 9.2–4, 6–7	The people that walked in darkness
3	Isaiah 11.1–9	The shoot from the stem of Jesse
(4	Isaiah 35	Let the wilderness be glad)
5	Isaiah 40.1–11	Comfort ye, my people
6	Isaiah 60.1–6	Arise, shine, for your light is come
7	John 3.16–21	Light has come into the world

A third model, similar to the first, differs in using the visitation story rather than the annunciation to Mary, for those who wish to save the latter for the Christmas Carol Service.

1	Isaiah 40.1–11	Isaiah's witness
2	Micah 5.2–4	Micah's prophecy
3	Luke 1.5–25	Zechariah's vision
4	Matthew 1.18–25	Joseph's dream
5	Luke 1.39–49	Mary's joy
6	John 3.13–21	The Father's love

The final model makes no use of the Old Testament, but instead unfolds picture by picture the story that leads up to the birth of

Jesus as Luke portrays it in the first chapter of his Gospel. It is not particularly suited to the candlelight setting. After four gospel readings, the First Letter of John provides a comment on which to finish.

1	Luke 1.5–25	The Annunciation to Zechariah
2	Luke 1.26–38	The Annunciation to Mary
3	Luke 1.39–49	The Visit of Mary to Elizabeth
4	Luke 1.57–66	The Birth of John Baptist
5	1 John 4.7–14	God is love

The use of *Benedictus* and *Magnificat* is strongly urged, with this fourth sequence particularly. Other sung material that has proved its worth includes the traditional Advent Mattins and Vespers Responsories, especially to the music of Palestrina, the Advent Prose (to be found in the English Hymnal, No. 733) and the Advent Antiphons (discussed in the previous section). The collect of Advent Sunday provides an appropriate final prayer. There is a good argument for not ending with blessing and dismissal, but leaving the service somewhat 'in mid air', heightening the expectancy of the event still to come.

Preparing the Community for Christmas

As has already been said, the weeks before Christmas provide the Church with an unparalleled opportunity to make contact with those outside its immediate fellowship. For once in the year, it is the *Christian* story that is in the forefront of people's minds, with whatever lack of real understanding it is perceived. There are at least four major liturgical ways in which the Church may capitalize on this situation for evangelism.

The first is by the *open air event*. Quite what this is will depend on the type of parish. A town centre parish may organize a 'static' happening in a shopping centre on a Saturday with carols and the dramatization of the Christmas stories. A suburban parish may employ lorries to transport a Christmas tableau around estates or organize a torchlight procession, led by a band, with carol singing and brief readings and prayers, with an efficient loudspeaker system, at 'stations' along the route. Better still if such a procession ends up by leading the people, who have gradually joined in, into the parish church for a very brief carol service. In a smaller community, well-organized carol singing on foot around the streets may suffice. But a unique opportunity is lost when the preparation and celebration of Christmas is all within the church building, for, even when the churches are full, as they often are at Christmas, it is still only a small percentage of the population who attend, except in the most rural and settled communities.

The second liturgical opportunity is the nativity play. Religious drama has declined somewhat in the last twenty years and fewer parishes have plays at Christmas and Easter, especially performances in which adults take part.[3] This is a sad loss, for the parish nativity play, often simply a pageant with readings and carols, was a marvellous teaching aid, drawing into the church friends and relatives of performers, as well as all sorts of members of the community good at lighting, sound, stage-building or make-up. It was a genuine point of contact with a wider cross-section of the parish. The revival of such occasions is greatly to be encouraged. A good director and a careful script are important, for the amateurish can be painful and a distortion of the story, but there is no great need for gimmick or sophistication. Young and old alike can bring both to performing and witnessing the story a fascination and reverence that responds to the simple but sincere.

There is also great possibility in the 'Crib Service', an occasion for children with their parents to *prepare* quite consciously for the Christmas event. It is probably a better teaching opportunity and more genuine preparation than the currently popular 'Christingle' services. Held either on the Fourth Sunday in Advent, or on the afternoon of Christmas Eve, the Crib Service is an occasion for the priest, starting with a bare crib, an empty stable, gradually to put into it, with the aid of the children who will be willing helpers, straw, manger, oxen, angel, Joseph and Mary, teaching, often by questioning, the story, interspersing it with carols. In another part of the church is a field with sheep and shepherds, and the question is asked, to build up the sense of expectation, 'Where will the shepherds be when you return on Christmas morning?' There

---

[3] The reasons for this decline are varied, and need not concern us here, though it is worth noting the irony that one of the contributory factors has been an increase in the emphasis on the dramatic in the formal liturgy.

can be also, far away in some corner of the church, kings with their camels, beneath a star. And perhaps the priest may show the children the *bambino*, though he does not yet place it in the crib, but tells them instead about the Midnight Mass and how he will place it in the manger then, trying to convey something of the atmosphere of Christmas night. The service ends with the children gathered around the crib where suitable prayers are said. Or this may be the appropriate occasion to switch on the lights on the church's Christmas tree, so that there may be some talk also of gifts and the singing of 'In the bleak midwinter'. The families may be sent home to get out or to make their own crib and to prepare it just like the one in church. With this sort of build up, the children are almost guaranteed to rush for the crib in church on Christmas morning to see the Christ-child in the manger.

The fourth liturgical/evangelistic opportunity is the Christmas Carol Service, discussed below.

The Christmas Carol Service

The main Christmas Carol Service in church may be held either as a preparation for Christmas on the Fourth Sunday in Advent or as part of the Christmas celebrations during the twelve days to Epiphany. Pastoral considerations will dictate which. In most parishes the *form* of the service has become an unchanging tradition, and there is merit in this. It is the Service of Nine Lessons and Carols, beginning with Genesis and ending with the Johannine prologue as the ninth reading. This form has found a special place in the English Christmas and there is not often good reason to tamper with it. But what is suitable for the principal parish carol service is not necessarily as appropriate for the multiplicity of carol services of different schools and organizations that many parishes have in the lead up to Christmas. Possible variations include the building in to the service of pageant, tableaux or play, the reduction in the number of scriptural readings in order to make room for some of the wealth of poetry on a Christian theme now available,[4] or

---

[4] Among modern poems, Elizabeth Jennings' *'The Annunciation'*, W. H. Auden's *'At the Manger, Mary sings'* and T. S. Eliot's *'The Journey of the Magi'*, as complements to the biblical passages, spring immediately to mind.

the introduction of a section around the tree of less liturgical material – the more secular carols and readings – before moving into the biblical sequence.

When using the traditional 'lessons and carols' format, it is worth considering the modification of one or two details. Eric Milner-White's Bidding, for all its beauty, sometimes strikes an archaic note, especially, for instance, at a school carol service. David Silk, in *Prayers for Use at the Alternative Services*, provides a modernization of it and an alternative form. The readings are best followed, not by the traditional 'Thanks be to God' by the reader, but by a period of silence for reflection and then the more usual 'This is the word of the Lord' and the people's response. Some of the readings, notably the annunciation story, lend themselves to the involvement of more than one reader.

The final reading may be read as a liturgical gospel, with, for instance, acolytes' candles, a procession, the people standing to face the reader and sung acclamations. But, where the Carol Service *precedes* Christmas, there is an argument for omitting the familiar John 1.1–14 passage, saving that at least for Christmas Day. Luke 2.21–35, the story of the presentation in the Temple, makes a satisfactory alternative climax, taking the Lucan account a little further and ending on a note of glory, reminiscent of the Johannine prologue. The Collect for Christmas Eve is better than that of Christmas Day when the service precedes Christmas. For this service, in which the 'word' is central, it is appropriate that, where there is a liturgical style to the occasion, the Bible should be *carried in* as part of the opening procession and placed on the lectern, which should itself be moved to a more central position than it usually occupies in most churches. The practice of the individual readers coming to the front and reading from their own small-print bibles, often of different translations, is at all costs to be avoided.

13
Christmas and Epiphany

The Celebration of Christmas

The celebration of Christmas begins with the midnight Eucharist of Christmas Eve and continues in an obvious way until Epiphany and, less obviously, until 2nd February, the Presentation of Christ in the Temple. The ASB calendar is at its least helpful at this season of the year. For, in what it employs by way of liturgical colour, proper preface, etc., it casts doubt on whether it is still Christmas or not as the Sundays in January take up traditional Epiphany themes one by one. Sundays after Epiphany are not quite the Anglican equivalent of the Roman 'Sundays of the year' of this season, for their propers tie them much more closely to the Christmas story. The propers are well chosen, but the confusion about liturgical season is unfortunate. Vagueness does not make for good teaching.

The parish is faced with two ways of resolving this. Either it can opt for a *short* Christmas season of twelve days, beginning on Christmas Day and continuing to the Feast of the Epiphany, with ordinary or *ferial* time beginning on the 7th January. Or it can choose instead a *long* Christmas season of forty days, continuing to the Feast of the Presentation, with ordinary time beginning on 3rd February. With this second arrangement, the Christmas cycle assumes a shape similar to the Easter cycle. The Christmas season moves to a climax at Candlemas, taking in Epiphany on the way, that feast day giving a new dimension to the season as it continues, just as the Easter season moves to a climax at Pentecost, taking in Ascension Day on the way, that feast day giving a new dimension to the Easter season.

There is a problem with this latter structure. Although the Feast of the Presentation often comes within a few days of the final Sunday 'after Epiphany', bringing the season to a conclusion in accord with the ASB structure, there is a clumsiness and confusion when the Ninth Sunday before Easter precedes

Candlemas. Though it can be hoped that in some subsequent revision of the calendar, 2nd February will be restored as the point where the Church changes direction, so to speak, from looking back to Christmas to looking forward to Easter, at present the forty day Christmas can only work tidily in one year in two. With the present rules, it has to be cut short a few days early if the Ninth Sunday after Easter precedes Candlemas. But, whichever length of Christmas season is envisaged, the old idea of the 'octave' makes little sense and the ASB does little to encourage it.

The Christmas season is not, of course, of such antiquity as the Easter season and, consequently, liturgical renewal has not unearthed liturgical distinctiveness for the season in quite the way it has for Easter. Nevertheless the season should have its distinctive ethos and flavour. There is a case for a Christmas greeting in church, for use throughout the season, equivalent to the 'Alleluia, Christ is risen. He is risen indeed. Alleluia' of the Easter season. The president could say 'The Word has become flesh and dwells among us' with the people's response 'O come, let us adore him', and there are other possibilities. Christmas has its equivalent of the paschal candle, in the Christmas crib, though its symbolism is not as rich. Blessed on Christmas night, as the paschal candle is lit on Easter night, it stands in the church *throughout the season* (for whichever duration has been decided). It is appropriate that there should be a 'station' there at the principal Eucharist of each Sunday. As the president and his assistants pass the crib during the Introit Hymn, there is a break between verses and a prayer is said.[1] It is better if, at least on some Sundays, this is a congregational prayer, and in parishes where there is a weekly notice sheet it can be printed on this.

But, though a crib in the church as part of the liturgy is a valuable symbol, for more evangelistic reasons the Church does well to have a crib *outside*, perhaps in a wooden box-shape shelter with a 'perspex' front. Of course there are problems to do with vandalism, and in some places this may be an impractical suggestion, but, where there is any possibility of

[1] There are suitable prayers in most anthologies. David Silk provides a variety of material in *Prayers for Use at the Alternative Services*.

it being mounted, it is worth the effort. If the 'inside' crib is to be blessed at the Midnight Mass, this outside crib might perhaps be blessed, and its light switched on, in the presence of children (who will be in bed at midnight) as soon as it is dark on Christmas Eve.

The liturgical colour of the season is white or gold. This should be maintained for the length of the season, whether for only twelve days, or through the Sundays after Epiphany, depending on which local custom is established. (The ASB advisory colours, with a change from white to green on the Monday after Epiphany, are best ignored.)

Christmas Eve and Christmas Day

For most parishes the 'Midnight' Mass of Christmas is the best attended service in the year. In many churches this is more of a headache than a cause for rejoicing, for often the church is too small, its provision of books inadequate and the fear of 'trouble' from those who have had too much to drink gives anxiety on a night which ought to be full of the joy and wonder of the incarnation. Careful planning can alleviate much of this anxiety. After each year's 'Midnight', careful notes should be made, for reference next year, about the additional seating likely to be needed, about the most efficient way of communicating a vast congregation and about keeping free necessary paths for access and procession. An 'on site' meeting of priest, wardens and sidesmen earlier in the evening will often be useful.

Well in advance of the festival, consideration needs to be given to which rite will be used. In some parishes this will not be a real question, for one rite is in constant use in the parish and no one would consider using any other. But there is a tendency in some places to *revert* at Christmas midnight to an older form than that used at the ordinary Parish Eucharist, the Prayer Book rite, for instance, instead of Rite A or B. The motive is a sort of courtesy to those once-a-year communicants who have not become familiar with the new. But it is a mistaken policy. For one thing, the Prayer Book rite, with its lack of seasonal material and its cross-dominated theology, is ill-suited to the celebration of the incarnation. Secondly, those who are so irregular in their churchgoing that they have not encountered the new rites will not, especially among the young, be so familiar with the old that they will find their way around the Prayer Book rite. Thirdly, it must be recognized that the old rites have failed to capture the imagination of the occasional communicant, else the occasions would have increased. Where the old has failed, the new must be given a chance to succeed.

There is, in any case, an argument for printing out the whole service, hymns and carols as well, if the parish has provision to do this economically. There is nothing worse than the sight of people struggling to find their way around unfamiliar books and probably having to share books as they do so. The additional material, specific to Christmas, such as the Blessing of the Crib, can then be included.

Though called the 'Midnight' Mass, this first Eucharist of Christmas usually begins earlier than midnight. There is no *right* time. 11.45 p.m. may enable one to reach the Gospel at midnight, 11.15 the Eucharistic Prayer. There is no real significance in the stroke of midnight, though clergy will sometimes have observed members of the congregation keeping an eye on their watch (or even whispering 'Happy Christmas' to one another at midnight, even though, where the service begins at 11.30, midnight tends to come half way through the Intercessions!). An earlier time than midnight is probably preferable for practical reasons. Some clergy take into account pub closing time.

It is all but impossible to have quiet in the church as it fills up with excited people. Perhaps one should not try. Nevertheless the service begins far more dramatically when it emerges from silence. The order of service could very reasonably ask for total silence for, say, three minutes before the service. In most churches this short period could begin with the dimming of lights or the turning out of most of them. Out of that darkness then comes (unannounced) the opening solo verse of 'Once in royal David's city' that has become so much a part of the inauguration of the English Christmas liturgy. As the hymn proceeds, president and assistants, with the choir if space permits, proceed to the crib, the president carrying the *bambino*. The hymn stops. He places the image of the Christ-child in it, blesses it and, with the assistants, kneels and says a prayer of adoration, preferably one in which the congregation can join, the text being printed in the order of service. The hymn then continues and the procession moves to chancel or sanctuary for the Eucharist.

The ASB propers include a collect particularly suitable for use at midnight or very early in the morning. A variety of lections is provided, but they are not divided, as in the Roman lectionary, into three separate sets of propers for midnight, dawn and daytime. The Isaiah 9 passage, with its talk of 'the people who walked in darkness have seen a great light', is obviously particularly suitable. The Luke 2.1–14 (15–20) Gospel is the one that relates most obviously to a midnight service, and in any case is more intelligible to the less committed, but, in parishes where there is no major celebration next day, the desire to read John 1.1–14 at midnight will be understandably strong. Because of time, many clergy do not preach at midnight, and certainly a full length sermon would be inappropriate, but a simple address provides a valuable opportunity not to be missed.

A long Gospel, an address, the Creed said and then prayers of Intercession provides a long sequence of *said* worship for the less than regular churchgoer. A short carol inserted at one point would break that usefully. Careful consideration will also of course have been given to the most efficient way of distributing the elements. There may be a need to use those not normally authorized to do so to assist with the administration. Extra communion 'stations' are valuable, but only if access to and from them has been thought out sufficiently well to ensure that the church is not locked in a kind of ecclesiastical traffic jam.

Christmas morning provides a problem in many parishes. A tradition has grown up in many places that almost every adult communicant attends the midnight Eucharist. Next morning, therefore, those few adults left and a fair number of children are all who are left to come to church. Where the service provided for them is the Parish Eucharist, it tends to be a rather 'low key' occasion, comparing unfavourably with an ordinary Sunday, which is very sad for those for whom this is their only celebration of a great and joyful feast. To avoid this, some parishes have a pattern that includes an early Eucharist, for those communicants who are left, followed by a non-sacramental Family Service. The trouble with this is that it divides families still further, and also leaves practically nobody to be present at the mid-morning service except children. It will probably be better to persevere with a mid-morning Eucharist, but rather than letting it be a poor version of Sunday, let it have its own distinctiveness. If it is to be principally a children's Eucharist, let it be designed as such (see Chapter 7). On this occasion there should be freedom to reorder the Ministry of the Word to make a good deal of the Christmas story, to sing carols and to process to the crib. It is the children who should process, not just the priest. They may appropriately leave gifts at the crib. In some parishes, there is no choir present on Christmas morning. If the adults really cannot be persuaded to come back, let there at least be a children's choir. These problems will ring no bells for those large parishes which can maintain a second full sung Eucharist to rival the Midnight Mass. How lucky those parishes are where numbers are such that people stay away at midnight because of 'overcrowding' in the church, and thus swell the numbers mid-morning. But not every parish is like that.

Nor must the needs of the elderly be neglected. The Church has no business reflecting the popular misconception that 'Christmas is for the children'. Both a midnight celebration and an early morning celebration may be unsuitable for some old people. If the mid-morning service is to be non-eucharistic or geared very much to young families, there needs to be a later celebration for the elderly. If this produces a surfeit of celebrations, it will often be the early celebration that is superfluous.

Few parishes have an afternoon or evening service on Christmas Day, as much for the priest's sake as that of the people, though there are parishes that have discovered that tea-time on Christmas Day is ideal for children, and a far more successful time than the morning. Most parishes will, however, probably continue to feel that Christmas *Eve* is a better day for a service at such a time. Where it is possible, however, it is good for the parish priest to go back to church at 6 p.m., or a time soon before or after that, to say Evensong. Nobody may come, but very often there is a handful of people who, for one reason or another, have been unable to come before, and who are grateful for such provision. A said office, a carol and prayers at the crib, all over in twenty minutes, is all that is needed. The priest will perhaps find it rounds off his own Christmas Day rather better than the last of many services in the morning can do.

Epiphany

In the churches of the East, the Feast of the Epiphany is given greater precedence than Christmas Day. This does not mean that in the East the story of the *magi* ranks above that of the birth of Christ; but it acts as a reminder to us that the Epiphany is about something much more than simply that story. In a way, that gospel reading on Epiphany has confused rather than clarified its meaning. The truth is simply that, as we move from Christmas to Epiphany, we move on from an emphasis on the *coming* of Christ, to an emphasis on his *revelation* or *manifestation*. They are two aspects of the same truth of the incarnation, just as resurrection and ascension are two aspects of the same Easter truth. The story of the *magi* has become attached to the Feast of the Epiphany because it is the first of the great 'manifestation stories'. The fact that another such story, the marriage at Cana, has long been the Evensong lesson at Epiphany illustrates how this feast really has a broader theme than is generally imagined.

There are not many feast days that in most parishes can be celebrated with a full Parish Eucharist after the day's work. But this is one of those days when, if it is possible, it should be attempted, especially if it is being regarded as the last of twelve days of Christmas. The Sunday lectionary only provides the story of the *magi* as the Gospel on the Second Sunday after Christmas (which only occurs in certain years) and only then in 'Year 2'.[2] To transfer its celebration from 6th January to the following Sunday will be to lose the lovely celebration of the baptism of Jesus authorized for that day. The Epiphany Eucharist appropriately begins, like the Sunday celebrations of

---

[2] In the ten years from 1981 to 1990, it will be read as part of the Sunday cycle only in 1984 and in 1987.

this season, with a station at the crib, in which the kings have now been placed, or with a procession to the crib bearing the figures of the kings to be put in place. If children are present it is effective to carry these figures to the crib one by one to the singing of the appropriate verses of 'We three kings of Orient'. The prayer at the crib on this day, and through until Candlemas if the crib is to remain on the Sundays following, reflects the manifestation theme.

The Sundays after Epiphany reflect the gradual unfolding of the truth of Christ – in his baptism, in the marriage at Cana, in the calling of the first disciples, etc. The unity and sense of development of this season need to be drawn out clearly. The presence of the crib as a reminder of how all these are extensions of the incarnation mystery is useful. There is also good reason for a special service one Sunday evening in January that draws all the Epiphany themes together. Like the Advent carol services discussed in the previous chapter, it can be a non-eucharistic liturgy, divided into sections, each consisting of a scriptural reading, that gives the section its theme, hymn, prayer, anthem (or psalm or canticle), non-scriptural reading and silence. Not all these elements need to be present. There are a number of possible themes in addition to those that form the gospel readings for the Sundays after Epiphany. The presentation is one, the appearance in the synagogue in Capernaum, described in Luke 4.14ff another. But the *great* manifestation is, of course, the crucifixion, and, carefully devised, an Epiphany liturgy can bring this out. For instance, it might have five themes such as these:

1 Revelation at Bethlehem (The Magi)
2 Revelation in Jerusalem (The Presentation)
3 Revelation at the Jordan (The Baptism)
4 Revelation at Cana-in-Galilee (The First Miracle)
5 Revelation at Calvary (The Cross).

If it were a processional service with stations, it might be so ordered that the first four marked the four points of the compass, and therefore the four arms of the cross, with the fifth at the very centre of the church, in the heart of the congregation, where might be raised a great cross, a moving climax to the service. Were it to be held on the *last* Sunday after Epiphany, and were the cross erected the one to be used on Good Friday (see Chapter 14), the service would then become a moment of transition from the looking back to Christmas to the pressing on towards Easter which the title of the following Sunday would proclaim.

The Presentation of Christ: Candlemas

2nd February is forty days after Christmas and is therefore the day of the Presentation of Christ in the Temple. The ASB provides the propers for this day, calling it by this title alone. The subsidiary and more common name 'The Purification of the Blessed Virgin Mary' is better avoided, for it places the emphasis on the secondary point of the story. It is as part of the 'manifestation' of the incarnate Christ that the feast has primary significance. The name Candlemas is common, but has no official place in either the ASB or the Roman Missal. The ASB also provides the Presentation Gospel in Year 2 on the First Sunday after Christmas, but not among the readings for the Sundays after Epiphany.

The traditional Candlemas ceremonies have no official place in Church of England liturgy, but are a powerful and dramatic symbol. Where the Presentation is regarded as the close of the Christmas festival, it brings that season to an appropriate climax. Not in many parishes will it be possible to gather sufficient of the congregation to hold the celebration on the evening of the feast day itself. In most parishes where it is to be observed, a Sunday will be preferred, before or after the feast, especially as the light ceremonies are particularly attractive to children who would be missing on a weekday night. But a transference to the Sunday brings its own problems. Only in a minority of churches is it possible to create sufficient gloom by turning off all the lights to give a real sense of light in darkness, and the symbol is a weak one in the semi-light. The problem of opting for a Sunday evening Candlemas liturgy (after dark, but, for the sake of the children, perhaps a little earlier than the traditional 6.30) is that only in the most adaptable parishes can the *Eucharist* be at that time. Other forms of service are less satisfactory, though a possible form, based on Evensong, is suggested below. Where the Presentation is observed at a principal Sunday service, the Year 1 eucharistic readings should always be used on the Sunday after Christmas to avoid repetition.

Before describing the form of the Candlemas ceremonies, a word of warning may be sounded. Candle ceremonies are appealing and popular. They can often be sentimental if the symbolism is not clear and the scriptural basis not emphasized. They can also be over-used. One candle rite for the Christmas cycle and one for the Easter seems enough. For Easter, it will, of course, be the Vigil (or its equivalent next morning). For Christmas, it could be an Advent liturgy, *or* a Christmas service *or* the observance of the Presentation, but it should probably not be more than one of them. Familiarity will indeed breed contempt, or, at least, rob the symbol of its power. Whereas both Advent and Presentation lend themselves to genuine development of the light theme, in the case of Advent because of the 'dawning light' sequence through from Old to New Testament, in the case of the Presentation because of the *Nunc Dimittis* material in the Gospel, the use of candles for the Christmas carol service or midnight Eucharist tends just to be for reasons of sentiment or 'prettiness'.

To return to Candlemas: the basic elements of the ceremony are the reading of the Presentation Gospel and the procession of lighted candles, possibly during the singing of *Nunc Dimittis*. Wherever possible, it should be a procession *of all the people* with their lighted candles, not a ceremony to be watched. At the Eucharist, the church begins in darkness. Notices normally given out before the service are left until later. Choir, president and assistants enter. If there is room, all the congregation gathers at the back of the church. Alternatively, and less ideally, the members of the congregation turn in their places to face the president. He greets them and explains what is to happen and its significance. Candles are then lit throughout the church, whether by servers or by ordinary members of the congregation who have been rehearsed. The acolytes', altar and sanctuary candles are all lit at this point. The source of light could well be the paschal candle, which will, in many churches, in any case be at the back of the church, where the president and his assistants stand, because of its proximity to the font. A hymn of light, essentially a familiar one that can be sung in semi-darkness, such as 'Thou whose almighty Word', may be sung during the lighting. The president then says a prayer of blessing after which, during the singing of *Nunc Dimittis*, the procession moves forward, the president and his assistants moving, as usual, to lectern, choir or altar, the people simply forward into their seats. At the words 'to be a light', all the church lights may be switched on full instantly. If a large procession is required, after *Nunc Dimittis*, a hymn, such as 'Of the Father's love begotten', may be sung as the procession wends it way around the church. By the end of the singing, all should be in their accustomed places. The president says the Collect. All, still holding their lighted candles, sit for the First Reading, sing the Gradual (which could well be the *Gloria*) and then stand with their lighted candles for the Presentation Gospel, after which they extinguish their candles and sit down for the Sermon. On this occasion the penitential section of the Eucharist is better used at the later point after the Intercessions. All the people's candles may be relighted during the Offertory hymn and held throughout the Eucharistic Prayer. The Roman Missal provides suitable words for the brief introduction and for the prayer of blessing, another form of which is found in *Prayers for Use at the Alternative Services*.

Where it is desired to celebrate Candlemas within an Evensong structure, the office proceeds as far as the First Lesson. After it should come the address. During *Magnificat* the candles are lit. Immediately after it the prayer of blessing is said and the Second Lesson follows. This should be the Presentation Gospel, read liturgically, the people standing, with their lighted candles, to face the reader. *Nunc Dimittis* follows immediately. The Creed, Lord's Prayer, Responsory and Collects follow, with the candles still lighted. Then comes a processional hymn during which all process with their candles, with a station at the crib, if it is still in place, a second one, where applicable, in the Lady Chapel to mark the secondary theme of the feast, and a third at the altar, where all may gather for the final prayer and blessing. That prayer may suitably be the Annunciation collect, linking as it does Christmas and Easter on this day when one finally gives way to the preparation for the other.

After the service, whether Eucharist, Evensong or another

form, the candles may be taken home and lit as a sign of welcome to Christ. Immediately after the service the crib is dismantled. Children who have been present will love to assist with this, and it will help them to learn about the Christmas season and the shape of the Christian year.

14
Lent and Holy Week

Lent: A Season of Preparation

The purpose of the Lenten season is to prepare Christian people for the annual celebration of the death and resurrection of the Lord. It was not originally, and is still not principally, a re-enactment of the forty days in the desert at the beginning of the Lord's ministry, and, significantly, the Gospel that recounts that story is not that appointed for the First Day of Lent. The thrust forward to Easter is always present in Lenten observance. The Lenten hymn has got it right: 'That with thee we may appear at the eternal Eastertide.' There is therefore a degree of nonsense about talk of 'preparing oneself for Lent', for Lent is itself the preparation. It is to be marked by study, prayer and fasting only in so much as they raise the sensitivity and expectation for the keeping of the paschal mystery.

A generation ago Lent was marked principally by additional services. The faithful were exhorted to make special effort to come to a weekday Eucharist or to attend a mid-week evening service, usually Evensong or Compline, with a spiritual talk different in style from the Sunday sermon. In addition, courses of sermons on related themes were arranged for the usual Sunday services. In the present day, the latter have continued, but the weekday services tend to have been replaced by study groups. What is really appropriate will differ enormously from place to place, but the principal aim should be to prepare for Holy Week and Easter, to heighten the sensitivity sufficiently that there is a genuine entering in to the experience of that week. It is that experience, more than a hundred additional Communions or study groups, that is likely to give people a leap forward in Christian perception and maturity, for it is that experience that is an entering into the central mystery of the faith. As far as Sunday sermons are concerned, the themes indicated in the lectionary provide a sufficiently dramatic build up to Holy Week to challenge the need always to dream up a special Lenten theme. A parish may also want to question whether Lent is the most appropriate time for study groups. Where they have no permanent existence, autumn may be as appropriate as Lent. The more old-fashioned approach – quiet weekday worship or devotional addresses on prayer – may have as much to give. But, of great importance is the need not to 'overload' people. It is sad when at the end of Lent people have had enough of extra nights out and feel they cannot find the time for Maundy Thursday, Good Friday and the Easter Vigil. These are the priority. Only where people are willing to go beyond these should an elaborate Lenten programme be planned.

The idea of 'giving up' things for Lent is also out of fashion, although, at the level of sugar and sweets, it has become very common. It can be a superficial exercise and a form of escapism from harder questions about real self-denial in the service of the gospel. But there is one sense in which this 'giving up' is important. The giving up of certain things in the liturgy during Lent is a prerequisite to a dramatically exciting Easter. Traditionally this has meant the omission of all alleluias in the liturgy (including in the hymns) and of *Gloria in excelsis* (on Sundays, though not on principal holy days), vestments of a solemn colour, whether violet or 'Lenten array', and the banishment of flowers from the church. All this is for the good and it needs to be matched by a carefulness on the part of the priest in choosing the hymns and the organist his voluntaries in accord with this mood. The air of preparation and penitence should give the liturgy its distinctive flavour through Lent in order that the return of all these things may give Eastertide a glorious ring. What is not given up is not appreciated.

It is this idea that has led in many churches to the custom of covering crosses, crucifixes, statues, etc., during Passiontide, or, in some places, throughout the whole of Lent. Again, this is a worthy custom and adds to the mood that the liturgy creates. With the ASB calendar, Palm Sunday, rather than the Sunday previously, is the time to do this. However, the original intention was not so much *cross*-covering as the covering of the excessively ornamental, decorated or jewelled. The cross itself is a symbol that should not be veiled through Holy Week. Either the covering should have a simple cross embroidered on it or the jewelled cross should be replaced by a simple wooden one. Banners may also appropriately be removed through this period.

The ASB calendar, in line with the Roman one, and indeed with the Book of Common Prayer, does not recognize the Fifth Sunday in Lent as 'Passion Sunday'.[1] There is no 'change of gear', so to speak, at that point. Instead Lent has been moving weekly nearer the passion in the choice of lections. The fifth week continues that process and brings us naturally to Palm Sunday. It has been a more gradual build up, but one that is more in accord with the emphasis on Lent, not so much as an exercise in itself, but as a preparation for Holy Week and Easter.

The rites for Palm Sunday, Maundy Thursday and Good Friday are discussed below and that for the Easter Vigil in the following chapter. The experience of Holy Week has become more and more significant for many Christians. Through the liturgy they are enabled to enter so fully into the experience of Christ that something of his death and resurrection rubs off on them, so to speak, as they go through Holy Week with him. Holy Week is not therefore principally about a calling to mind of the past, moving as that past story is, but a reliving of it, making it part of the present, and finding oneself changed by it. The services of Holy Week are not therefore principally teaching aids, but experiences into which one enters.

Christian people have many demands on their time. In ordering its worship, as much as the rest of its life, a local church has to be careful not to overtax busy people. Lent may sometimes be better observed by *fewer* parish meetings than by *more* services or study groups. Nevertheless, and despite the additional problem of family responsibilities over a holiday weekend, the Church does need to urge Christian folk to give Palm Sunday, Maundy Thursday, Good Friday and Easter absolute priority. A half-hearted observance of these deprives the Christian of the most exhilarating and moving religious experience the Church can provide. To attend on only one or two of those days is like hearing some, but not all, the movements of a symphony. Pleasure there may be, but there

---

[1] The Roman Church gives this name to Palm Sunday; the ASB omits it altogether.

cannot be real understanding, real entering in, without the experience of the whole.

In order to help people to find time for these four great movements in the symphony, the diary of Holy Week should not be overloaded in other ways. Something approaching an absolute ban on meetings and organizations is needed, though by parish consent rather than priestly edict! In most parishes it will be a mistake to hold extra services on the Monday, Tuesday and Wednesday of Holy Week, though there may be a long-established tradition that should not be undermined. Compline is *not* a suitable service for such occasions. Because it has *no* seasonal material, it cannot have that distinctive Holy Week ethos that the Eucharist or Evensong can. The Joint Liturgical Group has provided special services for these three days.

In Chapter 12, something was said of the importance of evangelistic liturgy in relation to Advent and Christmas. There is a similar need for Holy Week and Easter, but a real problem in meeting it. The liturgy is central for the churchgoer in this of all weeks, and should be so. His participation in it is essential for his growth. It has already been noted that extra impositions should not be put upon him at this time, for he has to go on being a member of a family and probably a worker at the same time, and these make very real and right claims upon him. Were the 'fringe' Christian or the very occasional communicant to come to the Maundy Thursday Eucharist or the Good Friday Liturgy, he might, if it were well done and supported by a prayerful atmosphere, be touched by it, or even drawn through it into deeper commitment, but people like him just don't go to the Maundy Thursday Eucharist or the Good Friday Liturgy. The more middle class of them possibly go to a Bach *Passion* or to the *Messiah*. And some of them would probably go to a Passion *play*, if it were well advertised and involved a lot of the locals. Both these means are marvellous evangelistic and semi-liturgical expressions of the Christian story which touch people in a way that the statutory services do not often have the chance to do. Every parish, weighing up issues of time and manpower, the spiritual needs of the congregation and the different, but equally spiritual, needs of the wider community, must solve this dilemma for itself. It may mean a great oratorio once every three years on the Fifth Sunday in Lent, all efforts into a Passion Play on Good Friday evening another year, and a massive publicity drive for the liturgy in the third year. There may be other solutions or, in some places, there may be none. But it is sad that, at present, whereas the Church draws people in at Christmas, Easter is becoming more and more a celebration only by the 'faithful'. This may in part be because Good Friday and Easter proclaim a harder truth. But the story of suffering, well told, will meet people's needs at a deep level and find a response.

If so much is to be made of Holy Week in the life of the Church, the parish priest must be ready for that. He must be prepared to clear his diary of everything that interferes with the liturgy (which will of course include his preaching) and the considerable amount of time that will be given over to rehearsal for each of the great services. Slap-dash, ill-thought out services will move nobody. If he is to ask his people to make their attendance a priority, he must make his preparation equally important and, inevitably, very time-consuming. But it is worth it.

Ash Wednesday

The First Day of Lent, Ash Wednesday, is a day on which many parishes are able to manage a Sung Eucharist. The contrast with the previous Sunday (for the three Sundays before Lent are in no way part of the season, as the liturgical colour, green, indicates) should be brought out – the hymns carefully chosen, the *Gloria* omitted, the organ, perhaps, silent except to accompany the service, flowers removed and the liturgical colour changed. But, traditionally, Ash Wednesday also has its own specific rite to inaugurate a season of penitence. There is no official Church of England order for this, though the American Prayer Book provides one.[2] But ever since the provision in the Book of Common Prayer of *The Commination*

---

[2] David Silk also gives an outline in *Prayers for Use at the Alternative Services*. At the time of writing, The Church of England Liturgical Commission is working on orders for Ash Wednesday and Holy Week, but these are unlikely to be authorized for several years.

Service, Anglicanism has recognized the need for special provision on this day.

In the American rite, after the Sermon a bidding is provided. It, rightly, lays stress on the significance of Lent as a preparation for the paschal mystery and gives something of its origins. It goes on to call the people to 'the observance of a holy Lent, by self-examination and repentance; by prayer, fasting and self-denial'. (It has already been noted that it may be counter-productive to exhort the people to too much additional devotion during the forty days of Lent.) Silence follows for a time and then, optionally, the blessing and imposition of ashes. The ashes are traditionally made from the palms of the previous year. The American rite continues with Psalm 51 (which may, of course, be sung during the imposition of ashes). The Litany of Penitence follows and then a long prayer for forgiveness (a modern translation of the Prayer for Absolution at Morning and Evening Prayer in the English Prayer Book). The Peace follows immediately and the Eucharist continues. There are two critical points that are worth making in this otherwise admirable rite. First, the American rite provides at the imposition of ashes only the traditional words, 'Remember that you are dust, and to dust you shall return'. But the modern Roman rite wisely places that sentence as an alternative to the more positive, 'Turn away from sin and be faithful to the gospel'. Secondly, the American rite omits the prayer of intercession in order to connect penitence with peace. The omission on this day seems unfortunate (and the Roman rite retains the equivalent Prayers of the Faithful).

Whereas in the American rite, the imposition of ashes is an optional alternative to words of penitence, in the Roman rite the imposition, with the singing of Psalm 51, replaces words of penitence. In the Anglican tradition the words should probably be retained and in an English setting this will mean a reversal of the order of some of the material in the Eucharist. In Rite A, the penitential section will clearly be omitted at the earlier point. But after the Sermon, the Creed being omitted, the special material is used. If the sermon has not included teaching about what is to follow, a short bidding, not unlike the American one, should be given by the president at the altar step. After a time of silence he blesses the ashes and all those who wish come forward to stand or kneel at the altar rail where he makes the sign of the cross on their forehead in ash saying one of the formulae above. He himself either makes the cross in ash on himself or another minister does so. Psalm 51, or another suitable psalm, hymn or anthem may be used during the imposition. The priest then washes his hands before leading the people in prayers of penitence. These may be introduced, in accordance with the ASB rubrics, by the Commandments, with the appropriate responses or at least by the full 'Comfortable Words', not often heard now with Rite A, despite their appearance in the text. Confession and Absolution follow and then, in the reverse order from the ASB rubrics, the Prayers of Intercession, after which the Eucharist continues as usual, the Fourth Eucharistic Prayer being particularly suitable on this day. In Rite B a similar order may be followed.

There is a suitable alternative to the use of the penitential and intercessory prayers in the use of the litany of the ASB, which combines both elements effectively, and which could be followed by a prayer of absolution before the Peace. The Prayer Book Litany, with some of the intercessory sections omitted, would be suitable with Rite B.

Mothering Sunday

Mothering Sunday is one of the liturgists' nightmares, for its observance cuts straight across the build up of the Lenten theme towards Holy Week. In the ASB lectionary, for instance, the Gospel is that of the Transfiguration. The ASB makes no real provision for the observance of Mothering Sunday, but a note in one of the tables of psalms and readings suggests the use of the propers for Pentecost 14 and provides other possible readings. But, however difficult it may be, Mothering Sunday must be adequately observed, for it is a point of genuine contact between Church and daily life, and can reach out to those on the fringe. Churches able to mount two major services on a Sunday will be able to retain the Eucharist for the Fourth Sunday in Lent, but with a Mothering Sunday ceremony attached, and to lay on a separate Mothering Sunday service for those not part of the weekly Parish Eucharist congregation. Churches unable to hold two morning services will have more of a problem. It may be one of the occasions for transferring the Eucharist to the evening (see Chapter 3 above).

At the Eucharist, it is impossible to mix the Transfiguration and Mothering themes. The Transfiguration theme should therefore be followed through the Eucharist and the service proceed as usual, but with the Intercession reduced to a minimum, because of what is to follow, or even omitted. After Communion, the president briefly explains the meaning of Mothering Sunday in his own words and then may be said this short litany, possibly with children reading the various suffrages, to each of which all respond:

Lord, receive our thanks and prayer.

For our mothers and fathers, R.
For the security of our homes and family life, R.
For the joy of all loving human relationships, R.
For your holy catholic Church, the mother of us all, R.
For your family in this place and for our life together, R.
For Mary, the Mother of Jesus, and for all who seek to follow her example of motherhood, R.
For all the members of our families who have died and now find their home in you, R.

The president then blesses the gifts that are to be given, whether flowers, simnel cake, or whatever. A hymn is then sung. 'O God in heaven, whose loving plan'[3] is particularly suitable. During this the gifts are distributed. Though it is principally the *children* present who will want to come forward to collect the gifts to present to their mothers, *adults* with mothers present should be encouraged to come forward, and mothers, of whatever age, present without their children, should, if possible, be included in some way in the distribution. The earlier prayer for the departed is also important in this service, for there is a need to be sensitive to those present whose mothers are dead. After the hymn the usual post-Communion prayer, blessing and dismissal follow.

Where there is to be a specific Mothering Sunday service, it may be built around the three themes, Mary the Mother of Jesus

---

[3] No. 74 in *One Hundred Hymns for Today*.

(linked with the Feast of the Annunciation), Mother Church and our own Mothers, though this is but one of several possible outlines. It is doubtful whether the traditional 'Jerusalem, the mother of us all' theme will cut much ice with the sort of congregation that would come to such a service.

Palm Sunday

The principal service of the day on Palm Sunday ought, in most places, to be the Eucharist, preceded by the Liturgy of Palms, though other possibilities are discussed below. For this principal service, the whole congregation gathers at a convenient place from which the procession can set out. This might be the church hall, or a second church within the parish, a suitable open air gathering point or at the church gate. Instructions about changes of plan in the case of inclement weather need to have been given. It is, of course, possible to have a procession *inside* the church, whether of all the congregation, or simply of the president and his assistants, but this is very much a second best.

The 'palms' are better distributed before the liturgy begins, unless the numbers are very small, in which case they may be distributed after they have been blessed. It is possible to buy palm branches, but they are exceedingly expensive. In most parishes palm crosses will be used, but, instead of or in addition to these, branches of local trees may be cut for use on this day. When all are ready, the president, in red vestments, greets the people and explains briefly the significance of what is to follow. The people hold up their 'palms' as the president blesses them. The Palm Gospel (Matthew 21.1–13) is then read with the usual gospel acclamations. With words such as, 'Let us go forth in peace, praising Jesus our Messiah, as did the crowds who welcomed him to Jerusalem', the procession sets out. The American Prayer Book and the Roman Missal provide suitable texts, though the American rite reverses the natural order by placing the blessing of palms after the Gospel, whereas it is appropriate that the people should hold the palms that have been blessed during the gospel reading.

The obvious hymn for the procession is 'All glory, laud and honour'. The order of the procession can vary with local circumstances, but, if a hymn is to be sung in procession, there is a strong argument for putting the choir *in the middle,* else the singing can become very ragged and out of time. A large crowd singing unaccompanied as it moves is not always very successful. If a band is available, it is worth seeking its help. But, where there is no band, to decide to walk in silence is inappropriate. This is not a Good Friday 'Procession of Witness'. (There would, in any case, be few enough to whom to witness easily on a Sunday morning.) It is an entering into the experience of Palm Sunday, and that has an ethos quite different from Good Friday. Let the people *sing.* Local circumstances will dictate the length of the procession. If the church hall is right next door to the church, the procession will hardly seem long enough. On the other hand, if it is more than half a mile it will so lengthen the liturgy that there will be a temptation to rush and make omissions in the Eucharist.

When the procession reaches the church, the hymn may change to 'Ride on! Ride on in majesty' or, if the entry of the people into the church is bound to be chaotic as everybody finds a place, this hymn may be sung as an introit when order has been restored. It is the right hymn to move the liturgy on from the atmosphere of Palm Sunday to a recollection of the passion. For the Eucharist leaves behind the *Hosannas* and moves immediately to the *Crucify!* of later in the week. The president says the Collect, a lesson is read and the gradual sung. The Gospel is the Marcan Passion. Three readers are needed. Traditionally the priest reads those parts that are the words of Christ. If there is a deacon, he is the narrator. A third voice is used for the other solo parts. The whole congregation joins in as the crowd, the priests, etc. This inevitably involves printing out for the people the entire text of the Passion with their own parts indicated. But once the parish has printed its Palm Sunday Liturgy it can last for several years. In some places, the congregation will be encouraged to *stand* throughout the Passion, but, after a processional walk, it will probably be better to allow people to sit, but to stand at the words, 'And they brought him to the place called Golgotha'. Silence is kept for a while at the end.

A custom has grown up in many churches of omitting the sermon on this day. There is no rubrical authority for this, and it has been a misguided trend. However briefly, the priest does well on this day to expound the passion story and to exhort the people to a holy keeping of the days that are to follow. But the Creed may be omitted and also the Prayers of Intercession. The Roman and American rites both omit the Prayers of Penitence, and certainly they are inappropriate at the beginning of the service. But in their traditional Anglican position they provide a suitable response to the reading of the Passion and to the sermon. Indeed the sermon may be used specifically to link Passion and Prayers of Penitence. The Eucharist then continues as usual, the Fourth Eucharistic Prayer in Rite A being particularly appropriate.

At early celebrations of the Eucharist on Palm Sunday, the second set of readings in the ASB (which include the Palm Gospel) may be used, and palm crosses blessed and distributed after the opening Sentence and Greeting. At services later in the day than the principal Eucharist, the palm crosses, already blessed, may be given out as people arrive.

In some parishes Palm Sunday afternoon may provide a more suitable occasion than the traditional Good Friday for a more public demonstration. A procession through roads and streets, gathering people, and especially children, as it goes, perhaps with a donkey, will catch the imagination of many people. It need not be restricted in its theme to Palm Sunday, though that will probably be its starting point. At the various 'stations' along the way, reading, prayer and even tableau may move the story on stage by stage until the Good Friday story is told. And because, for some of the participants, this will be their only liturgical experience over Holy Week and Easter, in some subtle way that does not anticipate too much the liturgy of Easter night and morning the sense of victory and triumph must be present. Palm Sunday has, in its own particular mood, the potential for presenting both sides of the coin, so to speak, of the Holy Week story.

Palm Sunday evening is often a time for special services. There will be places where this is right, but in others it will be an overloading. There is even a case for cancelling a sung evening service. After the Liturgy of Palms, the faithful disperse until the Eucharist of Maundy Thursday. There is certainly an argument for giving the choir an evening off; it will be working 'overtime' later in the week.

Maundy Thursday

Where pastorally appropriate, there should be just one celebration of the Eucharist in the parish on this day, though sometimes the presence in the parish of older people unable to go out at night makes an earlier celebration necessary. The main Eucharist should be held late enough for all to be home from work, but sufficiently early for all but the youngest children to attend – seven o'clock, or perhaps half an hour later in commuter parishes. (The clergy's attendance in the morning at the Eucharist for the Blessing of Oils and Renewal of Vows is discussed in Chapter 10.)

The liturgical colour for the Eucharist of the Last Supper is white and the *Gloria*, which has been omitted on the Sundays of Lent, is nevertheless said or sung today. The bells may be rung before the service and the organ played, but thereafter they are silent until the *Gloria* of the Easter Vigil, except that the organ is used as necessary for accompaniment. The Eucharist proceeds as usual until the Sermon. The Second ASB collect is preferable at this point in the service.

After the Sermon may follow the Footwashing. The gospel account of it has already been read. Suitable anthems may be sung during the ceremony. Where the choir is of sufficient competence, John Ireland's 'Greater love' is highly appropriate. Before the service seats have been placed in a convenient place in the front of the church. By tradition there are twelve, but it is better to have half that number and room for the ceremony, than twelve and be crowded – the space available will dictate. Those whose feet are to be washed will, of course, have been chosen and briefed before they come to church – if for no other reason than the need for them to be suitably clothed; ladies in 'tights' present a problem! The Roman rite restricts this ceremony to men, but few Anglicans will think that appropriate. This is no mere play-acting of the Last Supper, but a deep expression of humility, love and service in the local Christian community. It is helpful, though not absolutely necessary, if those chosen are *representative* of the church community – not all young, or all old, or all women. A record should be kept of those chosen, so that different people are invited each year.

After the Sermon, the president withdraws to the vestry,

takes off his chasuble and returns carrying a bowl. He needs two assistants, priests or deacons if they are present, but otherwise lay people, one carrying the jug of water, the other the towel. Meanwhile those whose feet are to be washed have gone to the chairs provided for them and removed footwear. The president goes in turn to each of them, kneels before them, takes the jug and pours water over their foot (or feet) into the bowl. He then takes the towel and dries them. As he gets up he may take their hand or greet them in some other way. When all have had their feet washed, the president and his assistants return to the vestry. He puts on the chasuble and enters the church again. Meanwhile those whose feet have been washed return to their places. The Footwashing rite may conclude with the singing of *Ubi caritas* ('Where charity and love are, there is God'), a traditional part of the liturgy of this day, available now in several translations.[4]

The restoration of this ceremony has not been as widespread as that of other traditional Holy Week practices. This is partly because it is argued that it cannot have the same meaning and significance in our culture that it did originally; it is therefore in some ways a false exercise. There has also been an unease about whether it can be performed in such a way that it is genuinely helpful to worship – it could so easily degenerate into a farce. It is certainly true that it is *different* from most of the rituals of Holy Week in that the real benefit is not to those who *see* it, but to those who *do* it. The mass of the congregation in the church will probably be unmoved by it – it is not visually impressive – or faintly amused (though that is more likely to happen if it is over-stylized and too solemn) or a little embarrassed. But for the priest it is a deeply moving experience to kneel in this way at the feet of those, over whom he presides, and yet whom he is called to serve. He would do well sometimes, not every year, to preach about the way it affects him deeply. Those whose feet have been washed will also know what it means to have it done to them. It is a most powerful symbol, once experienced, of the relationship of leadership to service in the Christian community, and a sacramental action of great significance.

The Eucharist then continues with the Prayers of Inter-

---

[4] Including Nos. 132 and 195 in *More Hymns for Today*.

cession. After Communion a single prayer is said. The usual post-Communion prayer is not altogether suitable, but the first ASB collect for Maundy Thursday may appropriately be used in its place. If the sacrament is to be 'reserved' for use on Good Friday (see the following section), or if a Watch is to be maintained before it, the elements are now taken to the appropriate place. Here local customs will differ considerably. In the Roman tradition, which some will want to follow, the sacrament is carried during the singing of *Pange Lingua* ('Of the glorious Body telling') to a side altar, decked with candles and flowers, and placed in a tabernacle, *which is then closed.* President and assistants remain kneeling before the sacrament for a while. In some churches, however, either because there is only one altar and one aumbry, or for other more theological reasons, it will seem most appropriate simply to place the elements without ceremony, and without additional candles, flowers, etc., in the aumbry, which is then locked. In yet other churches, where there is to be no Communion from the reserved sacrament next day (and this will be the majority of Anglican churches), what remains is simply consumed after Communion and the aumbry, if there is one, left open and bare until the first Eucharist of Easter, though in this case some clergy will want to keep consecrated bread in another private place in case of emergency in the following forty-eight or so hours. If *Pange Lingua* is not sung at this point in the service, its use during Communion (or with the first part at the Offertory and the second during Communion) is particularly appropriate.

The stripping of the altar now follows. The Roman rite no longer orders the recitation of Psalm 22 during this and, indeed, other words said or sung are appropriate, or it may be done in silence. Nevertheless the psalm is very suitable, especially when there is a choir to lead the singing of it (but without *Gloria Patri* at the end). Careful rehearsal by servers, or by those members of the congregation who are to do this, is needed, if it is not to be a fiasco. Slowly, silently and reverently they extinguish the candles, remove the vessels, candles and books used for the Eucharist, and then the crosses and the altar coverings. The priest meanwhile stands at the front of the congregation facing the altar. As the various assistants complete their tasks they come to join him there. The lights are gradually lowered as the psalm proceeds. When it ends and the task has been completed, president and congregation all kneel in silent prayer, the remaining lights being switched off, save for one shining on the bare altar and one by the door to allow people to see as they leave. All remain in silent prayer until the president and his assistants, with the choir if there is one, get up and leave silently and without ceremony. In many parishes it will be more realistic to encourage people to remain for a time in prayer now, rather than to return later to take a turn at a Watch. There is something to be said for the fact that we both watch and pray with our Lord, but also desert him and flee, like the disciples, to our homes, leaving him alone in the darkness. Nevertheless a formal Watch may be organized, though there is no need for it necessarily to be 'before the Blessed Sacrament' where that is not the tradition. The Watch before the bare altar and the stripped sanctuary is as appropriate. The Roman rite does not allow a Watch beyond midnight.

At some point, whether late on Thursday night or early on Friday morning, when the church is deserted, other items not removed during the formal stripping should be taken away, among them the paschal candle and coloured hangings. If possible all crosses and crucifixes are removed or covered, in order not to detract from the cross that will form the heart of the Good Friday Liturgy.

Good Friday

The old Anglican pattern for Good Friday consisted in many parishes of up to four services. Early in the day a faithful few attended 'Ante-Communion' – usually the Prayer Book Communion rite up to and including the Prayer for the Church. This service was often preceded by Matins and the Litany. Mid-morning there was a Children's Service, normally of the 'hymn-sandwich' variety, but, in some circles, the Stations of the Cross. At twelve noon began the Three Hours Devotion, a service of preaching, with hymns, silence and prayers, but the minimal use of Scripture. There was little congregational participation and no liturgical movement. The people 'knelt at the foot of the cross', not literally but spiritually, and also sat at the feet of a 'conductor', often imported for the occasion. A minority stayed for three hours, the majority came and went at one o'clock and two o'clock. In the evening there was often a sort of Evensong-type service, often following a Procession of Witness, and often ecumenical.

This pattern has been breaking down in recent years for a number of reasons. The first has been a decline in the attendance at the traditional Three Hours. For one reason or another people have seemed less willing to sit quietly for a long period to listen. This is, no doubt, in part because other worship has changed so drastically and the Three Hours has somehow become marooned in a liturgical past. For another reason, there has been an increasing dissatisfaction with patterns that totally separate adults and children in worship. Families want to be together, at least for part of the time in worship, and, for instance, a ten o'clock Children's Service followed by a twelve noon adult liturgy makes for problems in the family. Another difficulty is the increase in Good Friday working. A church that puts its principal act of worship at midday will, in certain urban areas, prevent some of its members from being present. However, the most fundamental objection to the old pattern is that the principal service, the Three Hours, is itself unsatisfactory on a number of counts. First, it makes very little use of the Scriptures, whereas one would expect an adequate Good Friday liturgy to be built around the passion narrative. Secondly, it is too cerebral a form of devotion for the majority, depending totally on listening and reasoning. Thirdly, it relies far too heavily on the ability of the conductor and ignores all liturgical insights about the active participation of the people.

For all these reasons, some reordering of the pattern has become necessary in most places and is probably desirable in all. Such reordering should restore primacy to the *Liturgy*, the content of which is described below. Depending on how much optional material is included, this service will last between one hour and one hour and a half. It could be used at 1.30 p.m. or 2 p.m. to finish at the traditional three o'clock. As such, it could be used on its own or preceded by an hour and a half of the traditional sort of address, silence, prayer and hymn sequence associated with the Three Hours. Alternatively it could begin at twelve noon, stop with the Liturgy of the Cross at one o'clock, give way to the more traditional preaching service until 2.30 and end with the conclusion of the Liturgy (optional reception of Holy Communion, and some commemoration of the burial) to end at three o'clock. The final option, where Good Friday working is common, is the liturgy in the evening. All these are possibilities, depending on local need. Where the Three Hours has retained its popularity, one of the options that retains both a three hour service, and a fair proportion of it given over to preaching, is probably best.

The needs of children will be one of the deciding factors in reordering the pattern of parish worship on Good Friday. Provision for children during Holy Week should be an important part of any parish's planning. The special liturgies of Palm Sunday, Maundy Thursday and Good Friday are quite suitable for children from the age of about eleven and, without complete perception, children younger than this may be caught up in the atmosphere of them and 'held' by the various ceremonies. But it is desirable that, during the week, there should be a time when they do things *at their own level*, as much as anything in order that they may learn more about the meaning of the liturgy in which they are taking their part. In those years when school holidays have begun before Palm Sunday a children's project for an hour a day on the first three weekdays of Holy Week could well be the answer. But often school holidays do not begin until Maundy Thursday. Good Friday, and the Three Hours, then becomes the obvious time for such an exercise. Local opportunities will vary, but a possible pattern would be:

12 noon   Adults gather in church for the traditional preaching service.
Children gather in hall for teaching and activities at their own level (they bring their lunch or else are provided with hot cross buns and fruit).

1.45 p.m.   The older children join the adults in the church for the Liturgy of the Cross, but the younger children remain in the hall to make the Easter Garden.

2.45 p.m.   As the liturgy moves to its climax, the younger children join those in the church, bringing with them the Easter Garden they have made, the reception of which is made part of the closing minutes of the liturgy.

3 p.m.   All disperse.

There is at present no authorized Church of England form for the Good Friday liturgy. It is possible to draw one up using nothing but the provisions of the ASB, but unless it includes a Eucharist (which the ASB does not envisage for it orders no proper preface), it will be somewhat barren. The liturgy needs either some form of the veneration of the cross or the sharing of Communion (or both) if it is to be satisfying, even though it remains true that the principal constituent of the liturgy on this day must be the Passion Reading. The American and Roman rites both provide additional material, but what follows is loyal, wherever possible, to the ASB text and rubrics.

The church is lit only sufficiently for people to read. The altar is bare as at the end of the previous evening. There is a chair for the president and a lectern. Choir, assistants and president enter in silence. The clergy wear red – alb and stole, but chasuble as well if there is to be a Eucharist; or a cope may be worn. The service follows the usual eucharistic form up to the readings. The penitential prayers should come at the beginning. If Rite B is the custom, these prayers should on this day be transferred to this early point. The Commandments or the Comfortable Words could well be used to introduce this section. Only the first of the Collects in the ASB is needed, the themes of the other two being taken up in the Prayers of Intercession later. An Old Testament Reading and an Epistle should probably both be read. It would be a pity if the liturgy did not include Isaiah 52.13—53–end. The Passion Reading from John takes the place of the Gospel and should be read dramatically in the same manner as described for Palm Sunday (above). After the Sermon, the Creed may be said and a hymn or anthem could be inserted here if appropriate.

The Prayers of Intercession follow. The ASB provision for other forms might be used in one of two ways. Either the ASB Litany (the full form, not that in the Appendix to Rite A) might be appropriately used, or else the Roman prayers for this occasion, which consist of a series of biddings with silence and collect to conclude each section. In this case, not all the sections need be used.

It is at this point that the Liturgy of the Cross should be

inserted. Although there is a tradition by which at this moment a cross is *unveiled,* it is preferable for the president and his assistants to go out of the church, or to the back of it, returning with a great wooden cross (whether a plain one or with the figure of Christ upon it) carried by president or deacon, and preceded by two servers with lighted candles. The procession moves very slowly through the congregation as the hymn 'Sing my tongue, the glorious battle' is sung. By tradition the procession stops three times and the hymn is long enough for these pauses to be of the duration of a whole verse. By the end of the hymn, the cross has been brought to the sanctuary where it stands on, above or before the altar, with the lighted candles beside it. All then kneel and the *Reproaches*[5] are sung, either to one of the traditional settings, or adapted very easily to Anglican chant, or said, as a devotion between priest and people. For most Anglicans veneration will probably mean no more than this kneeling in their places, the priest on his knees before the cross, but some will follow the older tradition of approaching in a kind of procession to kneel momentarily at the foot of the cross, or along the altar rail. After the Reproaches, this part of the service is brought to an end by silence and a concluding collect.

This may mark the end of the Liturgy, though there are possible further sections. Or it may mark the end of the first part, where, during a three-hour service, for instance, an hour or so of the traditional preaching style is to be inserted, the conclusion of the Liturgy following later. The two possible additions, now or later, are, first, either the Eucharist itself or Communion from the Reserved Sacrament, and some commemoration of the burial of Christ.

Except in Evangelical circles, there has been no tradition of a celebration of the Eucharist on Good Friday in Anglicanism since the influence of the Oxford Movement. Nor does Roman Catholicism permit it. It has been argued that on this day all eyes should, so to speak, be on the one great sacrifice of Calvary. Neither the Book of Common Prayer, nor the Alternative Service Book, forbid a celebration, and such

---

[5] The text of the *Reproaches,* a quite beautiful devotion, may be found in the Roman Missal and in the Holy Week Services of the Joint Liturgical Group.

practice is becoming more common. If it is to happen, the veneration is followed, appropriately, by the Peace ('He has reconciled us to God in one body by the cross'), and then the Eucharist continues in the usual way until the Communion. The final section should be thought out with some care. The usual post-Communion prayer does not seem altogether appropriate and the blessing might be omitted.

In some more Catholic circles in the Church of England, the tradition has been followed, not of a celebration, but of Communion from the 'pre-sanctified' bread (and sometimes wine) from the Maundy Thursday Eucharist. The Church of England has never yet sanctioned the use of the consecrated elements in this way and, in some ways, the practice does not accord with Anglican ethos.[6] But, where it is the custom, the veneration is followed by a simple rite consisting of Lord's Prayer, possibly *Agnus Dei*, Invitation to Communion and the sharing of the pre-sanctified elements.

But there is much to be said for the established Anglican practice of abstaining from Communion from Maundy Thursday until Easter. There is a sense of entering into the experience of Jesus: 'I will no more drink of the fruit of the vine until I drink it new.' With such a view, the Liturgy of the Cross becomes a *substitute* for the Liturgy of the Eucharist on Good Friday and provides a fitting climax to the rite.

The other possible addition to the rite (and this is not, on the whole, found in the traditional rites of Christendom) is some commemoration of the burial of Christ. This would of course be inappropriate until three o'clock, but it does complete the story of the day and is more satisfactory if people are not to return to church until the Easter Vigil. He who has not been buried in the liturgy cannot easily burst the grave. All that is required is the reading of John 19.31–end with the collect of Easter Eve and suitable hymnody. Where the liturgy has coincided with a children's project that has included the making of an Easter Garden, it may be borne into the church ('Were you there when they crucified my Lord?' being sung, very quietly, with 'Were you there when they laid him in the tomb?' as the final verse).

---

[6] It cannot be known at the time of writing whether the Holy Week services on which The Liturgical Commission is working will include this provision, novel to Anglicans in England.

Even the youngest of children will not spoil the atmosphere at this key moment if they see themselves as guarding the tomb.

A word must be said in conclusion about acts of witness on Good Friday. Christians rightly want to draw attention to the solemnity of this day and to witness to their faith before those who regard it as just another ordinary day. There are ways to do this, and ways to be avoided. The aggressive loud speaker or the protesting banner will often do more harm than good. A simple but colourful dramatic presentation of the story in the shopping centre or along a route will invite interest at very least. It may be the moment for the Church to re-learn the value of 'street theatre'. If there is to be a handout, let it not so much bemoan the misuse of Good Friday – it will be too late for that – but warmly invite the recipient to the Easter services.

15
The Great Fifty Days of Easter

The Celebration of Easter

The resurrection is celebrated in the Church's calendar in three ways: first and foremost by the great celebration of Easter Day itself, secondly by the weekly observance of Sunday as a 'little Easter', and thirdly by a glorious season of fifty days, from Easter Day until Pentecost. All three should have about them a paschal note. It is a pity that the Anglican liturgical revisers allowed the Sundays between Easter Day and Pentecost to go on being called 'Sundays *after* Easter', rather than 'Sundays *of* Easter', for the title preferred in both Prayer Book and ASB encourages the misconception that, whereas Lent lasts a full forty days (plus six Sundays), Easter lasts barely a week. By the Second Sunday after Easter many parishes are 'back to normal'. There is no distinctive paschal flavour to the worship. This is a grave impoverishment, not only because it deprives the people of the opportunity for rich and joyful celebration over a period of weeks, but also because it isolates Ascension and Pentecost from the paschal mystery of which they are part.

In order to understand the Easter festival, it is necessary to realize that originally death and resurrection were celebrated not in successive seasons, as separable units, but as one great mystery. There was no Holy Week or Good Friday. Easter was a celebration of both sides of the grave, as the Vigil service moved through the night of darkness to the morning. This sense cannot really be recovered in the life of the Church, and it would be foolish to try, but it is helpful to realize that talk of 'the paschal mystery' is about death *and* resurrection. Baptism, as an entering into that paschal mystery, is, similarly, an experience of death *and* resurrection.

There is another sense in which we have lost the sense of the wholeness of the Easter mystery, and that is in relation to the

Ascension and the Giving of the Spirit. The Easter faith is more than simply that God raised Jesus. It is also that Jesus has been taken into glory and the Spirit has been poured out. These are inseparable parts of the one mystery and the Johannine perspective unites them at a single moment in time on the first Easter Day (John 20.1–22). The liturgical cycle has followed the Lucan perspective in drawing out each of these three aspects for separate emphasis on different days. But the Easter season is to be seen as a gradual unfolding of the mystery, not as the successive celebration of a number of independent truths. On Ascension Day, the Church says not: 'Here ends Easter. Here begins Ascension', but: 'Now add to your picture of the resurrection this further aspect of the truth. Christ has gone up on high . . .' Thus the ASB is right to subtitle the Sunday after Ascension 'Easter 6', and in the Roman calendar this Sunday is designated one of the Sundays 'of Eastertide'. On the Feast of Pentecost, the fiftieth great day of Eastertide, the last aspect of the paschal mystery is celebrated. The Giving of the Spirit brings the celebration to its climax. This emphasis is quite different from the old picture of the three feasts, each with its 'octave', but it is more primitive as well as theologically more sound. It is not that in so doing the Church is opting for the Johannine, rather than the Lucan chronology, but that by this means the total significance of what it means to be baptized and to be 'in Christ' is more fully understood and experienced.

During Eastertide, the ASB makes provision for a special Easter form of greeting at the Eucharist. It may be used at other services also. The priest says, 'Alleluia. Christ is risen.' The people respond, 'He is risen indeed. Alleluia.' There is also an Easter form of invitation to Communion. It also permits the addition of a double alleluia to both the Dismissal and its response. Where the Dismissal is sung, this needs preparation by organist and choir. The Easter forms should be used daily until and including Pentecost. They are also suitable at 'paschal liturgies' outside Eastertide, that is at Baptism, Confirmation, Funerals and *Requiem* Eucharists. The 'Easter Anthems' may be used daily at Morning Prayer, but also deserve wider use on a regular basis during Eastertide at the Eucharist. The paschal candle, lit at Easter, burns during all Eucharists and other principal services through the season until the last service on

Pentecost Sunday. Thereafter it is moved to the font until the following Maundy Thursday, but is moved into the chancel to stand by the coffin at funerals. During Eastertide it stands *in a prominent place*. This need not necessarily be by the altar, if another position, such as the chancel step, is more obvious. For weekdays, when services are in a side chapel, it may be moved into the chapel, or else left burning in the main body of the church visible to those making their way to and from the chapel.

The Easter Garden has become an important part of the Easter celebrations in many Anglican parishes. As has already been indicated, it can be put in position at the end of the Good Friday Liturgy and the stone sealed, but only during Holy Saturday should it be decorated with flowers. It may be blessed at the Vigil and the stone rolled away. Thereafter it may remain, preferably until Pentecost, providing that it can be renewed when its greenery wilts and flowers wither. If it is in a suitable position, a 'station' may be made at it during the Introit at the Eucharist on the Sundays of Eastertide and on Ascension Day, and a suitable prayer said, in much the same way as the pause at the crib at Christmas. Suitable prayers for use at the Easter Garden are provided in *Prayers for Use at the Alternative Services*.

But perhaps the most important point of all is that the priest remembers, in planning the hymnody and in preparing his sermons, that it is Easter all the way for fifty glorious days. In too many churches the paschal flavour is disappearing before the season is half completed. The alleluias should not die away until Pentecost evening. No longer should it be true that Anglicans are better at keeping Lent than celebrating Easter. The fifty great days should feature in their thinking as much as the forty days of prayer and fasting that precede them.

The Easter Vigil

The Easter Vigil has been one of the great rediscoveries of modern liturgy. In some parishes it has become the crowning glory of the liturgical year, yet in others it does not feature at all. There is no doubt that it can be a very powerful experience for the participants, but it also has the danger of being an esoteric rite for the few. It is beset with problems. At what hour should it be? How does it relate to the principal Eucharist of Easter morning? What order should be followed? For there are basic differences between, for instance, the Roman order and the proposals of the Joint Liturgical Group, mainly in relation to the lighting of the paschal candle. Liturgical scholars are not even agreed on its status and use in primitive centuries. Is the reintroduction of something so beset with problems worthwhile?

In the experience of the author, the answer must be Yes. He has seen first his own understanding of the paschal mystery, and then that of a parochial congregation, transformed by exposure to the Easter Vigil. Its symbolism is so rich, and the way in which the Easter mystery gradually unfolds so enlightening, that it is always worth the considerable effort both of devising a form suitable to the needs of the local community and also of striving to make it part of the experience of an increasing number of Christian people. Of course there are parishes where it will not be possible to celebrate what is in fact the First Eucharist of Easter during the night or very early in the morning, and in the next section the use of Easter Vigil material at other points instead is discussed. But, assuming for the time being that a Vigil is possible, when should it be?

We are talking of a service that must last a minimum of one hour and a quarter, but which, for its effectiveness, should preferably last up to two hours. (There is of course the possibility of a far longer Vigil, right through the night, and this is discussed later.) The ideal is to begin in darkness and end in daylight. There are parishes where there are sufficient people with the imagination and enthusiasm to rise for a 5.30 a.m. service. The problem is that, in most parishes, they will be a minority, and the riches of the Vigil will be lost to most. Midnight, though a traditional hour, does not have the appeal that it does at Christmas. Though not ideal, nine o'clock at night has worked in many parishes. It is then dark when the Vigil begins and, by the time it ends, at about eleven o'clock, it feels like the middle of the night. Local and pastoral circumstances must decide the issue of time.

It is impossible, within the compass of this book, to give very detailed suggestions about the way the Vigil should be ordered. It is a great feast of colour, light, movement, and song, calling for the use of every skill at the church's disposal if it is really to excite. It is an opportunity for a greater degree of active participation by the people than is often possible, with a variety of responsibilities from the reading of lessons to the ringing of bells and the lighting of candles. Fanfares may be sounded at appropriate points.

In the Roman rite the service begins with the Liturgy of Light. (In other rites this comes later after the Liturgy of the Word.) There are two ways of presenting this Liturgy of Light. The first one has the congregation seated in a darkened church. At the appointed time the doors of the main porch are opened. The president and his assistants are gathered in the porch. The president greets the people and explains to them the purpose of the Vigil.[1] He then lights and blesses the new fire, in the porch, and then blesses the paschal candle which he then lights from the fire. The deacon (or another priest or, if there is no other priest, the president himself) raises high the candle and sings 'Christ our Light' to which all respond 'Thanks be to God'. Then all enter the church, led by the deacon with the paschal candle.

The alternative, and better, way to begin the Vigil, when possible, is for all to assemble outside at a proper bonfire, from which the procession, led by the deacon with the lighted candle, enters the church.

The same acclamation and response is sung twice more as the candle is borne through the church and all other candles, including those held by the members of the congregation, are lit from it. The candle is placed on its stand by the deacon who now goes to the pulpit or lectern for the Easter Proclamation, *Exsultet*. The people, with their lighted candles, face the deacon. The *Exsultet* is a most beautiful song, but it requires a good singing voice. If necessary the singing of it should be delegated to a layman. Or else it may be turned effectively into a spoken dialogue between deacon and people.

The service now moves into its second phase, the Liturgy of the Word. For this the members of the congregation extinguish their candles, but the other candles in the church remain alight. A lectern, near the paschal candle, is used for the readings

---

[1] All appropriate texts for the Vigil are to be found in the Roman Missal, the American Prayer Book and *Prayers for Use at the Alternative Services* where they are not in the ASB.

which follow, but additional candle light may be needed at it if the paschal candle stands very high. After an introductory bidding by one of the clergy, there follow a number of Old Testament passages, each followed by a psalm or a period of silence and a collect. Hymns or songs may be inserted between the sections. The Roman rite provides seven readings, the American rite nine, but except at an all-night Vigil, probably only three of these will be selected. These must include Exodus 14.15—15.1, the account of the Exodus. After the last Old Testament reading a hymn may appropriately be sung ('Guide me, O thou great Redeemer' would be a suitable choice) while the candles of the people are relighted.

The hymn over, the organ, which until this moment has been used only for necessary accompaniment, thunders out with a great noise that leads after a time into *Gloria in excelsis*. Meanwhile the church bells ring out, and other bells and musical instruments may be sounded, and all the lights in the church are switched on fully. The effect should be electric and a gasp almost audible. The congregation, holding their lighted candles, lustily sing the *Gloria* and the president then says the Collect of Easter Day. The congregation then sits for the Epistle reading (Romans 6.3–11, especially if Baptism is to follow, or one of those provided in the ASB), sings the Gradual and stands for the Easter Gospel. The Marcan account is suitable, saving the more elaborate accounts for the morning. After the Gospel, the people extinguish their candles and sit for the Sermon.

After the Sermon the Liturgy of Baptism will follow. At the very least this consists of the Blessing of the Baptismal Water and the Renewal of Baptismal Vows, but it may, and, where possible, should, include Baptism and, if the bishop is the president, Confirmation may be administered. There is no moment in the year when the significance of baptism is more clear. The threefold parallel of Exodus, Easter and Baptism has been powerfully shown through the scriptural readings. If there is a child or adult whose baptism can appropriately happen in this context, it will be an unforgettable experience for all involved. The procession moves to the font. Traditionally a Litany, including prayer for those to be baptized, is sung as the procession moves there. The paschal candle is carried to the font in the procession. The president then proceeds with the

Baptism in the usual form, beginning with the Decision and continuing to the Welcome (see Chapter 6). At the Blessing of the Water he may lower the paschal candle into the font. The Roman rite also provides for the Blessing of Water when there are to be no baptisms immediately. Because of the teaching value of the Blessing of Water in relation to the Exodus and Easter mystery, in preparation for the Renewal of Baptismal Vows which is to follow, and in anticipation of baptisms later on Easter Day, this blessing makes a good deal of sense.

It is unlikely that the Easter Vigil will often be a suitable occasion for a major Confirmation. But if there are a few candidates and the bishop is present, he may appropriately confirm them *around the font*, immediately after the Giving of the Candle to the newly baptized and before the Welcome.

With the president still at the font, there follows now the Renewal of Baptismal Vows. The ASB provides the form for this.[2] The president may sprinkle the people with the baptismal water as a reminder of their own baptism. This leads immediately into the Peace. The form, 'We are the Body of Christ . . .' is more suitable than the ASB Easter form when it follows the Liturgy of Baptism. The Eucharist then continues as usual, with the use of the Easter Invitation to Communion and the Easter Dismissal. At some point before the end, a procession to the Easter Garden, where it is blessed, is appropriate. Indeed such a blessing could precede the Blessing of the people and the Dismissal, which could then take place at the Garden. The bells, silent before the Vigil, should ring out as the people leave.

There will be parishes where an all-night Vigil is possible, if not every year, then as a special project occasionally, perhaps by the young people of the parish. In such a case, the form of the Vigil itself would be much the same, but with opportunity to 'slacken the pace' and meditate more fully on each of the elements. A break might be taken between the different sections. Non-biblical material might be introduced.[3] But one basic and significant addition can happily be made. Between the Old and New Testament readings can be inserted Holy

[2] On pp. 276f.
[3] Alice Meynell's poem 'Easter Night' deserves a place in every Easter Vigil, as does Edmund Spenser's 'Easter'.

Week material, and especially the Passion, restoring the Vigil as an experience of the *whole* paschal mystery, death as well as resurrection. The early period of the night could be spent in preparation for the Vigil – getting the church ready, choosing the material and rehearsing it. After a break, the Vigil itself might begin at two o'clock if it was to last until a little before dawn.

In some parishes a full Eucharistic Vigil in the night or at dawn will seem impossible, but there will be the possibility of a curtailed Vigil on the Saturday evening, in effect the Liturgy of Light, the Old Testament sequence of readings and the Liturgy of Baptism. In some places this may work quite well, but there is a strong argument for the *unity* of the rite and that, if a second best has to be settled for, it should mean the integration of elements of the Easter Vigil in the Easter Day morning Eucharist. Only the element of darkness is lost in such an arrangement.

Easter Day

The Eucharist of Easter morning has a different ethos from that of the night Vigil. The Vigil Eucharist is the paschal mystery, the commemoration of God's mighty deliverance, and, though it proclaims powerfully Christ's victory over death, does not dwell on his Easter appearances or reunion with his followers. The Sunday morning Eucharist celebrates this glorious reunion. Darkness, dawn and daylight mark a gradual unfolding of the mystery and an ever-increasing joy. Those who have been present at the Vigil, providing that it has been in the evening or at midnight, should therefore be encouraged to be present and to communicate again at the morning Eucharist. When there has been a dawn Vigil, this cannot so easily apply. A dawn Vigil will presumably take the place of the traditional 'eight o'clock', leaving one further Eucharist later in the morning, for those who cannot come early. Where there has been no Baptism at the Vigil, whether at night or at dawn, it is desirable that there be one at the principal Eucharist of the day. It is also possible (and has much to commend it) to repeat at every celebration on Easter Day the Renewal of Baptismal Vows. This may be placed between the

Absolution and the Peace, and the Creed consequently omitted.

Where there has been no Vigil, the principal elements from it should, as far as possible, be incorporated into the main Eucharist. This would begin with the Easter greeting at the back of the church followed by the blessing and lighting of the paschal candle (but probably dispensing with the new fire), a procession through the church and the placing of the candle on its stand with acclamations. The Easter Garden could be blessed now or at the end of the service. Three readings should be used, the first being the account of the Exodus, and the Liturgy of Baptism, precisely as in the Vigil, used between sermon and Peace. Prayers of Penitence could be omitted altogether. The Renewal of Vows provides that element.

The giving of eggs (real ones as much as chocolate ones) has become the custom in many churches. Where this is linked with teaching, it is a happy custom. Since the significance of eggs is linked with the bursting from a shell that the empty tomb typifies, they could well be distributed to children at the end of the liturgy from the Easter Garden, the children having first gathered round for both Garden and eggs to be blessed. But it is important not to 'overplay' either Garden or eggs to the detriment of the great Easter symbol, the paschal candle. If children are to take something home, in some ways a better symbol is a candle (in a jam jar) lit from the paschal candle that they can carry home still alight, then to be extinguished but relit for a few minutes each Sunday until Pentecost.

An Easter Carol Service

At some point during the Great Fifty Days it may be appropriate to hold an Easter Carol Service to draw out some of the great themes that belong to this season. As with the Advent and Epiphany services already described, services can be devised, consisting of a series of sections, each of which includes at least a 'controlling' scriptural passage, carol or hymnody and collect, but possibly also other music, non-scriptural readings, silence and responsories. In Eastertide such services would also incorporate the Easter greeting and dismissal. Four distinct sequences suggest themselves.

The first takes up the dominant theme of the Vigil and is particularly appropriate where the Vigil has not been celebrated. Musical material from the Vigil might well be included. The five stages are:

1	Exodus 14.19–31	The Escape through the waters of the Red Sea
2	Joshua 3	Crossing the Jordan into the Promised Land
3	1 Peter 3.17–4.6	Christ goes through the deep waters of death
4	John 20.1–18	The Resurrection
5	Romans 6.3–11	Identification with Christ through Baptism.

A second sequence is a straightforward presentation of the Easter material in the final two chapters of St John's Gospel. The material could be combined in a different way from this:

1	John 19.38–42	The Burial of Christ
2	John 20.1–9	Peter and John at the Tomb
3	John 20.10–18	The Risen Lord appears to Mary
4	John 20.19–23	Easter Day evening
5	John 20.24–9	The Appearance to Thomas
6	John 21.1–14	By the Lakeside
7	John 21.15–end	'Simon, do you love me?'

The third sequence meditates on eucharistic passages in the New Testament, especially those that relate to the resurrection:

1	John 6.22–40	'I am the Bread of Life'
2	Luke 22.7–19	'I will no more drink . . . till I drink it new'
3	Luke 24.13–35	Known in the breaking of bread
4	John 21.1–14	By the Lakeside
5	Revelation 3.14–end	'I will come in and sup with him'

A fourth sequence, a useful one for teaching the total meaning of the paschal mystery, invites the use of Ascension and Pentecost material as well, and therefore makes for greater musical possibilities. It takes, in their Lucan form, the three elements of resurrection, ascension and coming of the Spirit and meditates on each in turn. It then uses the Johannine equivalent, in which all three elements are united, as a liturgical

Gospel to sum them all up and to show their essential unity:

1   Luke 24.1–11   Resurrection
2   Acts 1.6–11   Ascension
3   Acts 2.1–11   The Coming of the Spirit
4   John 21.11–22   The Johannine parallel.

The Gospel (fourth reading) would precede or follow a sermon, or else this short explanation might precede its reading:

> We have heard in the writings of the Evangelist Luke, in his Gospel and in the Acts of the Apostles, of the three mysteries of our faith that Easter celebrates:
>
>> God raises Jesus from the dead: Resurrection.
>> Jesus is exalted at the right hand of the Father: Ascension.
>> The Spirit is poured out upon the Church: Pentecost.
>
> It is these three mysteries, bound inextricably together, that the Church celebrates and proclaims, from the first hesitant *Alleluia* of the darkness of Easter night, through the fifty days, until the last *Alleluia* dies away on Pentecost evening. Hear now of these same mysteries, all of them part of the Easter experience, as the Evangelist John tells of them.

These four sequences by no means exhaust all the possibilities for the Easter season.

Ascension and Pentecost

Ascension Day is the fortieth day of Easter and Pentecost the fiftieth. There is no particular liturgical ceremony associated with either feast day, though the liturgy is in both cases enriched by the new theological emphases that the feast brings to the Easter season.

The tradition of an early morning Sung Eucharist on Ascension Day has declined, in some parishes because of its impracticality. But it is a loss, for early morning seems a far more natural time than mid-evening to celebrate the return of Jesus in glory to his Father. The practice of extinguishing the paschal candle after the Gospel at the Ascension Day Eucharist is a mistaken and unfortunate one, not only because it destroys the unity of the Great Fifty Days, a theological as well as a liturgical unity, but also because it gives a wholly misleading symbol of the *absence* of Christ. There is no sense of 'Now he's gone' once Ascension Day has arrived. In a way there wasn't that sense even in the experience of the earliest Christians.

Whitsunday, or Pentecost, the last great day of Eastertide, should have about it a sense of *climax*. To all the joyful celebration of Easter is added the marvellous truth, 'His Spirit is with us'. The liturgical colour is red. There is no ceremony for the final extinguishing of the paschal candle. But it would be appropriate, at the end of the last service of the day, to gather around it and to sing a hymn that draws out all the truths that Easter has proclaimed. ('We have a gospel to proclaim' is an obvious choice.) After it, the Blessing is given and the Easter Dismissal sung or said. The candle is then extinguished and the service ends. If children have been present, they will learn something, and enjoy themselves, if they are allowed to help move the candle to the font and dismantle the Easter Garden.

The ASB is unhelpful in its provision for Pentecost week. Although it recognizes no octaves, and although it orders that Easter elements should cease on Pentecost, it nevertheless provides Holy Spirit readings for the Office throughout the week and suggests red as the liturgical colour. There is a sense of a '50 + 6' season, which is unsatisfactory. In the Roman calendar 'ordinary' time begins on the day after Pentecost, and the colour is immediately green. The Holy Spirit readings would have been better provided in the days leading up to Pentecost. Subsequent revision may remedy this. Meanwhile a degree of illogicality and confusion must be tolerated.

16
Holy Days

Keeping Holy Days

The Alternative Service Book has revised and enriched the calendar of saints and other feasts to be celebrated in the Church of England. Among the 'Greater Holy Days', it has added St Joseph, St Mary Magdalen, The Transfiguration and The Blessed Virgin Mary, and transferred to dates outside Advent and Lent the feasts of St Matthias and St Thomas (in line with the Roman calendar). St Mary Magdalen and The Transfiguration were, of course, accorded 'red letter' status from 1928, but do not have this status in the Book of Common Prayer. The Feast of The Blessed Virgin Mary is a recognition that both the Presentation and the Annunciation are principally feasts *of our Lord*, rather than of his mother, though the choice of 8th September (the traditional date of the *Nativity* of Mary), rather than the universal 15th August, was an unfortunate alteration on the floor of the General Synod. The feast commemorates not one aspect of the nativity story, but the whole significance of Mary's place in Christian thought, as the ASB propers for the day indicate.

The list of 'Lesser Holy Days' is extensive, though considerably less than that in the old Missals based on Roman usage before the Second Vatican Council. The parish may be selective in the names it commemorates. Some are more suitable than others to an ordinary parochial context. But the choices made should be, in the best sense, 'catholic'. A calendar in which, for instance, all post-Reformation figures of either Catholicism or Protestantism had been omitted, would be a narrow and impoverished one. These lesser holy days may variously be observed either by a 'full service', whether Eucharist or Office, where collect, sentences, liturgical colour, etc., are 'of the saint', and, in the case of the Eucharist, lections, psalmody and preface also, or by a simple mention in the prayers while retaining as the primary theme that of the previous Sunday. These holy days add variety to the Church's worship, but, far more significantly, they come as regular reminders of the heritage into which we enter when we come to worship. It is not just that the saints whom we commemorate once worshipped in similar fashion, but that, every time we worship, we participate in some small way in the worship of heaven of which they are part. To the priest saying his office alone, or to a small village congregation gathered for a Eucharist, this can be an enormous encouragement.

Nevertheless the celebration of the great Christian saints must not be allowed, as it has sometimes done in the past, to obscure the shape of the liturgical cycle or to destroy the ethos of a particular season. Too many holy days, accorded a 'full service' in Advent or Lent, for instance, will interfere with the distinctive and developing moods of these seasons. The same is true of the celebration of Sunday. At several points in the year the intrusion of a greater holy day into the Sunday cycle will all but destroy it. The ASB lays down careful rules for transferences when holy days and Sundays coincide. When a parish wishes to transfer a holy day, falling on a weekday, to the nearest Sunday, it should bear in mind the danger of distorting the liturgical cycle. As a general rule, it is an unfortunate move, except sparingly in the weeks 'after Pentecost'.

How are holy days to be celebrated on weekdays? In a parish where there is a daily Eucharist, there is no problem, but such churches are a minority. The tradition of Holy Communion on greater holy days is, however, a very widespread one in the Church of England, and there cannot be many parishes where it is not possible. But surprisingly few churches have adopted the custom, that seems to work well in the parishes that have incorporated it into their programme, of having an *evening* celebration on greater holy days. The wise priest will have an eye to these days when planning the dates of PCC, Standing Committee and the like. Could not such meetings often begin with a brief celebration of the Eucharist?

In commemorating a saint, the priest cannot safely assume that the congregation knows much about him (or her). The Eucharist should begin with the Introit Sentence and Greeting, and then 'Today we celebrate the Feast of St N. who . . .'

A useful guide is *The Cloud of Witnesses,* by Martin Draper. This provides such introductions for the lesser holy days, with other material, including subjects for intercession.[1] It also makes provision for a non-scriptural reading, usually either drawn from the particular saint's writings or about his life. This may be read at the Eucharist – after the Gospel, for instance, or during the preparation of the Offertory, or after Communion – or it may be incorporated into the office as an additional reading. Because the office employs the semi-continuous reading of the biblical books, the scriptural readings do not relate to the saint on a lesser holy day, but the use of this additional reading compensates for this. At the Eucharist, in choosing the readings from among those provided in the 'common' of saints, the priest must exercise care. Not all in a particular section are suitable to every saint. To take an extreme example, John Keble may be commemorated on 29th March with material 'Of Any Saint', but Proverbs 31.10–end ('A good wife who can find?') is hardly appropriate!

The Patronal Festival

There are only a very few churches without a 'dedication', in most cases to a saint, but in some cases to 'a mystery' – Holy Cross, Holy Trinity, etc. – or to Our Lord himself – St Saviour, Christ Church, Emmanuel. In most churches it is clear *when* the Patronal Festival or Feast of Title is. In a few cases this is not so. Churches dedicated in honour of Our Lord himself may opt for one of several dates. 1st January, The Naming of Jesus, is sometimes suitable, especially if the dedication is 'Emmanuel', but it is a Bank Holiday. The Sunday after the Ascension, with its emphasis on the kingship of Christ, is a good occasion, though some parishes dedicated to 'Christ the King' will prefer to opt for the Roman feast of that name, and its propers, on the Sunday next before Advent (not, however, without destroying the pre-Christmas liturgical cycle). Other parishes will opt for the Transfiguration on 6th August, but it is a difficult date at the height of the holiday period.

---

[1] The collects provided are not within the ASB rubrics, though they could be used as post-Communions, nor are the scriptural passages where they differ from those in the ASB.

Churches dedicated in honour of the Blessed Virgin Mary have a considerable choice. Her major feast, on 8th September in the ASB calendar, has the merit of beginning the autumn's activity on a festal note. But where this date is not thought suitable, 31st May, *The Visit of Mary to Elizabeth*, will often be suitable, except when it falls on a Bank Holiday Monday.

Parishes with obscure dedications will normally be able to discover the date of their saint in one of the reference books.[2] Parishes with a Patronal Festival at a very inconvenient time, whether the middle of August or late December, will often discover another traditional date associated with their saint, whether a date in the East, or a date of his *translation*, or even of his birth instead of his death, more convenient for celebration. But, in any case, if the universal Church can transfer feasts because of their inconvenience, so can the local church where circumstances dictate it. The loss, of course, in unilateral transference, is in solidarity with the rest of Christendom celebrating that day.

The ASB indicates that a parish should regard its Patronal Festival (or Feast of Title) as a *greater* holy day, even if it is not one in the national calendar. This means that, in addition to its celebration at the Eucharist, proper psalms and lessons should be chosen for Morning and Evening Prayer. Since all the 'commons' of saints provide at least nine lessons and three portions of psalmody this is not difficult. Parishes often wish to extend their Patronal Festival to the following Sunday. This is understandable enough, and normally the right thing to do, but at certain times of the year, especially in Advent and Lent, the liturgical cycle would be so interrupted by such an intrusion that it is better to concentrate all efforts into a great Eucharist on the evening of the feast itself. In any case, it is desirable that there be a celebration on the feast day itself. Priorities have gone sadly wrong when, on the Patronal Festival, there is a party, or fair or a barbeque, but no Eucharist, though by all means let these precede or follow the liturgical celebration.

It is too easy for a whole number of different days in the parish's year to end up being about the same thing. Somehow Patronal Festival, Feast of Dedication, stewardship renewal,

---

[2] *The Oxford Dictionary of Saints* is particularly valuable.

and other occasions too, all come down to a renewal of the congregation. Sermons begin, 'What matters is not this building, dedicated to St N. but you, the people in it . . .' and the preacher launches off on an over-familiar theme. If all these different occasions are to say something distinct, and not to be mere reverberations of each other, it needs to be drawn out that the Patronal Festival is about the patron saint. 'Who was he?' 'What is to be learnt from his life?' 'What kind of flavour can it give to our community that we are under the name and patronage of St N.?' Questions such as these give the Patronal Festival a point of its own (but see also *The Feast of Dedication*, below).

All Saints and All Souls

One of the rediscoveries of modern liturgical theology is the *unity* of all the departed, and indeed *our* unity with all of them, in the communion of saints. The Book of Common Prayer, with its talk of being 'knit together in one communion and fellowship', had that insight, yet subsequent Anglican theology and practice has, until recently, reflected an increasing acceptance of the Roman distinction between 'saints' and the majority of the dead. There is no scriptural basis for this categorization.[3] The Book of Common Prayer made no provision for an All Souls' Day distinct from All Saints'.

There is, however, both practical and psychological difficulty in commemorating all the departed on one occasion. Over the years All Saints and All Souls have developed their differing ethos. All Saints' Day, with its white vestments, has been a glorious celebration of the company of the saints, with the great heroes very much in mind, but with an awareness also of the countless number of saints whose names have been forgotten. But All Souls' Day, at least until the recent reforms, has had a mark of penitence and solemn intercessory prayer about it, supplication for the dead, the naming of local individual departed ones, black or purple vestments, an absence of light and colour, very much a day of the *Kyries* rather than the *Gloria*. Liturgical reform has altered this considerably, for funeral

---

[3] I have discussed this very fully in *The Communion of Saints* (Alcuin Club/SPCK 1980).

liturgy (and All Souls' Day is really an extension of that) has taken on a *paschal* flavour that has left it very different. Nevertheless the problem remains in part. There is, for many, a sombreness about the day, which does not match entirely the joy of All Saints' Day. The problem is accentuated when the parish, for the best pastoral reasons, has invited those recently bereaved to share in the liturgy of this season at a service in which names will be read out.

Several solutions are possible and each parish must discuss the one it finds most satisfactory. In one place it may be decided to persevere with two separate celebrations on successive days, conscious of the connection between the two, but preserving their individualism as well. The main problem with this solution is that, in dividing forces, there will be danger that both occasions will be less than successful. This will be particularly unfortunate if it means that those specially invited, most of them not regular churchpeople, do not find the whole eucharistic community waiting to welcome them.

In another place, one service only may be held, on All Saints' Day. At it all the Christian dead, the great saints and those who have died recently locally, will be recalled together. This is a better solution. It is certainly theologically sound, but liturgi-cally difficult to 'pull off'. The liturgy on this day needs a distinctly pastoral dimension if the bereaved are present, and this is not easily incorporated into the ethos of All Saints' Day. But it is not impossible, and the attempt will often be worth-while. Certainly it is a better way forward than holding the one service only on All Souls' Day, and allowing the character of that day to shape the liturgy completely. For then the congre-gation misses out on the marvellous meditation that All Saints' Day provides on our unity, especially in worship, with the whole company of heaven. A book of pastoral liturgy would not be complete without a plea that All Saints' Day be accorded great honour, if for no other reason than the truth it proclaims that all liturgy is simply a reflection of the worship of heaven. We are but a small part of a mighty enterprise.

Another solution has already been mentioned in Chapter 11. It is that the annual service for the bereaved to remember their dead should be held, not in November, but during Eastertide. At a purely practical level, May is better than November for old people to go out in the evening. It has also been suggested that that service need not necessarily be eucharistic, whereas on All Saints' Day the Christian community would obviously not want to worship in any other way. With the particular pastoral concern of the recently bereaved removed, it would be possible to bring together the emphases of 1st November and 2nd November in a single celebration on All Saints' Day.

There are a number of points of detail to be noted. When All Saints' Day falls on a Sunday, it takes precedence over the Eighth Sunday before Christmas, but in order that the pre-Christmas liturgical cycle should not be unnecessarily interrupted, one of the Old Testament lections provided for the Eucharist on All Saints' Day is the 'Fall' story (Genesis 3.1–15). A rubric in the ASB provides for a 'first Evensong' of All Saints' Day on the previous day by choosing psalms and readings from among the eucharistic provision. Liturgy of the departed is always paschal liturgy and, therefore, at All Saints or All Souls Easter greetings and acclamations are suitable and the paschal candle may be lit. Where the 2nd November propers are used ('The Commemoration of the Faithful Departed'), the singular-form Collect needs to be amended from 'with our *brother* N.' to 'with our departed brothers and sisters'. The form of prayer at section 60 of the ASB Funeral Services is suitable as a eucharistic Intercession.

A local Sanctorale

To its calendar of Lesser Holy Days, the Alternative Service Book attaches a rubric that 'diocesan, local, or other commemorations may be added to these lists'. The use of the word 'other' would seem to authorize, for instance, the use of any festivals from the Roman calendar that do not actually conflict with Anglican provision. The 'diocesan' provision envisaged is a diocesan supplementary calendar, issued by the bishop, suggesting names of significance locally, but which were not of sufficient note outside their own area to warrant national commemoration. In some dioceses this provision has been made, but not yet in all.

But the rubric clearly implies that commemorations, more local than diocesan, may be permitted. In a town of any size, for instance, there will be well-known names of Christian benefactors, founders of educational or similar institutions, or men and women who have gone out from the community to serve the Church overseas. Or there may have been parish priests in the past of notable holiness or scholarship. But names must not too easily be added to the calendar, for, however much the Church of England eschews formal canonization, to be named in a calendar is a step along a path to recognition as a 'saint' in a technical sort of sense. The ASB provision should therefore be used sparingly and suitable criteria discussed. This matter is much more fully examined in my *The Communion of Saints* and questions about criteria for inclusion are carefully considered. Despite the dangers, there is great profit in a local *sanctorale*, thought through by Parochial Church Council or Worship Committee, for it helps Christian people to think about the meaning of Christian sanctity, to see that it is something lived out in the local community, and to experience that closeness with those who have gone before that belongs to Christian worship.

The Feast of Dedication

The Dedication Festival is listed as one of the Greater Holy Days in the ASB calendar. It is kept on the anniversary of the date of the church's dedication or consecration. If this is not known, it is kept on the first Sunday in October, though it may legitimately be kept on any known date connected with the church building, if that is more convenient.

A word of warning has already been given about the tendency to give several different festivals, including the Feast of Dedication and the Patronal Festival, the same ethos and theme. Yet each is justified only by its difference from the other. The distinctive theme of the Feast of Dedication is its celebration of the church *building*. The sermon that dismisses the significance of the building, and goes on to preach about the rededication of the people, has missed the point. Of course, it is true that 'the church is the people' and the building is but a tool in the task they undertake. But an incarnationalist religion does not despise places where God's presence is sought and where, in response to prayer, he chooses to make himself known. The

Feast of Dedication is the day for thanksgiving for the place of the church building in the Christian community's life. It may well also be the opportunity for questioning or reassessing that place. But there is room in the Christian year for a liturgy about bricks and mortar, and the Feast of Dedication should not be 'spiritualized' into something else.

In many a church, or, perhaps, *around* many a church, outside as much as in, the Feast of Dedication is the opportunity for a procession, involving all, that halts at various places to pray, to be reminded of the past, or to see with fresh eyes a sight of beauty too often taken for granted. Whether it be a Norman pillar, a stained glass window, the font or a memorial, it will have a meaning and a message to be drawn out with a word of reflection and prayer. This sort of procession need not be restricted to an ancient and beautiful church. The Victorian and the modern have much to show to the discerning eye. The procession, having wound its way around church and churchyard, ends at the altar where the building can be recognized for what it really is, a great canopy under which the Church celebrates the rite that makes both the people and the building a church.

17
Other High Points in the Year

New Years and Fresh Starts

References have been made at several points in this book to the danger of repeating too often acts of rededication of various types by the congregation, and at this point these references may all be gathered together. There are many opportunities during the year to 'look back over the last year and pledge ourselves for the year ahead' and some clergymen seem unable to resist any of them. The danger is not simply that such rededications become monotonous (or even farcical), but that the whole idea of a solemn undertaking loses its power, and promises that should be made after sober reflection are made lightly with no real sense of commitment. Renewal of promises can even be sprung on unsuspecting congregations without warning. One day a congregation will, rightly, rebel!

The most fundamental of promises in the Church are those made at Baptism and again in Confirmation. It has been argued in Chapter 6 that the renewal of these is a solemn business, not to be sprung on people and certainly not to be added to every Baptism. The time for this solemn renewal is at Easter, whether at the Vigil or during the Eucharist of Easter morning. That is probably sufficient. But a case can be made out for one further occasion, on the day of the parish's principal rite of initiation in the year, when the bishop comes for the Confirmation. Within that context, the renewal takes on the flavour of an act of support for, and solidarity with, those then to be admitted to full participation in the Church's life. Other occasions should be resisted.

But reaffirmations are not always about *belief*. Often they are about commitment to the Church's work, and certainly there is an argument for underlining very occasionally both corporate commitment as a community and also the individual's personal commitment. But special ceremonies are only an *underlining* of this, for the offering of life, personal and corporate, is part of what is very clearly seen to be happening every time the Eucharist is celebrated. To have too many special rites to bring this out is no substitute for good teaching about the Eucharist, or for the way the Eucharist is ordered.

The occasion in the year most suitable for a corporate renewal of commitment to the Church and to each other is a Sunday soon after the Annual Church Meeting. That is the point in the year when, from a business point of view, the parish looks back and plans forward, and the liturgy should be in touch with that reality. On that Sunday, new officers may be blessed for their work and a blessing sought for all the parish has in mind for the year ahead.

But there is also frequently a call for the personal rededication of the individual's commitment to the Church's work. This is normally related to what, in most parishes, has come to be called 'Christian stewardship'. A Sunday in the year is often given over to this theme (it is discussed in the section that follows). Let this be the occasion for personal rededication. A renewal of baptismal vows, a corporate rededication and an individual one add up to quite as much reaffirming as will do anybody any good. Let Advent Sunday be set free from being the beginning of a new year to being a key moment in the unending liturgical cycle. Let New Year's Day be what it is, the Feast of the Naming of Jesus. Let the Patronal Festival be about the patron saint, and the Dedication Festival be about the church building. Let the beginning of September be the beginning of September, not yet another 'new year'. All these occasions have their distinctiveness. They should not be merged into some vague recurrent excuse for starting again.

Christian Stewardship

The majority of parishes operate some sort of scheme by which the members of the congregation are asked to make promises about what they will give to God, normally through his Church, in terms of their time, ability and money, and in many parishes this is known by the shorthand description of 'Christian stewardship'. The understanding of it varies a good deal from place to place, and the degree of commitment it elicits varies as much, but these are not the concern of this book. Where a parochial visitation to increase giving is undertaken, there will often be a call for a service of commissioning. Guidance about such a service is provided in the final chapter. At the end of the visitation the whole enterprise, and each individual's pledge, is offered to God. Liturgical provision needs to be made for that too. In many parishes, and rightly so, this is not the end. Each committed person is encouraged to review their commitment annually, and so there develops an *annual* service of offering. This is the occasion which, in the previous section, was advanced as the most suitable of all those in the year for a personal act of rededication.

When should it be? Logically it should be around the anniversary of the original 'campaign'. But this can present problems. If all that is intended for the Service of Offering and Rededication is a brief insertion of a prayer and a pledge into the ordinary liturgy of the day, then there is no real problem. But if the occasion is to be 'built up' and the rededication theme is to take over the service, with the Sunday lections and other propers replaced, then careful thought has to be given to the suitability of the Sunday. That sort of treatment of the Sunday cycle will make no sense at all for long periods of the year. The solution may lie in delaying the first rededication after a 'campaign' to a suitable time of year, and only then making it an annual occasion.

There are two Sundays in particular that suggest themselves very strongly for Stewardship Rededication. One is the Eighteenth Sunday after Pentecost, which normally falls in late September or early October. This Sunday is suitable because its theme in the Alternative Service Book is 'The Offering of Life' and its readings are 'tailor-made' for Christian Stewardship. There is therefore no interruption at all in the liturgical cycle.

The other attractive possibility is to combine Stewardship Rededication with the occasion in April or May when the new officers are blessed after the Annual Church Meeting. In this way what, in the end, is a rather false distinction between corporate and individual commitment, need not be drawn, for what is offered to God is both the parish's life in the 'vestry year' ahead and also the commitment of each individual to it.

There is no better time to invite the individual to reassess his personal commitment than when he is being made aware of the church's needs and hopes through the business, including the financial business, that is done at the annual meeting.

As to the form of any such rededication, it would be a theological impoverishment not to place it within the Eucharist. Within that service it would be a liturgical nonsense to divorce it from the presentation of the bread and wine. The best procedure is probably for the written promises to be brought to the altar at the Offertory, with the eucharistic elements, and an extended 'Offertory prayer' to follow. In this way, the people grasp more fully that this point at *every* Eucharist is, in a sense, a bringing of their time and their ability, as well as their money, to be used in God's service. The prayer might suitably be something like this:

President: Blessed are you, the Almighty Father,
     Lord of all creation:
All: For all that we have is a gift from you.
President: Blessed are you, Lord Jesus Christ,
     the Saviour of the world:
All: For you bid us share in your self-offering and sacrifice.
President: Blessed are you, Life-giving Spirit,
     who binds us together in love:
All: For you fill us with joy in the Body of Christ.
President: Blessed are you, Father, Son and Holy Spirit:
All: Yours is the greatness, the power, the glory,
    the splendour and the majesty,
    for all eternity.
    Take our hands, and work with them.
    Take our lips, and speak through them.
    Take our minds, and think with them.
    Take our hearts, and set them on fire.
    With love for you and for all mankind.
    Blessed are you, Lord God, for ever and ever.

Popular Festivals

The clergy in rural areas will sometimes bemoan the fact that Remembrance Sunday and Harvest Thanksgiving are the high points of the liturgical year in their villages, and nothing they do seems to alter the fact that these two days matter more than Easter and Pentecost, if not more than Christmas. In response to their complaint, the urban clergyman can sympathize or urge his rural brother to preach clever sermons on both occasions that appear to be about Remembrance Sunday and Harvest Thanksgiving, but are really about the Church's Easter faith (the connection is easy enough to make with both)! But there is a serious lesson to be learnt by every priest and parish from this rural experience, and priest and parish ignore it at their peril. It is that people respond to the Church when what it is doing relates to what they are engaged in and to the community of which they feel part. In a genuine village (not so much a commuter village, where half the people 'play at villages', which may include attending Harvest Thanksgiving), the harvest really matters. Good crops represent the income and livelihood of many of the inhabitants and therefore the prosperity of the community. In a settled village, without too much dramatic movement of population, the surnames read out on Remembrance Sunday are the same as those of the people standing in the church or round the memorial cross. There may be few left who actually remember those who died personally, but the village has a corporate memory of which they are part.

In the town, very often the priest, and maybe the church community, rather despise such occasions. Many clergymen so resent the popularity of Harvest Thanksgiving that they play it down as much as they can. It is certainly true that neither Harvest nor Remembrance Sunday has the same power to pull the crowds that it did, and this is not surprising, for the annual crop is not of immediate concern to the suburban or urban dweller, and the names on the War Memorial are quite different from the names of the present-day population. For all that, the parish does well to build on what interest there is in these festivals, for they are points of contact with the community, and, in anonymous urban and suburban areas, anything that helps *create* a sense of identity and community is valuable. If a War Memorial does that it becomes a tool of the gospel.

But, more importantly, the lesson to be learnt from the rural communities is that there must be liturgies that touch people in their daily and communal living. If this isn't, in a new community, at Harvest Thanksgiving or Remembrance Sunday, when is it? That is the question to which the local church has to address itself. It may be that a Festival of Work, an industrial and urban equivalent of the Harvest, is one answer. It is unlikely to 'catch on' immediately, but Harvest Thanksgivings did not become universally popular overnight. It may be in the development of the 'Civic Service', or its more local equivalent, understood as something much wider than simply an annual service for mayor, or council chairman, and council, to become a genuine celebration of the whole local community.

Books on liturgy usually ignore such services, for the purist has no time for them, but, unless the Church of England wishes to follow the way of a sect, it must be constantly on the look-out for occasions of ministering to its whole parish, and that must include the institutions in it and the places where its people work. Some will protest that their parish is not like that, for a commuter parish has no institutions, except schools, and everybody works elsewhere. But it is precisely in those parishes that a sense of corporate identity and community most needs to be developed by the Church, for there are few other bodies to do it. If that is the ministry the Church is to exercise, liturgy will surely be an important part of it.

The Harvest

The Alternative Service Book provides a full range of propers for 'Harvest Thanksgiving' (which is, undoubtedly, a better name than the more popular Harvest *Festival*). Apart from full provision for the Eucharist, including a note that the liturgical colour should be that of the season, almost invariably green, it gives a wide range of lections and psalmody, which may be used at Morning and Evening Prayer, or at specially devised Harvest services. No date is specified and the local church will choose its own. The most popular dates, towards the end of September and at the beginning of October, are several weeks beyond the real end of harvesting, and rural communities, recognizing this, often opt for an earlier time. Too close proximity to the Ninth Sunday before Christmas is unfortunate, for the creation theme of that day overlaps in its choice

217

of lections, and even of hymnody, with the Harvest. It would just be possible to combine the Harvest with that Sunday, but it would be a very late Harvest, and would rather restrict the creation theme to a narrow application. Where the Eighteenth Sunday after Pentecost (usually in late September) has not become the annual stewardship rededication (but see an earlier section of this chapter), its theme and propers are suitable to Harvest thanksgiving.

The form of the Harvest service presents a problem. The Christian community would in general be sorry if it were not eucharistic. The presentation of the harvest loaf at the Offertory for use at Communion is a well-established custom, and there is no better time for harvest gifts to be presented than at the same time as the bread and wine (and presented, incidentally, as much by adults as by children, if they can be persuaded). Yet, as has been argued above, this season is one of the most productive points of contact with the wider community, part of which would not cope with the Eucharist. For them a different sort of liturgy needs to be devised, or the office modified. In some places the solution has been an evening non-eucharistic service on a Friday night, followed by a Harvest supper, with the Harvest Eucharist the following Sunday morning.

What has been said of the Harvest applies in the main also to the Rogation Days, observed on the three days before Ascension Day. In practice the traditional services or processions associated with this time must, in most communities, be on the Sunday, even though that obscures a little the development of the paschal theme. Clergy will vary in their attitude to prayers for good weather and fine crops. There are those for whom some of these petitionary prayers provide real theological problems. But few would dispute the value of a carefully devised service to seek God's blessing on the community. The ASB provision of Rogation prayers and readings would form an exciting basis for a service, and a service that prayed realistically about the mutual dependence of town and village, commerce and agriculture, employment and leisure, would greatly help Christian people to understand their environment and to be discerning about the changes to which it is being subjected. For whether at Rogationtide, Lammastide or Harvest, these are vital issues about which Christians should think and pray, whether they live in urban or rural communities.

Remembrance Sunday

Remembrance Sunday is the Sunday nearest 11th November. It usually coincides with the Seventh Sunday before Christmas. The ASB provides suitable psalmody and readings.[1] A difficult responsibility falls to the priest on this day. It is to allow people freedom to express their loss, or their pride or their resolution in a natural way, and yet to bring Christian perception to bear. The Christian Church is not pacifist, though it has a reverence for the pacifist tradition as a costly loyalty to the way of the cross, but it has been increasingly unhappy with any sort of patriotism or nationalism that seems, either to build up a sense of the nation's pride, glory and victory, or to deny the fundamental brotherhood of all mankind under the fatherhood of God, with its consequent recognition of our own part in the atrocities and sicknesses of our world. The expectations of, for instance, the local British Legion and of the local Christian community about an appropriate form of service for Remembrance Sunday may differ considerably. This issue cannot be 'fudged'. Christian ministry in this area is at a watershed and a degree of tension is inevitable, and perhaps may be creative. The sensitive parish priest will go as far as he can in accommodating those who desire a traditional sort of parade service, but he will be right to set limits on what is acceptable, for the Christian gospel does have correctives to offer to the way many people perceive issues of war, peace and patriotism. He will, however, be on surer ground if he has secured the support of his Worship Committee. He will also be less likely to cause unnecessary offence if he, and some of his lay people, are willing to sit down with the representatives of other organizations to devise the service together.

It is unlikely that the best form for such a service will be eucharistic. If the Remembrance Service is at about eleven o'clock, as is often the case, the Eucharist may well be able to precede it, depending on local circumstances, or be transferred to the evening. In devising the service, a good deal of useful material may be drawn from the 1968 ecumenical form, which has not been superseded.[2] Although the Eucharist in full is

[1] On p. 984.
[2] David Silk provides the heart of it in *Prayers for Use at the Alternative Services*.

219

not suitable in many settings, the first part of it may well be. For, using Rite A, it begins with Penitence, which may be introduced by a specific bidding relating to war, goes on to employ the Scriptures (the Remembrance Sunday selection may be used or the propers 'For the Peace of the World'), and after the Sermon provides for Intercessions, at which point the commemoration of the dead, including Last Post and Reveille, might be included, and ends, appropriately, with the Peace. It is just possible, in some communities, that at that point the congregation might go to the War Memorial, for the prayers customary there, after which it might be dismissed, while the regular communicant churchgoers, with others who chose to come back, return to the church to complete the Eucharist. This would, however, not work very smoothly, except where the War Memorial was situated ideally in relation to the church.

Where the Eucharist is a separate service from the Remembrance Service, it is better to use the appointed lections for the Seventh Sunday before Christmas. The theme of Moses, the liberator, enables the preacher to bring in a Remembrance Day dimension, but the liturgical cycle, the development of which is particularly important at this stage in the year, is not broken. The same argument therefore applies in those churches where there is no Remembrance Service as such, or attendance by particular organizations. Though special intercessions may be said, or material from the 1968 form be appended as a sort of prologue or epilogue to the Eucharist, the propers are better those of the Sunday than those for the Peace of the World (the use of which on a Sunday is in any case contrary to the rubrics).

When the Bishop Comes

The visit of the bishop of the diocese, or of one of his suffragans, is a high point in the year in any parish. The entire Christian community should be urged to be present, not in order to impress the bishop (who will know that a 'three line whip', so to speak, has been issued) but because the bishop is the symbol of unity among all Christians, and those in communion with him should be present to make him welcome.

The procedure if the bishop is coming to preside at Confirmation is described in Chapter 6 and no more will be said of that here. But, whenever the bishop comes, if it is for a parochial occasion, rather than because the church is being used for some civic or community event, consideration should be given to making that service the principal Eucharist of the day. The bishop cannot possibly visit all his parishes on a Sunday morning. Some must be content with an evening visit. But few parishes can be so rigid that the Eucharist on that day cannot be moved to the evening. It is a general, but not invariable, rule, that where the bishop is, there the Eucharist should be celebrated.

When a bishop is present, within his diocese, at the Eucharist, he is, almost invariably, the president. Of course, for his own soul's health he will sometimes be present when another priest presides, but this will be in his own chapel or when he chooses to slip into the back row of a congregation. When he visits a parish, other clergy do not have the privilege of presiding, for in doing so normally, in the absence of the bishop, they do it as his deputy. By 'president' in this context is meant what the ASB means, the function of being the principal celebrant – greeting the people, giving the Absolution, saying the Collect, the Peace, the Eucharistic Prayer, etc. The old-fashioned idea of 'presiding at the throne', which in practice meant sitting to the north of the altar, absolving, probably preaching, and blessing, but delegating the 'celebrating' to a priest, is a theological nonsense. If it is objected that the parish's ceremonial is too complicated for the bishop to master, then the ceremonial had better be simplified for the occasion.[3] A bishop from another diocese, or a retired bishop, may, as a courtesy, be invited to preside, but he does not do so by right.

A word has already been said (in Chapter 1) about the practice of concelebration. Though there is no theological sense in a group of priests reciting the Eucharistic Prayer together, there is symbolic point in the bishop being surrounded by his priests when he presides. Their ministry is an offshoot of his,

---

[3] Cathedrals are, by tradition, a partial exception to this rule. There the dean or provost often has rights and privileges over against the bishop, that a parish priest in his church does not have. Cathedral chapters rightly guard their privileges jealously, but on a diocesan, rather than a 'domestic', cathedral occasion, the bishop presides. It has to be said that, in any case, theologically, rather than historically, the Cathedral anomaly cannot be justified.

and there is a special relationship between him and them, which can be expressed symbolically at least by their being grouped around him during the Eucharistic Prayer and what follows it, and also, if the space and architecture of the church permit, by their sitting grouped around him in a similar fashion throughout the service. This applies to all the priests of the diocese who are present. To have some, but not others, associated with the bishop in this way makes no sense.

If the bishop is to make a solemn entry through the midst of the people at the beginning of the service (and it is appropriate that he should) or, indeed, if he is to be received at the door, it is unfortunate if he has to wander about the church in full view before the service begins. He should be met at the gate, by priest or warden, and conducted to where he is to robe by a route that does not take him through the body of the church, unless this is unavoidable.

There should be careful consultation with the bishop in advance, usually through his chaplain or secretary, about the form of service. A telephone conversation is no substitute for careful notes, or an annotated script, that the bishop can read just before the service. Detail will be helpful, even down to notes on when the people stand, kneel, or sit, and what they have to be told. No two parishes are exactly alike in what they do. The bishop will do his best, but he will need to be briefed.

The advance consultations will reveal whether the bishop is bringing a chaplain. If he is, it will be the bishop's chaplain, rather than anybody local, who is responsible for holding the bishop's mitre, staff, etc. If there is a chaplain, he will usually be another priest who, though willing enough to fade into the background, should be drawn into the liturgy in an appropriate way. If there is no chaplain, the bishop will probably value the assistance of one or two lay people, whether servers or not, to act as his chaplains, or, if there is a deacon or another priest, he may do this. But the bishop should be consulted about what help he wants. The last thing he will want is anyone who will 'fuss' about him. A bishop who is being fussed will not be relaxed, and a bishop who is not relaxed will not give of his best. The old custom of carrying a bishop's staff in front of him, as if it were a processional cross, has, thankfully, almost disappeared. The bishop walks with his staff in his hand. Most bishops have also simplified considerably the number of times that they take off and put on the mitre, and will not welcome over-fussiness at this point in particular.[4]

It is appropriate for a bishop within his diocese to be welcomed with a special greeting at the door, especially if it is his first visit. Something along these lines would be suitable:

Priest (or Warden): Right Reverend Father in God:
we welcome you to our parish of St N.
to preside at our Eucharist
and to share our fellowship.

All: Welcome, Bishop N.
We greet you as our chief pastor and teacher and
as a fellow worker in the Lord's service.
May the Lord be with you.

Bishop: I thank you for your welcome and your prayers.
May the Lord bless you
and make you a blessing to others.

The Introit Hymn would then follow immediately. The tone of this greeting, or of any less formal greeting, is important. The bishop is to be made welcome, but he is not a guest 'from the outside', so to speak. It is his church and he is 'our' bishop. It is for that reason that the churchwardens, with their wands, by tradition walk immediately in front of the bishop, the parish priest preceding them, the bishop's chaplain(s) following the bishop.

Perhaps the important principle for a parish to remember, when planning for a visit by the bishop, is not to overdo things, not to pull out stops that haven't worked for years. Just as the wise parish will want the bishop to be natural and relaxed, and will try to avoid fussing him with unimportant details, so the bishop will want to find a community that enjoys its worship, and is natural and relaxed about it. Getting the choir to sing an anthem just beyond them, or fleeing to *Ritual Notes* to discover how the parish used to treat a bishop, does no good, for it puts the parish itself on edge, though organizing a spring clean of the church and a tidy up of the vestry will do no harm at all.

[4] Most bishops wisely take a more pragmatic view, and advocate greater freedom and simplicity, than the recent Alcuin Club/Church Union guide to episcopal ceremonial. Parishes would be wrong to imagine that most bishops live by it!

Ecumenical Occasions

It has not been within the compass of this book to discuss the many occasions in the liturgical year where there might be an ecumenical dimension. But it would be sad, for instance, if in a town parish, where churches of other denominations are situated within the parish boundaries, there were to be no united worship through the whole of Holy Week. The once-a-year meeting together is, however, of less value than a regular, perhaps once a month, sharing in one another's worship.

Ecumenical services divide very clearly into two categories. There are those where the churches work together to produce a service for a civic or community occasion, and there are those where Christian communities meet to worship together to express and enhance their unity. The former type, civic or community occasions, present the greater problems. If the 'Established Church' decides the form of service, and merely invites representatives of other churches to take part, the Anglican bias in the service can be too strong for these days. If the service is drawn up ecumenically, it can be a shapeless and unhelpful order, combining haphazardly elements of several traditions, without any overall unity. At a local level, clergy and ministers, if possible with lay people too, need to sit down together to talk through their various understandings of worship and to discover the common principles behind all their traditions.[5] With this exercise done (though it might need repeating after further experience of differing traditions), when an occasion for devising a common form arose, the order that emerged, while incorporating material from every tradition, would have an integrity all its own. Studies along these lines should be a priority for Clergy Fraternals and Councils of Churches, which all too often discuss everything but worship.

Where an ecumenical service is simply a gathering together of different Christian communities, without the constraint of presenting an ecumenical face to outside bodies, the 'one off'

---

[5] They could well be aided in this by a consideration together of Chapters 1, 2 and 5 of this book!

service is often best left as a genuine experience of the regular worship of one communion, the host church each time 'doing its own thing', so to speak. Before the service a few words might be said to explain its *rationale* and special care should be taken to ensure that the order of service is in a form that all can easily follow, but once the service has begun, let it be a genuinely Anglican one, or Methodist one, or Roman Catholic one. This will probably mean that, except in the reading of lessons, the other denominations present have little part in the leadership of the liturgy, but the presence in the 'sanctuary' of their leaders will be adequate expression of the *acceptance* of others. To participate in such services is a necessary pre-condition to understanding another Christian communion, and thus to unity. To enter into the worship of another tradition with openness and sensitivity is in any case to have one's own spirituality enriched.

Where ecumenical services are held on a regular basis, the more difficult exercise of finding a genuinely ecumenical form must be undertaken. There is value in acceptable common forms that are more than mere compromises. But they will emerge only from long hard experiment and reflection, offered prayerfully to God, and within communities of Christians who have developed a genuine concern for one another. In devising such services, three simple points may be borne in mind.

First, worship *expresses* the unity of Christians, but it does not need to be constantly obsessed with that as its theme. Christians grow in unity when together they reflect on the goodness of God, or the life of the Spirit, or the needs of the world, not when they think about unity, though, of course, the liturgy, whether in an ecumenical context or not, always has words and symbols that reflect and enhance the unity of the worshippers. Christian unity should not be the *theme* of every united service.

Secondly, what has been said previously about *presidency* applies also in ecumenical worship. The great danger in united services is that, because everybody must have his part, nobody is in control. The service is divided up among so many clergy that even a single prayer gets divided into two! Continuity of leadership, and not *too* much delegation, is important to the smooth running of worship. Associated with this danger, at least in urban areas, is the *clericalization* of worship. There are so many priests and ministers to be given a role that lessons about the part of the laity in liturgy are, on ecumenical occasions, forgotten.

The final point is the most simple of all. One of the liturgical riches that we share, and which transcends denominational divisions, is hymnody. There are a great many hymns that we all sing. There are also a great many tunes that we all know. Nevertheless other denominations always seem to use the words we know to the tunes we don't, and, less seriously, the tunes we know to the words we don't! Careful consultation about tunes as well as words is strongly to be advised before an ecumenical service.

Processions

To process is a liturgical act. It is one of the ways in which the body is used in worship, and should be a *religious experience*. It is difficult to see how the traditional wander round the church during an extra hymn and back into the choir stalls can be that for the choir, let alone for the rest of the congregation who remain in their places during this exceedingly long hymn. In order to decide what form a procession should take, it is useful to think of it as a symbolic liturgical pilgrimage. A pilgrim is one who undertakes a journey, along the way of which he may encounter many things, but always there is the object of his journey in mind, that thing that he will see or do when finally he arrives. There is both direction and purpose in what he does.

So with liturgical processions. First of all, they are something which people *do* rather than *watch*. Of course this is not always possible, but ideally the procession is an activity in which all present participate. Watching the priest, servers and choir do an ecclesiastical perambulation is not the same activity at all.

Secondly, they are journeys that *start from one point and end at another*. On Palm Sunday, for instance, the procession may begin in the church hall or at another church and process *to* the parish church. At the Easter Vigil, the procession may begin outside at the new fire, but process into the church with the lighted paschal candle. On other occasions, the processional route may be more restricted. At Candlemas it may begin in the open space at the back of the nave and process to the chancel. On other occasions it may begin with the people coming out of their places, but end with them grouped or crowded around the altar. But the principle in all these is the same. A procession sets out and arrives. It does not merely end up where it started.

Thirdly, *something happens when the procession arrives.* Something is celebrated or some climax is reached. This is true, for instance, of the regular Gospel and Offertory processions at the Eucharist. It is also why a solemn processional *entry* of the ministers at the Eucharist makes sense – they are on their way to do something significant – but their exit at the end need have no elaborate procedure. It is certainly true of the Palm Sunday, Easter Vigil and Candlemas processions. The people are on their way to celebrate the Eucharist. If on other occasions, such as Dedication Festival, there is a procession around the church, inside or out, and it ends at the altar, prayer should follow, at least a collect, and a blessing, so that there is some climax, however brief.

Of course there are places where there is no room for a procession by all inside the church. In such cases watching a procession may be all that is possible, except on certain occasions when all can process outside. There are, in any case, some processions – like that at the Offertory – in which only *representative* figures move on behalf of the whole congregation, and the traditional procession of choir and clergy at a Festal Evensong is merely an extension of that representative principle, but where that sense has been lost it is best recaptured by processions of all present. The procession to the crib at Christmas or the garden at Easter does not justify a procession of the whole congregation, but here *children* might exercise that representative function of going with the priest to say a prayer at crib or garden.

Pilgrims, it was noted, encounter things of interest and beauty along the way and stop to look at them. Processions have that element too. It was suggested in Chapter 13 that a Candlemas procession might stop at the crib and in the Lady Chapel. On the Feast of Dedication the procession might stop at the lectern and at the font. Processions from outside might pause at the door or at a great cross in the churchyard. At each such station a pause for thought might be followed by an appropriate prayer before the procession moves on.

18
Welcome, Commission and Blessing

Welcoming a New Priest or Deacon

When a new parish priest is instituted, a special service, usually involving the bishop and the archdeacon, is held. Because a diocesan order of service is almost invariably provided, such an occasion need not be considered here. But a parish very properly wants to give a welcome to other new members of its staff, whether a newly ordained deacon, or a priest who has come to share in the parish's ministry, or a licensed layworker. Such a welcome at the Parish Eucharist is entirely appropriate, but the form it takes should be considered carefully. The occasion is not one of *commissioning*. That is the bishop's task and he will have done it, either in the ordination or in granting his licence. It is an occasion of welcome, acceptance and pledge of solidarity. Anything that looks like an ordination (for instance, the wardens presenting a new deacon to the parish priest who blesses him) is to be avoided.

The constituent parts of such a welcome could be:

(a) The parish priest presents the new minister to the people,
(b) The people extend their welcome and promise their prayerful support,
(c) Symbols of his ministry among them are presented by lay people,
(d) The new minister greets the people,
(e) He exercises his new ministry as the liturgy proceeds.

Quite apart from the welcome given to the new deacon or priest, the occasion is a useful teaching one. In presenting the new minister, the parish priest is able to say succinctly what his function and ministry is. 'A deacon is called . . .' enables him, in the words of the Ordinal or similar words, to give useful teaching. The symbols that are presented reinforce this. There are three obvious areas in which the minister has a clear role – the teaching ministry, the pastoral ministry and the sacramental ministry. For a new priest, obvious symbols would be a Bible for teaching, a stole for pastoral care and a chalice and paten for the sacraments. In an ordination these are given by the bishop, but here *by the people* as an indication that they will *accept* these ministries exercised among them. For a new deacon, the New Testament and the stole are obvious symbols. A symbol of his involvement in sacramental ministry is more difficult. Where baptismal water is blessed, not at every Baptism, but annually at the Easter Vigil, a jug of baptismal water might be presented. Or the Oil of Healing, where the deacon will share in that ministry, might be appropriate. Or the lavabo bowl, jug and towel as a symbol of his function as a servant and assistant to the president in the liturgy.

It is also important that in the words that accompany the giving of symbols the picture of ministry that is given is one of sharing, both the sharing among all the priests and deacons in the parish, but also among the whole Christian body. The texts that follow are for use in welcoming a deacon, but need only a little adaptation for use with a priest.

> We give you this gift
> as a sign of your share in the teaching ministry of our church.
> Be among us a preacher and a teacher.
> Share with us the task of discerning God's word in our day
>   and of proclaiming it in the community.
> Be among us a man of prayer, of study and of reflection.
>
> We give you this gift
> as a sign of your share in the pastoral ministry of our church.
> Be among us as a counsellor and a pastor.
> Share with us the task of serving our neighbours
>   and of spreading God's love and compassion in our community.
> Be among us a man of healing and reconciliation.
>
> We give you this gift
> as a sign of your part in the sacramental ministry of our church.
> Share with the priests who minister here
> the privilege and joy of leading the people
>   in the celebration of the sacraments.

> And let your life as a deacon find its focus
> in your ministry as a deacon at the Eucharist.

A new deacon will exercise his new ministry by reading the Gospel, preparing the elements and administering the chalice, a new priest, perhaps, by presiding at the Eucharist.

Ministries and Tasks

The renewed emphasis in the Church on the variety of ministries, and the emergence within parishes of those with particular expertise and training to exercise specific ministries, has raised an important question about authorization and commissioning for their tasks. Dioceses and parishes are not yet in accord over the way to proceed, so it is difficult to prescribe. Not all these ministries are of the same kind. There are some, for instance, that involve training for a ministry that may go outside the parish into the rest of the deanery or beyond. Here both the question of authorization and of commissioning belong to the bishop, though he may, wisely, delegate the latter to the rural dean in order to avoid any thought of quasi-ordination that episcopal commissioning might give. But what of ministries to be exercised totally within the parish, whether or not they have had to receive episcopal authorization? Should there be a special service?

One school of thought will firmly say 'No' in almost every instance. Every Christian, the argument will run, has been given gifts and is called to exercise his ministry. There is no reason why the 'lay pastor' should be commissioned any more than the 'flower arranger'. Both exercise a ministry in accordance with their ability, yet we should find a service of commissioning of Flower Ladies a strange occasion. Commissioning, the argument will continue, far from enhancing the ministry of the whole people of God, undermines it by creating special categories of ministers. This view needs to be taken with the utmost seriousness and, even when a parish judges that there are occasions when it should be disregarded, it serves as a deterrent to the temptation to be constantly drawing up services of commissioning.

One of the problems, however, with a rigid policy such as

this is that it does not take seriously enough the need for those who go out from the church to minister in its name to have some form of *validation*. Everybody knows, for instance, that most non-churchgoing parishioners expect the vicar, with his clerical collar, to call, and nobody else will do. Gradually they will grow used to lay people visiting, or even bringing the sacraments, but it will help them if such people have some authority, designation or status.

'Jesus *sent out* the seventy (or the seventy-two) into all the towns . . .' An argument can be made for a distinction between gifts and functions *within* the Body, for which there should be no commissioning – baptism is the authorization for those – and ministries on behalf of the Church *to the wider community* beyond, for which some simple form of commissioning would be appropriate. To judge the question, to commission or not to commission, by this yardstick could be a useful guide for the parish, though there will be the inevitable 'grey areas' that need talking through.

This does not, of course, mean that other ministries, within the Body, are not given mention in the liturgy. Whenever anybody undertakes a new task within the Church, it is right that they be prayed for in the Eucharistic Intercessions. The Church asks a special blessing on them then, and any cycle of prayer in the parish ought to be sufficiently inclusive to ensure that all the ministries that are exercised, however humble, are brought to God in prayer on a regular basis.

When there *is* to be a commissioning for a particular ministry, whether short or long term, the procedure can be quite simple. Prayers for those to be commissioned are offered at the time of the Intercession. After Communion, but before the final prayer, blessing and dismissal, those to be commissioned come to stand before the parish priest. He spells out very simply the task they are to do. He asks them whether they believe they are called to do it and whether they will undertake it sensitively, and they reply. He asks the other members of the congregation whether it is their will that these people should exercise this ministry on their behalf, whether they will see this ministry as part of the whole ministry in which they all share, and whether they will support them with their prayers. The people respond graciously and warmly. The priest then blesses them and

231

sends them out in the name of the Church. The Eucharist is then brought to its usual conclusion without delay. It is not appropriate to call in the bishop for such a commissioning. It is something done for or by the local church and has no implication outside the parish.

Gifts

In the course of the year there will be occasions when gifts given to the church, whether a new Bible, chalice, embroidered kneeler, are to be used for the first time. The parish priest has to consider in what way any such gift is to be dedicated or blessed. The most simple answer is the most satisfactory. It is that the gift is blessed *in being used*. Its holiness is not dependent on words that are said over it. In some cases it may depend in part on the loving labour that has made it or the costly sacrifice that has bought it. But, in the main, its holiness is in proportion to the reverence attached to it as part of the 'holy things' of the church's worship. There are many gifts that are appropriately simply put into use. Where some outward sign is required, however, it is not inappropriate for the gift to be brought to the altar at the Offertory, carried by the donor unless it is anonymous, or, if it has been made locally, as for instance vestments or embroidery might be, by the craftsman or craftswoman. It is then placed on or near the altar, unless it is something that can actually be *used* there and then at the Eucharist.

But there are occasions when a silent presentation of the gift is not enough. The priest will judge that the donors would appreciate something more. Particularly will this be the case when the gift is in memory of somebody, or in commemoration of some event or anniversary. The blessing of inanimate objects has often been a cause of controversy in the Church. (In the Roman Missal, for instance, the conflict is indicated by alternative prayers of blessing on various occasions. At Candlemas the priest *either* blesses the candles *or* the people who will carry them; so, on Palm Sunday, with the palms.) The religion of the incarnation takes seriously the part the material plays in conveying God's gifts to his creatures, and so there is no need to be over-scrupulous about this. Our prayer is really that the gift may, by God's grace, be a blessing to us. In praying that, we recognize that however much we, naturally, focus on the gift, God's grace will be focused on us. The prayer might therefore appropriately run like this:

> Bless us, O Lord our God,
> as in your name we bless this gift.
> We dedicate it to your glory,
> + Father, Son and Holy Spirit,
> and in memory of N.
> As we have worshipped you here on earth,
> so may we come, with him, to share the worship of heaven,
> where you live . . .

Where the gift is for use in worship, the prayer might be slightly reworded to strengthen the sense of fellowship with the departed when we use, in our worship, the gift that is being blessed. The usual Offertory sentence or prayers would follow.

There are, of course, occasions when these suggestions would be quite inadequate and a whole service would be built around the dedication, though even then a prayer on this model might form the heart of the rite. The blessing of an organ would call for a great musical service. The blessing of a stained glass window would provide its own theme, depending what the window depicted. By tradition the consecration of an altar is reserved to a bishop, who would then normally preside at a celebration of the Eucharist at it. But diocesan rules and orders of service must be respected on such occasions.

A word may be said about that most frequent of all gifts in church – the regular 'collection', the presentation of which can, in some Anglican churches, very often involve more elaborate ceremonial than any other part of the liturgy. Two points may usefully be made. First, the practice of presenting the eucharistic elements and the collection separately is unfortunate. Though they may reasonably arrive at the altar at different points in the hymn (for it is not sensible to delay the preparation of the altar until the collection has been taken), they should be offered together and the words, 'Yours, Lord is the greatness . . .', if they are said, said over all the gifts. Thus, for instance, to present the bread and wine and to say the Offertory sentence before the hymn, and then to present the collection at the end of it, is mistaken.

Secondly, a simplification of the procedure for its presentation (at all services, not just the Eucharist) would be welcome. The Anglican genius for passing the plate from sidesman to warden, to server, to priest (and sometimes even to bishop), is faintly ridiculous and the great elevation that follows more so. There is no need for all these intermediaries in the presentation of the people's offerings. No priestly gesture of blessing or elevation is required to validate the gifts. It would be far simpler if those who have taken the collection came forward, either together, or separately as they finished, and placed their plate at the foot of the altar. A plate is suitable for this. A 'collection bag' is not, and its disappearance in favour of a basket, so common on the continent, would be a great blessing.

Postscript

It has been inevitable that sometimes in the chapters of this book the word 'priest' or 'president' has been used as a sort of shorthand for the whole local church. 'The priest must decide . . .' nearly always ought to read, 'The priest and the people together must decide . . .' The participation of the whole local church in the planning of its worship, as well as in the execution of it, has been fundamental all the way along. For the days are past when a priest can talk of 'taking a service' or 'conducting worship'. His function is that of presidency, but that is only one of many functions in the liturgy. He has this role, and it is one to which he has to bring all the expertise, sensitivity and prayerfulness that he can summon, but it remains only a part of the whole.

Nor, in the end, can the local church, even acting corporately, think of itself as 'making' or 'devising' worship, however much we have to use such terms in our everyday discourse. All that the local church can do is to *participate* in worship. For, as the Church unravels the principles that lie behind our different traditions, we have reinforced for us the truth that worship is the characteristic activity of the *whole* Church. There is never anything new in liturgy, simply the rediscovery of something that has always been there. The local church often has to struggle to make that rediscovery for itself, but in the end what it is doing is simply participating more fully in an *eternal* reality. For even the unending cycle of worship of the Universal Church around the world is not the whole story. Constant worship exists independently of this world and of the Church militant. Worship is the essence of the life of heaven. All that we do is to participate in it, feebly and fleetingly. We never 'make' worship, let alone 'conduct' it. We simply join ourselves to it. With angels and archangels, and with all the company of heaven we sing

> Holy, holy, holy Lord,
> heaven and earth are full of your glory.

Index

There are no entries in this Index for *The Alternative Service Book 1980*, The Church of England, the Eucharist, Hymn, Officiant, Prayer, Reader or Reading because references to them occur throughout the text.

Except in the case of the author's own books (*The Communion of Saints* [1980] and *The Eucharist* [2nd edn. 1981]), liturgical books mentioned in the text are indexed by the name of the author, rather than the title of the book.